Islam, Democracy, and the State in North Africa

Indiana Series in Arab and Islamic Studies

GENERAL EDITORS

Salih J. Altoma, Iliya Harik, and Mark Tessler

Islam, Democracy, and the State in North Africa

EDITED BY JOHN P. ENTELIS

INDIANA UNIVERSITY PRESS

Bloomington and Indianapolis

The paper used in this publication meets the minimum requirements of American National Standard for Information Sciences—Permanence of Paper for Printed Library Materials, ANSI Z39.48-1984.

Manufactured in the United States of America

Library of Congress Cataloging–in–Publication Data

Islam, democracy, and the state in North Africa / edited by
   John P. Entelis.
      p. cm. — (Indiana series in Arab and Islamic studies)
      Includes bibliographical references and index.
      ISBN 0–253–33303–2 (cloth : alk. paper). — ISBN 0–
      253–21131–X (pbk. : alk. paper)
      1. Islam—Africa, North—History—20th century. 2.
Islam and politics—Africa, North. 3. Africa, North—Politics and government. 4. Islam and state —Africa, North.
I. Entelis, John P. (John Pierre), date. II. Series.
BP64.A4N6428 1997
320.961′09′048—dc21   97-410
1 2 3 4 5 02 01 00 99 98 97

Contents

Contributors

Lisa Anderson, Dean, School of International and Public Affairs, and Professor of Political Science, Columbia University.

Dale F. Eickelman, Ralph and Richard Lazarus Professor of Anthropology and Human Relations, Dartmouth College.

John P. Entelis, Professor of Political Science and Director, Middle East Studies Program, Fordham University.

Clement M. Henry, Professor of Government and Middle East Studies, The University of Texas at Austin.

Mark Tessler, Professor of Political Science, University of Wisconsin–Milwaukee, and Director, University of Wisconsin–Milwaukee and Marquette University Joint Center for International Studies.

John O. Voll, Professor of History, Center for Muslim-Christian Understanding, Georgetown University.

Susan Waltz, Professor of International Relations, Florida International University.

John Waterbury, William Stewart Tod Professor of Politics and International Affairs in the Woodrow Wilson School and Director, Center for International Studies, Princeton University.

I. William Zartman, Jacob Blaustein Professor and Director, African Studies, The Nitze School of Advanced International Studies, The Johns Hopkins University.

Acknowledgments

This book is the result of a two-year lecture and publication project on "The Crisis of Authoritarianism in North African Politics: Transition to Democracy?" that I directed at Fordham University. The project was funded by a generous grant from the United States Institute of Peace. I would like to thank the many people of USIP who assisted me in the project's successful completion, especially Dr. David R. Smock and Dr. Hrach Gregorian. Nancy McCarthy, director of Fordham University's Office of Research, was invariably helpful and supportive. I was assisted in the smooth administration of the project by the superb work of my former administrative assistant and daughter, Joëlle Entelis. My current administrative assistant, Carolyn E. Cocca, a scholar in her own right, provided invaluable editorial guidance and was a source of continuous inspiration and support.

Parts of my chapter appeared in an earlier and very abbreviated form in *Current History* (January 1995). Lisa Anderson prepared her chapter while she was a member of the School of Social Science at the Institute for Advanced Study (1993–1994); she was supported by a grant from the National Endowment for the Humanities. Earlier versions of Dale F. Eickelman's chapter were presented under the auspices of the Sabbagh Lectures at the University of Arizona, Tucson, March 24, 1994, and at the Department of Public Affairs, George Mason University, April 6, 1994. He especially wishes to thank Adeed Dawisha, Deborah Hodges, Mark Katz, Thor H. Kuniholm, and James Piscatori for comments on earlier versions, and David Kaiser for explaining recent developments in the history of science. His discussion of recent political developments in Morocco is based on field research supported in part by the John Simon Guggenheim Memorial Foundation (1992) and the Moroccan-American Commission on Educational and Cultural Exchange (1992–1994). An earlier version of Mark Tessler's chapter was presented at a workshop on "Political-Religious Movements and Development in the Near East," organized by the United States Agency for International Development and held in Washington, D.C., in June 1992. Parts of Clement M. Henry's chapter appeared in his book *The Mediterranean Debt Crescent*. I. William Zartman gratefully acknowledges the research and writing assistance of Karim Mezran.

Introduction

JOHN P. ENTELIS

Both the politics of North Africa and the way the region has been studied in the modern period can be broken down into six relatively distinct phases. The first phase involved the region's struggle for national liberation as Morocco, Tunisia, and Algeria successfully overthrew French colonial rule to achieve full independence by 1962. The scholarly analysis of this period was fairly uniform in its portrayal of the inevitability and necessity of the decolonization process.

The second phase was an era of optimism and hope on the part of both scholars and statesmen, who envisioned a sustained period of "modernization" involving expanded social opportunity, sustained economic growth, and cultural diffusion or "Westernization." Although this phase of "political order in changing societies" was blatantly authoritarian, the overall benefits were deemed sufficiently important to justify such "benign" political control on the part of "charismatic" leaders such as Morocco's King Hassan II, Tunisia's Habib Bourguiba, and Algeria's Ahmed Ben Bella.

By the late 1960s and early 1970s, however, this benign form of Maghrebi authoritarianism had become increasingly "malignant" as the Arab police state (*mukhabarat*) deepened and widened its control over society, suffocating all forms of independent political expression. Most analysts of this third period accepted the mukhabarat state as a given and focused their study on elite maneuvering at the top rather than the growing discontent emerging at the bottom. As long as modernization policies were being pursued, Western interests assured, and regional stability maintained, statesmen and scholars alike felt it unnecessary to impose an alternative political paradigm that responded to populist needs, democratic aspirations, and calls for cultural integrity.

The increasing tension between state repression and expanding populist aspirations reached unbearable proportions when, in the early and mid-1980s, national, regional, and global economies suffered simultaneous failures which seriously compromised the so-called "welfare contracts" that had regulated state-society relations since independence. A worldwide "crisis of authoritarianism" ensued, bringing into question all forms of authoritarian control, including that operating in North Africa. Most academic observers and policymakers alike were unprepared for this crisis, which took the form of societywide uprisings, wildcat strikes, political turmoil, upsurges in civil society activity, and the rise of populist political Islamic movements. No event better captured the centrality of this crisis than the nationwide riots which broke out in Algeria in October 1988. These "events" constituted a kind of "turning point" which many foresaw as the end of one historic phase—authoritarianism—and the beginning of another—democracy.

The fifth period was a relatively brief moment (1989–1991) when the Maghreb had its initial experience with liberalization and democratization. In all three countries, movement toward genuine political change seemed to be occurring, reflecting broader liberalization processes taking place elsewhere in the region and the world—the fall of the Berlin wall, the collapse of communism, and the spread of democratic practices in formerly authoritarian regimes in the Third World. Zine el-Abidine Ben Ali's so-called "constitutional coup" presaged the opening of political life in Tunisia, as did the introduction of multiparty politics and competitive elections in Algeria in 1990. Even absolutist Morocco seemed intent on liberalizing its otherwise elite-manipulated political process. Serious observers of these developments, although initially surprised, were generally enthusiastic about this phase, at least until Islamist political groupings began to profit from such openings. Confusion, contradictions, and contortions quickly supplanted coherent analysis as models of democracy proffered elsewhere now seemed inappropriate for this region; theories of both political culture and political economy were put forth in explanation.

The last and most recent phase in the evolution of North African politics has been characterized by the reemergence of political authoritarianism not unlike that of the second and third phases—an army-dominated mukhabarat state. In each instance, liberalization has been curtailed and democracy derailed as military-backed regimes in Rabat, Algiers, and Tunis have used all possible means to maintain their stranglehold on society while faithfully following the advice of foreign patrons in liberalizing their economies. The distinguishing characteristic of this most recent phase of Maghrebi politics is the way in which authoritarian regimes have been kept alive "by the unwillingness of external donors to sever the aid tie, usually for strategic as well as humanitarian reasons" (Haggard and Kaufman 1995: 36). Nowhere have "predatory personalist rulers" been as adept in resisting reform and clinging to office as those currently in power in North Africa, usually "through continued access to external aid, repression, and careful maintenance of select patronage relations" (Haggard and Kaufman 1995: 36). The academic discourse on this phase has been controversial if not combative, with no single approach providing satisfactory explanations for how and why the Maghreb continues to defy the "laws" of democracy experienced elsewhere: authoritarian governments collapse in the face of failures of the political economy and are replaced by incipient liberalizing regimes which, although experiencing initial chaos, eventually consolidate into systems of institutional pluralism.

This book is concerned with describing, explaining, and critically analyzing the last three phases of the development of North African politics by focusing on those attributes that best illustrate the paradox described above. In the nine chapters that follow, the interaction of Islam, democracy, and the state in North Africa are analyzed from the competing but also complementary perspectives of political culture and political economy. Voll, Eickelman, Entelis, and Waltz direct their attention to the cultural components of possible political change, with special focus on the Islamic and human rights dimensions. Tessler's contribution examines the link between political culture and political economy as an explanation for socioeconomic crises and the rise of populist Islam. The chapters by Anderson, Waterbury, and Henry take an explicitly economic approach in their attempts to elaborate the dynamic relationship between political economy and political democratization. Zartman concludes with a contribution devoted to the international dimension of democratic transition in North Africa.

Political Culture

The crisis of authoritarianism in North Africa is not simply a struggle over tactics or a conflict within existing political elites, argues John O. Voll in his chapter, "Sultans, Saints, and Presidents: The Islamic Community and the State in North Africa." Rather, it is part of a much broader, global set of transformations in which the very nature of the basic structures is involved. The nature of authority and the conflicts over the identification of authorities are contested concepts in the emerging era; as a result, the fundamental struggles are conflicts about worldviews rather than simply conflicts among competing elites or economic classes.

Voll argues that, within this context, the crisis of authoritarianism in North Africa is a crisis of Westernizing, modernizing authoritarianism. The failures of liberal secularist authoritarianism in Tunisia and radical secularist authoritarianism in Algeria were failures of "ideal" models of the "successful" gradualist and the "successful" nationalist-radical revolution. The so-called "traditional" political system of the Moroccan monarchy is the only North African political system to survive intact since the achievement of independence.

As a result of global and regional transformations, according to Voll, the whole discourse of modernization and Westernization has come into question. The rise of more populist movements affirming Islam and the global pressures for democratization combine to force a reconstituting of religio-political discourse in North Africa. The result is a contestation of the basic concepts of political life, with Islamic movements emerging as significant factors, both in the political struggles and in the development of viable political conceptualizations for North African states and societies.

According to Dale F. Eickelman in his chapter, "Muslim Politics: The Prospects for Democracy in North Africa and the Middle East," there is a powerful background understanding among both Westerners and Muslims that "Islam," or what some people presume to be Islam, determines the identity and conduct of Muslims in a way in which other world religions do not. This implicit assumption came to the fore during the crisis that culminated in the forced resignation of Algeria's President Chadli Benjedid on January 11, 1992, and the military's cancellation of elections the next day.

Such objectifications of Islam as a religion and as a civilization permeate U.S. policy and public discourse, and one political scientist, adapting arguments current in the 1930s, has argued that "non-Western civilizations" have increasingly become political actors. Such essentialist arguments deflect attention from internal and historical differences among the carriers of traditions in a civilization and the often vigorous internal debate among those carriers. Civilizations, like cultures, are better seen as contested, temporal, and emergent.

The issue of contested cultures and civilizations is especially important, Eickelman writes, in assessing the prospects for democracy in the Arab world. Few maintain that being Arab inhibits democracy, but some readily impute antidemocratic sentiments to those who are Muslim. Sometimes the problem is definitional, as when democracy and democratic sentiments are defined principally in terms of votes and elections. Rather than focus principally on standard indicators, it is possible to focus on alternative measures of the growth of democratic attitudes and an understanding of "just" rule and governance.

Thus, politics are "Muslim" when they relate to a widely shared, although not doctrinally defined, tradition of ideas and practice. Muslim groups calling for democratization in such countries as Jordan, Egypt, Tunisia, and Morocco indicate how some Muslims, as self-conscious religious actors, use the instruments of existing political systems to magnify their political voice and intensify pressures for reform. From this perspective, Eickelman argues, Muslim politics is a struggle about people's imaginations—cooperation in and a contest over the symbolic production of political symbols and the control of the institutions, formal and informal, which serve as the symbolic arbiters of society. Politics as Leviathan is thus decisively abandoned in favor of politics as decisionmaker. In spite of the fascination of Western commentators with "Islamist" discourse, there is a rising tide of Muslim moderates responding to what they see as the bankruptcy of traditional religious and political discourse.

Likewise, mass higher education and mass communication have begun to have a profound effect on how people think about political and religious authority and responsibility by facilitating conceptual innovations and creating new networks for communication and action. Since midcentury, there has been an expansion of mass education, and this has created profound changes in the images and vocabulary by which politics are conceived. Mass education and mass communications have engendered a changed sense of authoritative discourse, have fostered the emergence of a sense of religion and politics as system and object that facilitate the incorporation of new elements, and have created altered conceptions of language and community.

To assess the varying prospects for democracy, Eickelman examines the timing of liberalization measures in Morocco since 1992, including expanded parliamentary and municipal elections, as well as, for comparative purposes, recent developments in Jordan and on the Arabian Peninsula.

These examples also suggest alternatives to thinking in terms of overall, misleading "paradigms." In the history of science, theories about such conceptual paradigms date from the 1960s; they have been successively abandoned since then, although parallel notions live on in thinking about foreign policy. Historians of science have abandoned the assumption that there is a fixed, hierarchical relation between theory, practice, and the means by which implicit and explicit changes in practice are assessed. As George F. Kennan and others suggest, it is time to discard the search for a universal paradigm of international politics to replace the collapse of that of the Cold War.

In North Africa and the Middle East, then, assessing the prospects for democracy entails listening to voices other than those of a Westernized elite and paying attention to the rich debates and arguments through which ideas of just rule, religious and otherwise, are re-imagined and re-formed throughout the Arab and Muslim worlds. Eickelman finds that the issue is not to decide whether such debates are occurring, but to recognize their contours, the obstacles, and the false starts (both internal and external) in making governance less arbitrary and authoritarian.

Nonviolent Islamic reformism and revivalism in Arab North Africa have a long history that dates back to the early days of colonial occupation and earlier, John P. Entelis argues in his chapter, "Political Islam in the Maghreb: The Nonviolent Dimension." *Salafiyya* (from *salaf,* forefather) movements emerged in all three countries of the Maghreb in response to external aggression and perceived threats to indigenous culture and belief. Today's nonviolent Islamic-based political movements are thus following in a recognized tradition of defying an authority that is demonstrably unjust, unresponsive, and undemocratic. They use the power of the mosques and the streets to challenge the authority of regimes viewed as illegitimate.

Such movements seek through prayer and preaching to mobilize popular support for a political program that promotes their ideas for the just and good society as defined for them by Islamic teaching. They further influence people through debates at youth centers, pamphlets distributed in poor neighborhoods, and work in the community. They sponsor mass rallies, large demonstrations, and public assemblies that are a testament to their impressive organizational abilities. While such efforts may at times degenerate into violence, violent action is not a structural component of either the movements' strategic thinking or their tactics. And if reformist movements have in both the distant and the recent past given rise to radical offshoots—especially when moderation has failed to achieve results quickly or broadly—the nonviolent reformers do not bear the responsibility.

Entelis breaks down Islamically based political opposition movements in North Africa into three separate but at times overlapping categories. One is comprised of the individuals and groups that reject the authority of official or state-sponsored Islam and instead promote nonpolitical action in education, culture, and social activities. They believe in "bottom-up" political change resulting from a strategy of acculturation, socialization, and education. At the core of their thinking is a renewed emphasis on the religious training and education of the young so as to ensure a devoutly Muslim political future.

A second group, equally committed to the goal of a more "authentic" Muslim society, calls instead for direct political action to attain it. Its members advocate the use of democratic and electoral means—political organization, mobilization, and participation—to bring about a nonviolent transfer of power in the nation. Reform of both state and society is at the heart of their political agenda.

The third category includes militant hardliners who want to transfer power quickly by any means, political or military, including violence, terrorism, and assassination. Its members subscribe to a puritanical belief system and most favor the imposition of Islamic law, strictly interpreted. It is to this group that the label "Islamic fundamentalism" best applies.

Different peoples and movements make up these three broad categories of Muslim activism directed against incumbent power. And while some individuals may undergo political transformation that causes them to move from one group to another, the distinguishing characteristic of each movement is its commitment to certain core beliefs of action: nonpolitical (religious), political (reform), and militant (radical). Entelis's chapter is concerned primarily with the second group of Muslim oppositional activists.

Despite the publicity militant Islam has received, the principal Muslim opposition movements in the Maghreb subscribe to a nonviolent transfer of national power. The three most popular and influential movements—Abdessalam Yassine's Justice and Charity in Morocco, Rachid al-Ghannouchi's an-Nahdah (Renaissance) in Tunisia, and the Islamic Salvation Front (FIS) in Algeria headed by Abassi Madani and Ali Benhadj—are in fact politically moderate, though all are banned.

Neither government oppression (in Tunisia), state terrorism (in Algeria), nor monarchical intimidation (in Morocco) has extinguished support for these groups, especially among people living on the margins but also among elites. Yet the situation is strained by extremist groups emerging within movements as well as those created outside them. For their part, government hardliners have instituted their own solutions, ranging from intensified political repression in Tunisia to expanded surveillance of suspected groups by Morocco's Interior Ministry to the application in Algeria of brutal force in the form of state-sponsored death squads. Human rights abuses and civil rights violations have risen dramatically in recent years, as reports from Amnesty International (1993 and 1994) and Middle East Watch (1994) have confirmed. In Algeria alone, between 40,000 and 50,000 people have died in the violence that has raged since the January 1992 military coup.

Should incumbent governments succeed in eliminating nonviolent Islamist groups, they will face a serious vacuum that can only result in greater political instability and social uncertainty. In short, while popular support for nonviolent Islamists in North Africa is holding, it is challenged daily—from above by recalcitrant officials and from below by fringe groups prone to violence. Should nonviolent Islamists be forced into submission or radicalized into violence, Entelis concludes, stability and democracy in the Maghreb will be unlikely anytime soon.

Soon after independence, governments in Morocco, Tunisia, and Algeria set up security agencies that effectively helped to silence political opponents and undergird the authority of the new regimes. In "The Politics of Human Rights in the Maghreb," Susan Waltz describes the origins and functioning of these agencies. She notes that even as Maghrebi governments acceded to the emerging international human rights regime by ratifying international covenants and participating in international human rights review mechanisms, at home they did not refrain from such practices as torture, "disappearances," political killings, and the imprisonment of dissidents. These practices were not necessarily widespread, but they were commonplace enough to effectively curtail political participation.

It was thus a development of some note that from 1987 through 1994 the governments of Tunisia, Algeria, and Morocco voluntarily undertook extensive domestic human rights reforms and concomitantly opened prison doors behind which some of the world's longest-held political prisoners had been jailed. In her chapter, Waltz offers an explanation for the wave of concern about domestic human rights practices and explores the significance of reforms undertaken by Maghrebi governments.

Although circumstances varied across the region, in each country pressure for reform was spearheaded by at least one politically independent human rights group. Human rights reforms were introduced first in Tunisia, where widespread fear engendered by a wave of political repression in Habib Bourguiba's final year of power left the Tunisian League of Human Rights as the only credible voice in politics. Reforms enacted by the new president, Zine el-Abidine Ben Ali, were part of an effort to capitalize on popular appreciation of the League and legitimize his own hold on power. Riots in Algiers in October 1988 pointed to the moral and political deficiencies of the FLN (National Liberation Front) government, and two new human rights groups pointed the way to reforms. Reform came more slowly to Morocco; but there, too, from the late 1980s, the Moroccan Organization of Human Rights began to argue for legal changes and political amnesty. In the process it rekindled the energies of two other existing, but moribund, human rights groups.

Waltz argues that pressures exerted by domestic human rights groups were matched, and reinforced, by influential actors abroad. International human rights groups, the international media, and finally, Western governments with close ties to Maghrebi governments each expressed concern about human rights practices and effectively championed local human rights defenders. In so doing, they lent strength to the Maghrebi human rights movement, and it was this combination of forces that effectively engendered the reforms.

The long-term significance of human rights reform in the Maghreb is not clear. Moroccan reforms are too recent to assess. But Algeria is in the grip of social and political chaos, and abuses by both Islamist groups and government security forces there have been widespread. In Tunisia, likewise, Ben Ali's government has reverted to old practices, harassing and imprisoning political opponents and human rights defenders in disregard of new laws limiting pretrial detention.

If skeptics may legitimately raise questions about governmental commitment to reform, Waltz suggests that there are two vantage points from which the reforms retain much significance. First, in taking up the discourse of human rights and in creating official human rights agencies, Maghrebi governments have helped legitimate the idea of universal human rights. Official discourse helps frame political debate and in this case opens the door to political accountability. Secondly, human rights (*huquq al-insan*) has become part of the lexicon of nearly all active social movements in the Maghreb and has thus anchored itself in the rudiments of an emerging civil society. While political commitments of those in power may wane, Waltz argues that to the extent human rights becomes embedded in discourses and political structures and to the extent that human rights ideals are supported by influential actors at home and abroad, human rights will remain on the Maghreb's political agenda.

Political Economy

In Mark Tessler's chapter, "The Origins of Popular Support for Islamist Movements: A Political Economy Analysis," Tessler addresses the reasons for the growing popular support for Islamist movements in many countries of North Africa and the Middle East. Further, he argues that the origins of this support are to be found primarily in the political and economic circumstances of these countries and only secondarily in the religious and cultural traditions of their inhabitants. This analysis stands in opposition to the assessments offered by Islamist leaders themselves, who usually insist that support for their movements derives principally from the religious faith of the Muslim Arab masses.

In developing the argument that support for Islamist movements derives primarily from economic and political circumstances, the author devotes most of his attention to Algeria, Tunisia, and Morocco, although some information about the other Arab countries is presented as well. The chapter also presents original public opinion data from Egypt and comparative data from Kuwait in order to shed additional light on the nature and determinants of relevant popular attitudes. These data are presented in the text and discussed more fully in an appendix.

The chapter is divided into five sections. The first section notes the existence of and examines the immediate causes for high levels of popular discontent. Particular attention is given to shortages and other inadequacies relating to employment, education, and housing. As a result of these problems, which affect almost all sectors of society but are most pronounced among the young and in the cities, a steadily increasing number of individuals is finding it impossible to fulfill their aspirations for social mobility and a better life.

The next section is devoted to the way that ordinary citizens understand the reasons for this situation. Tessler argues that many believe their problems are grounded in existing patterns of political economy; accordingly, they attribute much of the responsibility for their plight to the political regimes by which they are governed. Noting the large and growing gap between rich and poor, for example, many North Africans complain that the burdens of underdevelopment are not shared equitably and that, despite economic difficulties, there are islands of affluence and elite privilege. Even more important, many complain that elite membership is determined in most instances not by ability, dedication, or service to society, but rather by personal and political connections—the result being a system where patronage and clientelism predominate in decisions about public policy and resource allocation.

The third section reviews perceptions about the regional and international dimensions of this situation. It notes that politically conscious North Africans frequently speak of a tacit alliance in support of the status quo among domestic, regional, and even international political actors. These perceptions are examined against the background of the 1990–91 Persian Gulf crisis, which produced intense opposition throughout the Maghreb to the U.S.-led coalition assembled to defend Saudi Arabia and restore Kuwaiti sovereignty. According to many observers, Saddam Hussein was lauded for his challenge to the existing order, whereas the anti-Iraq coalition (which included Arab as well as foreign governments) was deemed an enemy of the people and said to be motivated solely by a desire to protect the interests of those in power.

The fourth section observes that many North Africans searching for an alternative to the status quo are turning to political Islam. Noting that Islamist movements are well-positioned to capitalize on popular discontent, he argues that many ordinary men and women support Muslim groups for instrumental reasons—to express dissatisfaction and exert pressure for political and economic change—rather than because they desire government based on orthodox interpretations of Muslim law. This analysis is supported by the presentation of original public opinion data. It is also grounded in a review of the Islamic resurgence during the 1970s and 1980s, beginning with a loss of public confidence in secular nationalism and pan-Arabism following the defeat of revolutionary Arab regimes in the war with Israel in June 1967.

The final section discusses organizational and ideological factors contributing to the growth of Islamist movements. One such consideration is the ability of Muslim groups to use mosques and other religious establishments to recruit and organize followers. Another is the operation of clinics, schools, and welfare programs in poorer neighborhoods, through which Islamists deliver social services and receive support for their cause in return. Yet another important factor is the absence of credible alternatives for articulating opposition to the status quo, particularly with parties of the political left losing their appeal following the end of the Cold War.

In concluding this political economy analysis, Tessler suggests that the popular discontent producing support for Islamist movements will begin to dissipate if, but only if, Arab governments display greater vision and dedication in addressing the grievances of ordinary men and women. For this to occur, these governments will have to work with increased honesty and effectiveness on behalf of their citizens; this in turn will require greater respect for human rights, a more equitable distribution of those burdens of underdevelopment that cannot be avoided and, above all, progress toward democratization and genuine government accountability.

In Lisa Anderson's chapter, "Prospects for Liberalism in North Africa: Identities and Interests in Preindustrial Welfare States," Anderson explores the role played by international political economy in the onset of liberal political reform in North Africa as well as the factors that impeded its realization. She notes alternative approaches for explaining stability and change—the primacy of culture and tradition, particularly Islam; international pressures; and the growth of voluntary organizations outside the purview of the state—but finds them inadequate and turns instead to reasons rooted in political economy.

Anderson argues that the changes in political systems in Morocco, Algeria, and Tunisia, from twenty years ago (despotic) to five years ago (multiparty systems), have come about due to the regimes' need for new sources of revenue. The subsequent reversal of this trend in the 1990s, she says, is due mostly to their fears of the strength of Islamic political movements. As an explanation for the initial liberalization, she outlines the differences between extractive states and those characterized by soft budget constraints (such as the North African states). In the former, wealth (and thus power) stem from the capacity to pay taxes to and effect concessions from the government. But in those with soft budget constraints, the state can depend on exogenous rents and does not need to rely on domestic taxes; therefore, the government lacks a reciprocal obligation to its citizens and buys acquiescence rather than bargaining for it. While in extractive states power derives from wealth, in the Maghreb wealth derives from power, which is best achieved through close ties to state regulatory and distributive agencies rather than to production itself.

In regard to the citizenry as a whole, such governments used their foreign-derived earnings to construct preindustrial welfare states characterized by generous distribution that made their citizens beholden to them for basic needs. The criteria for the particulars of distribution, Anderson writes, tended to be noneconomic and identity-based, spurring the formation of political cleavages in such societies and raising the importance of identity-based political movements over interest-based associations. This encouraged organization around familial, patronage, or ideological commonalties rather than shared economic interests.

With the depleted external revenues of the 1980s, these regimes turned to a new strategy for securing revenue—by loosening their links with foreign patrons and creating the potential for demands from (and obligations to) various sectors of domestic society. Political liberalization was intended to win over Western aid donors as well as those domestic constituencies likely to be targeted for taxation. But, according to Anderson, what was supposed to be little more than a sop to a timid and largely dependent bourgeoisie, a device to broaden and solidify the regimes' support, soon posed a serious challenge to those regimes.

While few of the societal class- and interest-based organizations were willing to contest government policies openly or to compromise their principles to secure access to the government, other groups were. Islamist movements gained supporters through passionate and symbolic appeals to those benefiting least from government distribution policies, for example, the poor and the young. While their protests were cast more in terms of moral outrage and personal identity than economics, some (such as Algeria's Islamic Salvation Front—FIS) were often better organized, more efficient, and less corrupt than the government. The FIS was also able to provide services that the government could not, and it out-performed a secular opposition that was too narrow in defining its political interests and ignored social and economic activities. Anderson argues, however, that many of the Islamic movements are not predisposed to liberal democracy, obtain resources from foreign patrons, and seek to build an alternative to the government rather than to participate in it. These movements can succeed by remaining vague but emotional in their appeals, while the government must defend its record.

In North African countries, alarm among elites at the growing strength of such Islamist political movements caused them to crack down, most severely in the case of Algeria in 1992. Anderson notes that the governments of Libya and Algeria, because of their oil and gas exports, have less need to develop a domestic productive capacity or to tax their constituencies; this not only narrowly circumscribes the social base of opposition but encourages a resort to symbolic politics. Tunisia and Morocco, on the other hand, are more dependent on their domestic economic constituencies and so have adopted more of the trappings of liberal politics—even though their reforms are more intent on broadening the base of support for elites than creating a truly democratic system. Anderson concludes that the legacy of the region's international political economy, the need for economic and political reforms, the weakness of associational life in civil society, and the seemingly disproportionate attention to identity-based movements do not foster bright prospects for future democratic reform in the region.

John Waterbury's chapter, "From Social Contracts to Extraction Contracts: The Political Economy of Authoritarianism and Democracy," is a complement to as well as a departure from Anderson's arguments and reflects the shift brought on by decreases in oil prices, worker remittances, and foreign loans that have laid bare the lack of viability of state-led, import-substituting industrialization built around a large public sector. This decrease in externally derived revenues and the weakening of the military establishment's grip on national wealth are spurring governments in the Middle East and North Africa to turn to their own citizens in order to finance the programs they regard as essential. In the mid-1980s, North African and Middle Eastern states began to adjust by curbing government expenditures, increasing the tax burden, narrowing the coalitional base of the regime, and allocating compensatory payments to crucial strategic allies and those most severely affected by the adjustment process. Waterbury argues that political liberalization should support the necessary process of economic reform by breaking down the state's monopoly on the allocation of resources and spreading the pain of adjustment; he also argues that such economic adjustment could be popular if preceded by a deep enough crisis. These governments would thus become more accountable and more inclined to bargain with their constituencies and less inclined to legislate merely by decree. Steps toward a new kind of contract, approximating a contract of extraction, must keep pace with the relative loss of political control caused by reform.

The political economy of authoritarianism and democracy, Waterbury argues, does not stop at a given country's border but is connected to international markets, sources of credit and arms, investment flow, strategic rents, and the instruments of international clientage and dependency. At a time when the collapse of the socialist economies and of the former USSR meant that the latter could no longer project its military power nor extend economic support to its potential Arab clients, North African and Middle Eastern regimes themselves fell into economic crises resulting from inherent flaws in their growth strategies as well as legitimacy crises that resulted from military failures and the loss of externally based income.

Waterbury also discusses the concept of praetorianism, which is not solely a function of the size of the military establishment or control over its resources but of its ability to preempt the political arena and repress and delegitimize its rivals. The level of armed conflict in North Africa and the Middle East has made the military's economic and political entitlements the single most important variable in determining the political economy of authoritarianism and democracy. With the exception of Israel and Turkey, North African and Middle Eastern countries are under the direct or indirect control of their military establishments, and these institutions will determine the pace of any transition toward democracy. In the days of import-substituting industrialization, such military establishments were the linchpin of dominant coalitions; but economic crisis has forced a reduction, however unevenly, in their entitlements. Even so, it is possible to have a high level of praetorianism while decreasing outlays to the military; Waterbury notes that armed conflicts are still occurring, even though the area's high-profile Israeli-Palestinian dispute is being resolved. He thus writes that the best that can be hoped is that the region's military establishments will do no more than hold their own.

Waterbury also explores the notion that taxation can constitute the implementation of a contract between government and citizen and broadens the argument to include all forms of extraction as "taxation" and all forms of accountability as "representation." But average tax burdens in North Africa and the Middle East are not noticeably low and have been increasing steadily, leading Waterbury to turn to other factors to explain the still low level of accountability: state reliance on state enterprise to lead development efforts, the use of indirect as opposed to direct taxation, or a lag between taxation and accountability. Further, state extraction can take different forms so that it is difficult to predict citizen reaction to different combinations and levels of taxes, sudden price shifts, diminutions of entitlements, inflation taxes, subsidies, or differences in the quality of public goods. Nonetheless, people do not generally perceive the inflation tax to be a tax, nor would there necessarily be an immediate reaction to price-setting that turns the terms of trade against specific sectors. Likewise, erosion of real wages and of subsidies may provoke strikes or riots, but more likely will cause people to migrate from the formal to the informal sector for second jobs or more easily obtained goods.

In such a system, capitalist interests may wield unusual leverage in bringing about government accountability. A government must trade policy concessions and economic incentives for much-needed investment that is lost because of a decline in outside rents. Such investment and entrepreneurship would stimulate growth, which would mean higher tax revenues for the government, and the government would in turn accept being held accountable by these private economic interests. In this age of computerized portfolio movements and currency transfers, the incentive for private money to bargain in the first place must come from a combination of factors: a strong preference for staying in the country, a disinclination to incur the costs of moving, and a lack of more accommodating alternative environments. In nearly all countries, private investment has been growing in relation to that of the public. Many North African and Middle Eastern states, argues Waterbury, have not only ceded pride of place to capitalist investors but in many instances have had to woo and legitimize them. While private owners of capital do not necessarily promote democratic accountability, they may, as a by-product of their bargaining, foster habits of interaction between governments and citizens that can lead to a transition. Waterbury notes cases of growing accountability in Jordan, Egypt, and Kuwait.

When such bargaining is recognized as legitimate, the state will have a difficult time denying the same legitimacy to bargaining with other interests in civil society, for example, Islamists, labor groups, human rights advocates, etc. At the same time, the state must curb entitlements to the majority while trying to serve minority (i.e., moneyed) interests. North African and Middle Eastern governments thus must try to arrive at contractual understandings with two constituencies whose short-term interests diverge. While private capital can be granted economic incentives, the bearing of social costs by citizens will undoubtedly create more demand for accountability; so far, much of this has been through Islamic movements. For the future, argues Waterbury, the major political challenge facing the regimes in the Middle East and North Africa is the transition from social contracts to extractive contracts under which the states must concede greater accountability in exchange for shifting the burden of social costs directly to their citizens. So far, the result has been a narrowing of the coalition that sustains regimes, rising unemployment (in the formal sector), and stagnant or declining per capita income. He concludes his analysis by looking at the specific cases of Turkey, Egypt, and Iran and their attempts to resolve their economic crises. Waterbury is cautiously optimistic about the chances that these and other countries in the region will at least make a break with the political status quo.

In "Crises of Money and Power: Transitions to Democracy?" Clement M. Henry observes that the political crises of the North African regimes have been accompanied by international debt crises reminiscent of the nineteenth century. But whereas the earlier crises resulted in colonial takeovers, the current economic crises may pave the way for political reform. In each North African country, with the exception of Libya, balance-of-payments crises led to structural adjustment, which included a substantial reform of the respective banking system. Henry argues that these reforms will generate substantial pressures emanating from the respective business communities for more accountable government and greater political contestation.

Drawing upon data from *The Mediterranean Debt Crescent: Money and Power in Algeria, Egypt, Morocco, Tunisia, and Turkey*, he focuses upon an independent variable—the structure of the commercial banking system, which has been little studied in the conventional comparative politics and political economy literature on political transitions. The financial reforms encouraged by the International Monetary Fund and the World Bank are designed to develop banking systems that are autonomous and competitive and that feature a substantial component of privately owned banks. To the extent that these reforms succeed, Henry argues, they will seriously endanger the patrimonial politics currently prevailing in North Africa.

Financial reform threatens the existing regimes in two ways. First, it tends to undermine their patronage networks. These networks rely heavily upon credit allocated by the political authorities. Whether a business is publicly or privately owned, the banks govern most, if not all, of its financial capital. A word from the ruler or his entourage is sufficient to make or break most businesses. Financial reform tends to limit these interventions and to oblige bankers to respect economic criteria in their lending practices. Secondly, as bankers acquire autonomy, that is, control over their finance capital, they may foster countervailing centers of economic power in the business community. These power centers do not, of course, oppose the state or regime per se; but their resources for collective action become available to contending centers of political power. Henry is not arguing that bankers themselves will play active political roles in a transition process. Intentionally or not, however, they will be the midwives, behind the scenes, of political change.

In examining Algeria, Tunisia, Egypt, and Morocco, Henry notes that any evidence for his argument can only be circumstantial at present because these countries have only very recently engaged in financial reform. The best evidence thus far is that the rulers anticipated potential countervailing centers of power in their respective business communities and either suppressed them (Tunisia and Egypt) or invested in them (Morocco). Henry still argues that the financial reform process is bound to continue, given North Africa's relationships with the international financial community, and that it will render the survival of its patrimonial regimes in their present form ever more problematic. He sees a major role for Islamic financial institutions in Egypt and possibly Algeria if the respective regimes decide to be more accommodating politically instead of destroying their mainstream Islamist opposition.

The book concludes with an analysis of "The International Politics of Democracy in North Africa" by I. Wiliam Zartman. According to the author, democracy is, by definition, self-reliance; and unlike other forms of government, it would seem to exclude international cooperation in its own support. However, democratic movements and governments have long cooperated with one another, and more recently notions of inherent democratic cooperation have encouraged the internationalization of self-rule. This is occurring at a time when North Africa is feeling the effects of two related waves of democratization and of political Islamization.

These waves tend to come in cycles. The beginnings of the democracy movement in North Africa took the form of a nationalist movement for independence, which promoted self-determination and self-government without specifying any particular content to the idea. Nationalist movements in the region cooperated to free their countries from foreign rule. But in the ensuing decades, self-government never went beyond the idea of government by nations of the country to an indication of criteria for government or procedures for choosing the governors. As the state grew in importance, dissatisfaction with the performance of the governors grew. The result now is a movement that specifies substantive criteria for proper government—the Islamist movement—and a movement that specifies procedures for involving the governed in the choice of governors—the democracy movement.

The resulting, potentially triangular conflict amounts, in fact, to two groups with their own international politics—the governments of North Africa and the Islamic movements, since the weak secular opposition parties have few international ties. The Islamic movements are each national products but have developed their own international politics of support, often reaching out to the same sources as the governments themselves. An interesting case was presented by the second Gulf war, where both governments and movements gave support to Iraq in different ways. The complicated arrangements on internal security policy are even more striking. There, the efforts of the governments to keep their Islamic extremists under control was a major motive in the creation of the Arab Maghreb Union in 1989 and security cooperation has continued. However, Morocco and Algeria have dropped their cooperation, again over the issue of state security relations, while Algeria and Tunisia, along with Egypt and Europe, maintain close security cooperation. On the Islamist side, data are much harder to come by, but arms supplies work their way from Iran, in particular, across Europe into Algeria.

Zartman concludes that, in a paradoxical way, the various pressures have increased pressure for democratization and have both increased inter-Maghrebi cooperation and been subordinate to inter-Maghrebi rivalries. Democratization takes many forms and has many effects, and it both drives international politics in the region and is subject to it.

References

Haggard, Stephan, and Robert R. Kaufman. 1995. *The Political Economy of Democratic Transitions.* Princeton: Princeton University Press.

Henry, Clement M. 1996. *The Mediterranean Debt Crescent: Money and Power in Algeria, Egypt, Morocco, Tunisia, and Turkey.* Gainesville: University Press of Florida.

Islam, Democracy, and the State in North Africa

1.

Sultans, Saints, and Presidents

The Islamic Community and the State in North Africa

JOHN O. VOLL

Crisis of Authoritarianism

A real crisis of authoritarianism exists in North Africa. Established regimes have been challenged and overthrown. The one-party state of the National Liberation Front (FLN) in Algeria is no more, and the secularist Neo-Destour state of Habib Bourguiba in Tunisia has ended. These authoritarian state systems have been replaced by relatively authoritarian military-based regimes that are unwilling to allow comprehensive, free, and open elections. Ironically, at least in the logic of older modernization theories, only in Morocco, with its sultan-king, is the political system the same as it was when modern independence was achieved. The vanguard radical party and the liberal secular presidency are no more. This is a time of epochal conflict and change.

The current conflicts are not simply struggles over tactics or strategies, or over the merits of varying paths to a shared goal of modernization. They are, in fact, struggles over the very concepts and perceptions of political life and the modes of conceptualizing polity and society. The revolutions underway now are struggles not for control over existing institutions so much as they are struggles to create whole new sociopolitical worldviews and polities.

The contemporary developments in North Africa are not isolated incidents or unique experiences. They are part of a broader global transformation that has been too glibly and too simply referred to as the emergence of a "new world order." The world is in the midst of transformations, and the intellectual methods and disciplines used to understand those transformations are in a state of flux. Scholars in the social sciences and humanities are working to understand and often to reconceptualize their understanding of what is happening in the world. This is reflected in the discussions of North African events as well as in presentations dealing with other parts of the globe.

Religion and the Modern World: A Reassessment

Some of the important dimensions of these changes involve the understanding of religion and its relationship to the modern (and post-modern) experience. Much of the research in the sociology of religion twenty and thirty years ago concentrated on defining what society would be like when religion inevitably disappeared. Looking back at a major symposium on the sociology of religion that had been held in 1970, scholars noted in 1979 that "much of the literature assessed there pointed to the declining importance of religion itself in secular society" (Long and Hadden 1979: 280).[1] However, by the early 1980s it was possible for a prominent sociologist of religion, Peter Berger, to write an analysis entitled "From the Crisis of Religion to the Crisis of Secularity" (Berger 1983). There has been a major shift in the issues that have to be dealt with, from analysis of the prospects of a "religion-less" society to an explanation of why religion continues to be such a powerful force in human affairs at the end of the twentieth century.

In the study of areas such as the Middle East and North Africa, the validity of many of the old accepted generalizations is now weakened or has been denied by developments. It is necessary to rethink and reconceptualize the basic nature of the processes of modernization and the dynamics of modern history. Religion is not fading away as a result of modernization. Just as the end of the Soviet Union did not mean the end of history, the so-called triumph of secularism as the world modernized has not meant the end of religion.

Even the basic units of world operations are being transformed. In 1945, the organization of the main actors on the global scene was an organization of actor-units that were similar in type. They could be brought together in a single organization, the United Nations, which was actually misnamed since it was an organization of states not nations. The major actors on the global scene were states; and the basic issues of politics, economics, religion, authority, and authoritarianism/democracy were viewed within the framework of the state structures which existed at that time.

In the present world of the rapidly changing Commonwealth of Independent States in the former Soviet Union, in the world of the former Yugoslavia, in the world of the mixture of old and new in the emerging European Community, and in the context of many other major political changes, the meaning and significance of "the state" has become a subject of serious debate. The disintegration of state structures that took place in Somalia, the various mixtures of majority and minority statuses in the regions of the former Yugoslavia, and other complex developments show that there are many different kinds of organizations, groups, and basic units that have significance. At a time when the main outlines of Marshall McLuhan's global village are finally becoming clearer in terms of electronic communications, ever-smaller identity groups—Bosnian Muslims, Somali clans, provincial language groups in France, among others—forcefully assert their right to some kind of separate existence. It is a time, in other words, when the basic natures of fundamental units and identities are being reconsidered, and it has been a long time since a reconsideration of such magnitude has taken place.

The basic units for analysis in political science and in history (in terms of global affairs) at the end of World War I and at the end of World War II were basically the same: the nation-state. To see a reordering of Western political thought similar to the present situation, one might have to look back as far as the reconceptualization of European international politics which took place in the years following the French Revolution and the era of Napoleon. Therefore, if we are going to be considering the crisis of authoritarianism in North Africa, we have to be willing to consider the possibility that there are a variety of authorities whose authoritarian position is being challenged, and that it is not just simply the old-fashioned, territorially sovereign nation-state which represents a conceptual unit that should be the basis of analysis. We have sultans, and saints, and presidents; we have an Islamic community (or Islamic communities) which may or may not necessarily be the same thing as nations or nation-states; and the global Islamic community is clearly not politically sovereign.

Clash of Worldviews

What we have is a battle of worldviews. We have a problem of definition. In more current terminology (or jargon), we face the challenges of trying to identify and then define the "hegemonic discourses" involved. It should be noted that these changing efforts to provide the dominant set of definitions exist both in the political power struggles of the region and in the scholarly debates describing those struggles. The crisis is not only one of trying to decide which group will control existing structures; the battle is to decide which worldview will define the fundamental structures of the social and political order.

The crisis has arisen because some authoritarian political regimes and their worldviews have failed in North Africa. However, it is essential to remember that the authoritarian regimes that have most visibly failed in recent years are not "traditional" ancient regimes. The authoritarianism that has failed is not the authoritarianism of traditional society. The authoritarianism that has failed is that of the regimes which are the products of the modernization of North African states that followed major Western models. It is, therefore, *Western* authoritarianism that is in crisis in North Africa.

To be specific, the Tunisian experience has shown that there can be such a thing as a liberal secularist authoritarian regime. Liberal secularist authoritarianism failed in Tunisia under Bourguiba. Radical secularist authoritarianism, on the one party/vanguard model, failed in Algeria. There is a crisis, but not a failure, in the more traditionally based political structure of monarchical authoritarianism in Morocco. Ironically, the state structure that one currently hears least about in terms of its being in a state of crisis is the *Jamahiriyyah* in Libya. This is the state we were assured was on the verge of collapse in the mid-1980s, especially since Ronald Reagan's policy of confrontation and attack was said to be undermining the ability of Muammar Qaddafi's regime to survive for any significant length of time.

There are important problems in perceiving the nature of this crisis of authoritarianism. The struggle is over the very concepts of political life and the way that people, both participants and scholars, think about society and polity. This is both a crisis in the politics of the region as well as for all political scientists and historians who deal with the area. Analysts in the West and in the Middle East and North Africa have real difficulties in coping with what has happened, especially in Algeria and Tunisia.

Algeria and Tunisia were model cases for the secular, social, scientific interpretation of the processes of modernization. There are important key similarities. They were relatively secular in orientation and they used religion only when it was necessary—for providing certain slogans of authenticity and for public relations. However, if one looks at the historiography of modernization in Tunisia and Algeria, there is an interesting contrast in the views of Bourguiba's Tunisia and the FLN's Algeria in the 1960s. Tunisia was the favorite of American modernization analysts. Bourguiba did everything that everybody said a leader should do if he was going to get it right as a liberal secularist. He was gradualist; he was not revolutionary. He was willing to compromise. He was even willing in the mid-sixties, under certain conditions, to have Tunisia engage in discourse with Israel. He worked in a variety of ways that made him a positive case study for liberal modernization. In describing the situation in Tunis in 1963, one of the best-informed American analysts observed that "political stability remains Tunisia's greatest asset and may provide the basis for development by relatively democratic methods of persuasion in an atmosphere of broad consensus. Tunisia has successfully channeled the nationalist enthusiasm for independence into a functioning concern for modernization" (Moore 1963: 40). From the perspective of the late 1980s, the remarkable development was that the result of the liberal secularist program of modernization was authoritarianism and failure.

The analyst committed to the virtues of liberalism and of secularism is thus forced to adopt a revisionism which says that Bourguiba really was not a gradualist or a liberal secularist or that he was not as effectively modern as he appeared to be. The alternative is to propose a very different conclusion, which accepts the possibility that liberal secularism may lead to authoritarian regimes. While some in the 1960s used to speak of the "authoritarian path to democracy" (see, e.g., Halpern 1963: 223–34), by the 1990s it is possible for others to speak of the liberal secular path to authoritarian autocracy. This situation means a challenge not just to the authority of liberal secular regimes but also to the authority of the liberal and secularist assumptions of scholars who saw such regimes as models for the appropriate mode of modernization in the second half of the twentieth century.

Algeria has some of the same characteristics, but it was favored by Western radicals and by a leftist interpretation. An effective and successful national liberation revolution took place in Algeria, and many analysts saw this as an advantage in building the "national" cohesion which was thought to be necessary for successful "nation-building" (viewed as the desirable goal in the 1960s). In the context of this revolution, for example, one scholar could write in 1963 that "partly because Algeria *in extremis* may have required a kind of positive nihilism, the Algerian motivation today is proudly anti-traditional, anti-intellectual, and anti-bourgeois. . . . What is clear is that 'proletarian-ization' offers greater possibilities for future mobility in political action and in breaking with tradition than is found in more stratified nationalist hierarchies. . . . Algeria gives every indication of becoming the most experi-mental, radical, and open-ended Arab sub-society in existence" (Gallagher 1963: 227–28). Algeria had a sound revolutionary base; it had a socialist orientation; it was in many ways, at least in the Middle East, the best-case scenario for the radical option of modernization. And it also produced an authoritarian failure.

It is not important to try to find the errors and mistakes of scholars who wrote two or three decades ago. Despite the assertions of some positivist social scientists, the social sciences are not predictive sciences, and political scientists and historians cannot predict an eclipse of governmental systems in the same way that astronomers can predict an eclipse of the sun. However, it is important to look at the foundations and assumptions of past analyses as a way of seeing how perspectives change and, perhaps, of learning the limita-tions of analysis. One might profit from looking at some of the best analyses of the late 1960s. In some cases, the predictions may have been wrong but the analysis provides important perceptions of the nature of the emerging polities. One such important and perceptive study is Elbaki Hermassi's book, *Leadership and National Development in North Africa,* which was ultimately published in 1972.

Hermassi looked at the three major North African states and in his conclusion clearly identified the three different approaches that characterized the elites of the political systems in Morocco, Algeria, and Tunisia. He said, if "the history of nations [were] determined only by ideational orientation, we would be tempted to say that the scripturalist orientation has predominated in Morocco, the gradualist orientation in Tunisia, and the mobilizational has triumphed in Algeria" (Hermassi 1972: 98). In the late 1960s, in the context of the time, the conditions in those three countries were such as to lead Hermassi to distinguish between those regimes that were capable of high levels of mobilization for development and those that were not. Algeria and Tunisia, in this analysis, were the most effective in this regard. He stated that it is "possible at this point to rank Maghrebi regimes, though schematically, in terms of political institutionalization, on the one hand, and economic productivity and welfare allocation, on the other. It is clear from the evidence presented that the Tunisian political system has so far displayed the greatest effectiveness" (Hermassi 1972: 211).

The conservative-scripturalist approach of the monarchy in Morocco, in this analysis, leads to short-term stability because it is obtained at the price of handing modernization projects over to the Minister of Interior (i.e., the person who controls the secret police), "for whom political considerations override economic exigencies" and the Moroccan "political system exhausts its energy in mediation and neutralization rather than devoting them to mobilization and change" (Hermassi 1972: 209). As a comparative conclusion, Hermassi stated: "If our hypothesis that legitimacy depends as much upon institutions as upon performance has any validity, we would expect the Moroccan monarchy, in view of its poor achievements in economic growth and welfare, to suffer diminishing legitimate authority. And we would expect that there would be increasing acceptance of the governmental authority of the Algerian regime" (Hermassi 1972: 211).

In the late 1960s, most scholars were convinced that programs of rapid mobilization and change were needed and that conservative programs of mediation and neutralization obstructed modernization and reflected weak political systems. Looking back with the advantage of hindsight, we can see that in a real sense the failures of the regimes in Algeria and Tunisia represent failures of the mobilization model. In addition, the failure of these regimes is also a failure of interpretation and theory as well as a failure of elites and political institutions. Conversely, the continued prestige of the monarchy in Morocco represents an affirmation of the positive effect on political stability and survival of rule through programs of mediation and neutralization.

The Democratic Revolution

A second dimension of perceiving the crisis of authoritarianism again involves analytical perceptions as well as the actual political experiences in Rabat, Algiers, and Tunis. This dimension consists of the global and regional experiences of contemporary democratization. Implied in the notions of authoritarian crisis and democratic transition is an opposition between authoritarianism and democratization—or perhaps better, "democratizationism." The presumed crisis of authoritarian regimes is that they are being challenged by prodemocracy groups and movements. Authoritarian regimes around the globe have come under attack from prodemocracy groups and many have fallen. The list includes the regimes of Eastern Europe and of the former Soviet Union. Samuel P. Huntington speaks of the great wave of democratization which occurred between 1974 and 1990 in what was "perhaps the most important global political development of the late twentieth century: the transition of some thirty countries from nondemocratic to democratic political systems" (Huntington 1991b: xiii). There is a crisis of authoritarianism on a global scale.

In analyses of Middle Eastern and Islamic countries, however, the perspective adopted and issues raised are very different. Huntington argues that Islam creates special obstacles to democratization: "To the extent that governmental legitimacy and policy flow from religious doctrine and religious expertise, Islamic concepts of politics differ from and contradict the premises of democratic politics" (Huntington 1991a: 35). This position is shared in varying ways by a number of other scholars. Martin Kramer, a noted Israeli scholar who has written important studies of pan-Islamic movements and "political Islam," recently wrote: "In an era of democratization, these lands of Islam remain an anomaly—a zone of resistance to the ideals that have toppled authoritarian regimes of the left and the right" (Kramer 1993: 35). This perspective may pass over some important aspects of what is identified as the global development of democratization.

The crisis of authoritarianism and the overthrow of authoritarian regimes involves many different elements which have been lumped together under the label of "democratization." The toppling of authoritarian regimes of the left and the right, in this process, starts with the existence of an authoritarian regime with rigorous thought control backed by an efficient secret police, and then involves the challenging of that authoritarian regime by massive demonstrations receiving the support of the majority of the population. The result is the collapse or overthrow of the regime and the establishment of a new political system advocating the ideals supported by that majority. If this is what is involved in the toppling of authoritarian regimes, then one of the early major popular overthrows of an authoritarian regime (of the right) in the contemporary era took place within the Islamic world—in Iran. And if we are discussing massive demonstrations and popular democratic opposition to a one-party authoritarian regime of the left, we cannot ignore Algeria.

One distinctive aspect of Islamic populist opposition to authoritarian regimes at present is that these often well-organized movements continue to be willing to operate within the existing political system to promote the democratization process. This is within a context where the regimes being opposed are less authoritarian than the communist regimes of Eastern Europe and are more willing to make some compromises. The process of democratization assumes a different form under these conditions. Jordan provides an interesting example of a country in which activist Islamists challenged monarchical authoritarianism. This did not produce a revolution. Instead, it provided the impetus for the beginning of a democratization of the system in which the king opened the way for Islamic activist participation in elections and then within the resulting parliament. The reduction of authoritarianism does not have to be violent to be effective and the opening-up of monarchical authoritarianism to more democratic processes does not present a picture of a "zone of resistance" to democratic ideals.

Dr. Essam al-Iryani in Egypt reflects a similar evolution. He was one of the intellectual leaders of the militant, activist Islamic student movement in the 1970s. Gilles Kepel's major study of "Muslim extremism" in Egypt describes his radical ideology and portrays him as an important figure in that movement (Kepel 1986: 152–55). Today, al-Iryani does not wear a robe or a turban but remains a major Islamic fundamentalist leader: He is a former member of parliament, the executive director of the physicians' professional association in Egypt, and one of the pillars of the operating-inside-the-system Islamic oppositional establishment.[2] There has been a series of challenges to authoritarian regimes in the Islamic world. Where the authoritarian regimes have resisted democratization, there have been major pressures and tensions; but where the regimes have been flexible, there have been gradual openings of previously authoritarian systems. In other words, either by revolution or accommodation there has been some form of democratization in zones where scholars such as Kramer feel it cannot happen.

The Islamic Challenge

The crisis of authoritarianism in Middle Eastern and Islamic societies takes an unexpected form, however, because the vehicle for the challenge is not Western secular liberal democracy. The vehicle for the challenge is Islam. As we look at these analytical problems in the context of North Africa, what is the opposite of authoritarian and what is therefore the causal element creating the crisis of authoritarianism?

The major opponents of authoritarianism seemed relatively clear and understandable for American observers in Eastern Europe. Havel in Czechoslovakia was a liberal radical playwright opposing the government, and people living in New York could not fail to understand him. Americans had a similar empathy with Lech Walesa of Solidarity in Poland. The two were liberal and radical secular democrats. What they advocated was what Americans expected should come out of anti-authoritarian revolution: multiparty, constitutional, parliamentary government—that is, something that looked like the political system in the United States or Great Britain. However, in North Africa, it is the variants of this very same Western set of models which are part of the crisis itself. This model, in both Bourguibism and "FLN-ism," can be seen as the starting point for the authoritarian regime—there is thus little appeal for advocating a repetition of the past. If opposed to the authoritarianism that the FLN created, why would one want to create a new FLN? If opposed to the authoritarianism that Bourguiba created, why would one want to bring to power another Bourguiba?

There are other options, which include holding open democratic elections and not utilizing the limitations of the systems of Bourguiba and the FLN. However, when this course was adopted in Algeria, it became clear that there was/is a popular viewpoint for an alternative to the existing FLN authoritarianism. The majority—in free and open elections—supported a distinctive alternative, but the Western world supported suspension of those elections. This was because the elections would have brought to power Muslim fundamentalists who would not be playing the game of politics the way the Western powers wanted them to play it. This means that in Algeria, as in other Muslim areas, the Western powers joined with authoritarian and semi-authoritarian leaders in supporting what John L. Esposito refers to as "risk-free democracy" in which "opposition parties and groups are tolerated as long as they remain relatively weak or under government control and do not threaten" the ruling group (Esposito 1992: 187). Virtually no one opposes free and open elections if they are sure that they will always win such elections. But democracy is never "risk free." Somebody that you do not like might get elected and, in fact, the ability of such people to win elections represents, in the minds of many people, the most important characteristic of proper democracy.

This situation creates a dilemma. True anti-authoritarianism in the view of the secular scholars and the leaders of the states necessarily involves either a process which would bring to power people and groups that they do not like or the creation of a continuing authoritarianism in order to oppose a potential new authoritarianism. This contradiction in the support for "risk-free democracy" is at the heart of the real crisis of authoritarianism in North Africa. This crisis involves a major struggle and a very significant transition in the whole polity. "The Crisis of Authoritarianism" involves the transition to battle over the fundamental definition of goals; even more, it is a battle to determine the very terms and concepts in which those goals are going to be expressed.

"Democracy" is a good example: How will democracy be defined and in what terms? Democracy is an "essentially contestable concept," that is, it is possible and inevitable that there will be a contest over the definition of the essence of the concept. "It is an inherently debatable and changeable idea. Like 'freedom', 'equality', 'justice', 'human rights', and so forth, 'democracy' is a term which, whatever its precise meaning, will always signify for many a cherished political principle or ideal, and for that reason alone it is never likely to achieve a single agreed meaning" (Arblaster 1987: 5). There is a matter of controversy because there is no necessary agreement on the essence of the concept of democracy.

This is not a struggle over tactics or strategy. It is not a struggle over gradualism versus revolution. It is not a struggle over "White Revolution" versus "Red Revolution." It *is* a fundamental struggle over the concepts and words to be used even in the debates. There is a distinctive dimension to this struggle as it takes place in North Africa, because there is a significant source of discourse that is independent of Voltaire and de Tocqueville and the Western European tradition. The Islamic tradition of political and social community and Islamic articulation of concepts and identities does not necessarily depend on what happened in Paris in 1789 or in England under the rule of King John. Islam provides a broad set of concepts for discourse that can go beyond the old European and North American models.

The Political Language of Islam

In thinking about democratization on a global scale, it is very important to go beyond the limits of the conceptual lexicon of the Western European political canon. In the North African contest, for example, it is important to remember that there are sultans and saints as well as presidents. In discussions of concepts, we are always limited by the constraints of translations and perceptions. "Sultan," for example, is not simply a direct cognate term for "king." When you say "sultan" in Rabat or in Fez, you are using a term that has a whole series of historical and cultural resonances that "king" does not possess. The relationship between the expectations involved in the utilization of these two terms defines important dimensions of the transitions taking place in North Africa.

The Arabic term used as the translation of "king" in modern Arab political discourse is *malik*, a term which has historic negative connotations. It involves a sense of personal ownership or property. In the first centuries of Islam, this title was used as an accusation against Muawiyah (ruled 661–80), the founder of the great Umayyad dynasty. He was said to have transformed the nature of leadership of the Islamic community from the true "successorship" to the Prophet, recognized by the title of *khalifah* ("caliph"), into "kingship." In the early Islamic community, malik "came to connote the temporal, mundane facet of government—the antithesis of khalifah and imam which signified piety and righteousness. The Umayyads were termed *muluk* [plural of malik] . . . by their opponents, who thus expressed disdain for an irreligious and worldly-minded government" (Ayalon 1987: 261; see also B. Lewis 1988: 53–56).[3] There was some use of the title by rulers in later medieval Islamic states, but it ceased to be of political importance until the first half of the twentieth century. At that time, dynastic rulers adopted the title as a direct translation of "king," as a way of indicating their adoption of European-style rule. In the 1920s and 1930s, a number of "kingdoms" were created. In the 1950s, the title "king" was taken by the leader of the newly created independent state of Libya.

In the Maghreb, the head of state in Morocco is now a "king." Under the French Protectorate (1912–1956), the title "sultan" had been retained for the traditional head of state. However, in the 1930s, Sultan Muhammad ben Yusuf became involved in the nationalist movement. After that, the modern-oriented nationalists rejected the title "sultan" "as lacking in modernity, replacing it in their slogans by the title of 'King' (malik)" (Waterbury 1970: 53). Following independence, Muhammad ben Yusuf formally assumed the title "king." Because of his traditional charisma as sultan and his special role as a catalyst and focus for nationalist mobilization in the 1950s, Muhammad V was the "one leader whose title to rule rested on sufficiently diverse mod-ern and traditional groups to satisfy all sectors of the heterogenous elite. . . . Morocco is unique in the Middle East and North Africa in that the struggle for independence centered around the capture, revival, and renovation of a traditional institution, the monarchy" (Entelis 1980: 35). This renovation involved the combination of the concepts of "king" and "sultan" as the identification of the head of the Moroccan polity. Without both of these dimensions, Kings/Sultans Muhammad V and his son, Hassan II, would have been less able to rule. However, for our purposes, it is essential to remember that these role-describing and role-perceiving concepts represent different dimensions of political power. For the modernized elite, Hassan II may be a king, but for the more traditional masses, the fact that he is also conceived in more historically Islamic and Moroccan terms provides an added dimension of support. It also adds a dimension of expectations that set Hassan II apart from European monarchs.

There is a similar importance in recognizing the conceptualizations that are involved in the leadership of non-monarchical systems in North Africa. Just as many people in Western Europe and North America have a different definition for the term "king" than people in Morocco, so also the meaning of "president" is complex. What do we think we are saying when we use the word "president," and is it the same thing that a Tunisian means when he or she uses the word *rais*? Does someone in the United States conceive of the term "president" in a way that makes it possible to use the phrase "president-for-life"? For most people in America the term "president" assumes that the holder of the office stands for election and has the possibility of losing his office. A president without a continuing electoral process is not within the political conceptual framework of most people in the United States. In Western political traditions, if someone holds the office of the chief executive "for life," he has a title that is different from "president." However, in Tunisia, Bourguiba *was* "president-for-life" and many did not see this as a contradictory concept. The term "rais" is not a simple Arabic equivalent for "president." Rais was applied traditionally to a person in a leadership position as the head of a group. It is linguistically related to the anatomical word for "head." While for some, it may be difficult to understand the concept of "president-for-life," the concept of a rais-for-life is credible. It is within this framework that one does not expect a state led by a president, using the conceptualization common in the United States, to become authoritarian; but a rais-led state might have authoritarian tendencies contained within the leadership concept itself.

Algeria also presents an interesting picture of multiple dimensions for leadership concepts coming out of its early experience of independence. The FLN created a modern one-party political system which also had a president and a cabinet form of government. However, it was observed very early on that the leader of the new state functioned as a *zaim* as well as a president. One scholar wrote in 1963, for example, that it is "one of the major ironies of the Algerian revolution that . . . the seven and one-half year conflict should come to an end bringing to power a zaim. The Arab concept of zaim embraces all of the qualities of a chieftain, a leader and father of the people" (W. H. Lewis 1963: 22). It is interesting that another scholar noted that the option of acting as a zaim, that is, as an active, charismatic "great leader," was open to the king/sultan in Morocco at this same time, but both Muhammad V and Hassan II chose instead to emphasize the role of the leader as arbitrator: "The [Moroccan] monarchy has used its power and authority for defense and has avoided bold initiatives. All the elements are present, however, to enable the king to adopt the role of zaim. . . . But the king has rejected the role of national leader. . . . Arbiter is the more familiar role" (Waterbury 1970: 155). In Algeria, the FLN leaders who were presidents, beginning with Ahmed Ben Bella and then Houari Boumedienne, became president-zaims with the potential and then the actuality of an authoritarian one-party state.

The conceptual resources of the Islamic political traditions in North Africa, then, contain a variety of concepts. There are both hybrid concepts such as the modern rais-president and there are more clearly traditional leadership conceptualizations. In this latter category there is the sultan who is the military umpire and honest arbiter in a segmented society, the "commander of the faithful." The current dynasty in Morocco came to power in the mid-seventeenth century at a time of anarchic crisis and represented an effective alternative to chaos. It provided coordination and mediation in a divided society. Now, it may be that the function of mediation and neutralization that Hermassi viewed as a weakness in the leadership mode of the monarchy in Morocco in the late 1960s was an important survival strategy that was contained within the Islamic community discourse. It may have appeared inappropriate if the effort was to create a territorially sovereign nation-state along a secular Algerian or Tunisian model. But the concept of a controlling, coordinating center in a segmented society is the key in this sense. A sultan is probably more effective than a dictator, and may be better than a rais or zaim.

There is also the leadership concept of the "saint." The saint represents an interesting option because the saint, as a leadership type, may be more easily transferable into the modern context than the pure "sultan." There is a powerful tradition of teachers with special charisma who created communities around them. These may or may not have had political or economic foundations, but clearly in the long run these communities had political and economic implications. Under certain circumstances, the pious leaders who led the devotional life of a group of followers would also step forward in times of political crisis to lead various types of revolutions. But even though the pious spiritual leader (and ultimately, revolutionary) who led the Algerian opposition to the French in the 1830s was successful in organizing opposition, saints generally have not been exceptionally effective in organizing large-scale political structures, especially when they have done it alone. The first, and only, king of Libya, for example, created an ineffective monarchy on what had been an effective spiritual base from the nineteenth century, the Sanusi order.

However, the tradition of informed political spiritual guides is a strong one which has reflections in the modern Islamic world. It is not unique to North Africa. However, most of the time, these spiritual guides have been most effective when they have been in the position of giving pious advice to strong military leaders. The foundation of the Saudi monarchy is such a dual framework. The great fundamentalist teacher of the eighteenth century, Muhammad ibn Abd al-Wahhab, did not become the "commander of the faithful." He became the spiritual guide to the "commander of the faithful." The current kings, who have remarkably few theological pretensions, are the

descendants of the commanders, not of the teachers. This is the model not
just in the Sunni world, but it is also the model identified and chosen in the
Shii political system as defined by the Ayatollah Khomeini. The Ayatollah
Khomeini was not the president of the Islamic republic and he was not the
prime minister—he was the spiritual guide of the republic. This type of
structure is most visible at present in the Sudan, where a military leader who
took over the government in 1989 had a certain amount of enthusiasm for
Islamic solutions, but no content for them. This content was provided by the
leader of the National Islamic Front, Dr. Hasan al-Turabi, who has no formal
position in the government but is reputed to be its major leader in the
country.

This tradition of powerful intellectual and spiritual guides fits into a pattern
that is familiar in North Africa, even though it seems rather strange to Western
social scientists looking at it. In Tunisia Rachid al-Ghannouchi looks like he
could fill this role to a certain extent.

Islamic Democracy?

In this context, Islamists provide at least one opportunity or one set of
opportunities for a new or different basis for discourse. In the writings of
Rachid al-Ghannouchi one finds an important substantive critique of the
modern Muslim experience. In his 1980 article, "Westernization and the
Inevitability of Dictatorship," he argues that in developing countries like
those in North Africa, where an elite speaks a different political language
from the masses, there will inevitably be an authoritarian dictator. In other
words, the processes of Westernization as experienced in North Africa in the
past century lead not to democracy but to authoritarianism. What is needed
in order to transcend that situation is a program that can bridge the gap
between the elite and the masses—and this can be provided by Islam.

Al-Ghannouchi does more, however, than simply say that "Islam is the
solution." People who criticize the Islamist movements in North Africa for
having no concrete program tend not to have read the works of people like al-
Ghannouchi very carefully. These groups offer programs that are at least as
specific and concrete as those offered by Bourguiba in the mid-1950s.
However, the battle at present is not over specific programs or particular
policies; it is to determine the basis for political discourse for the next
generation. In this struggle, the Islamists provide a clearly comprehensive
vocabulary and set of conceptualizations for later use in promulgating specific
policies and programs. They are an opposition that has a broad and comprehensive basis for discourse, for argumentation, and for developing programs.
In that framework, al-Ghannouchi's observations—for example, of the inevitability of dictatorship in the context of Westernizing modernization—

provide a way of mediating between large-scale political structures that can operate in the contemporary world and create ties to broader masses. They may even provide a viable path out of the current crisis of authoritarianism and toward a political system which involves a higher sense of popular participation.

There is a crisis of authoritarianism in North Africa. It represents the Maghrebi version of the late twentieth-century struggles, visible throughout the globe, for increased popular participation in the political system. However, those authoritarian regimes overthrown in recent years in North Africa have not been traditional autocracies or communist police states. Rather, the authoritarian regimes which had emerged in Algeria and Tunisia by the 1980s were the products of the liberal and radical Western programs of modernization. The development of such authoritarian regimes in relatively secular, Westernizing regimes creates a special problem both for political leaders and for Western analysts. The simple solutions offered to the anti-authoritarian revolutionaries of Eastern Europe, the former Soviet Union, and Latin America have little appeal to the majorities in the Maghreb states, since the call to create Western-style secular states is a call to repeat the experience that led to the authoritarian regimes. Liberal secularism has little appeal even in principle and lacks a sense of authentic legitimacy for many in the Middle East and North Africa.

At the moment we are seeing an epochal transition. The current conflicts are no longer simply over tactics or various strategies of modernization. There is now a struggle for control of the very concepts of political life, for control of the way people think about politics, and the way that we can talk about polity and society. What we are seeing now in this crisis of authoritarianism is the battle for hegemony over discourse. If you can control the words, you can control the polity.

Notes

1. Long and Hadden, 1979: 280. The papers of the symposium appeared in *Sociological Analysis* 31, nos. 3–4 (Fall and Winter 1970).

2. This portrayal is based on an interview with Dr. al-Iryani in January 1993, but his status in the doctor's syndicate has changed as a result of an increasingly repressive policy of the Egyptian government with regard to all of the Islamic groups, whether extremist or moderate.

3. Ayalon 1987: 6: 261. This article is an important source for the discussion of the history of the term's usage. See also the discussion in B. Lewis 1988: 53–56.

References

Arblaster, Anthony. 1987. *Democracy.* Minneapolis: University of Minnesota Press.

Ayalon, A. 1987. "Malik." *Encyclopaedia of Islam* 6.

Berger, Peter L. 1983. "From the Crisis of Religion to the Crisis of Secularity." In Mary Douglas and Steven Tipton, eds., *Religion and America: Spiritual Life in a Secular Age.* Boston: Beacon.

Entelis, John P. 1980. *Comparative Politics of North Africa.* Syracuse: Syracuse University Press.

Esposito, John L. 1992. *The Islamic Threat: Myth or Reality?* New York: Oxford University Press.

Gallagher, Charles F. 1963. "Language, Culture, and Ideology: The Arab World." In K. H. Silvert, ed., *Expectant Peoples: Nationalism and Development.* New York: Vintage.

Ghannouchi, Rachid al-. 1988. "Al-Taghrib wa hatimiyyah al-diktaturiyyah." Reprinted in *Maqallat,* part 1. 2nd ed. Tunis: Matbaah Tunis Qartaj.

Halpern, Manfred. 1963. *The Politics of Social Change in the Middle East and North Africa.* Princeton: Princeton University Press.

Hermassi, Elbaki. 1972. *Leadership and National Development in North Africa: A Comparative Study.* Berkeley: University of California Press.

Huntington, Samuel P. 1991a. "A New Era in Democracy: Democracy's Third Wave." *Current,* no. 335 (September). (Reprinted from *Journal of Democracy* [Spring 1991].)

———. 1991b. *The Third Wave: Democratization in the Late Twentieth Century.* Norman: University of Oklahoma Press.

Kepel, Gilles. 1986. *Muslim Extremism in Egypt: The Prophet and Pharaoh.* Trans. Jon Rothschild. Berkeley: University of California Press.

Kramer, Martin. 1993. "Islam vs. Democracy." *Commentary* 95, no. 1 (January).

Lewis, Bernard. 1988. *The Political Language of Islam.* Chicago: University of Chicago Press.

Lewis, William H. 1963. "Algeria: The Plight of the Victor." *Current History* 44, no. 257 (January).

Long, Theodore E., and Jeffrey K. Hadden. 1979. "Sects, Cults and Religious Movements." *Sociological Analysis* 40, no. 4 (Winter).

McLuhan, Marshall, and Bruce R. Powers. 1989. *The Global Village: Transformations in World Life and Media in the 21st Century.* New York: Oxford University Press.

Moore, Clement Henry. 1963. "'Bourguibism' in Tunisia." *Current History* 44, no. 257 (January).

Waterbury, John. 1970. *The Commander of the Faithful: The Moroccan Political Elite—Study in Segmented Politics.* New York: Columbia University Press.

2.

Muslim Politics

The Prospects for Democracy
in North Africa and the Middle East

DALE F. EICKELMAN

Making "Islam" an Actor

Dan Quayle, who has never been accused of Islamic expertise, said in a May 1990 speech, "We have been surprised this past century by the rise of Communism, the rise of Nazism, and the rise of Islamic fundamentalism" (Quayle 1990: 5–6). The parallelism is staggering, but Quayle got one thing right: There is a powerful background understanding that makes "Islam," rather than its Muslim adherents, an actor on the stage of world history. It assumes that "Islam"—or what some people presume to be Islam—determines the identity and conduct of Muslims in a way that other world religions do not.[1]

These implicit assumptions last came to the fore during the crisis that culminated in the resignation of Algeria's President Chadli Benjedid on January 11, 1992, and the military's cancellation of elections the following day. Aware of the mounting crisis, the U.S. press opened its pages to op-ed columnists concerned with the policy implications of "political Islam." Paul Johnson (1991), for example, argued that "European civilization" is facing its "third major invasion" from the forces of Islam, which are concentrated in a 4,000-mile belt of tension running from North Africa to China. This invasion by demographic growth and labor migration is said to equal the threat posed by the expansion of Islam into Europe in the eighth century and the rise of the Ottoman Empire in the late sixteenth and seventeenth centuries. Like Samuel Huntington (1993b: 34), who writes of the "bloody borders" of the crescent-shaped Islamic bloc that extends from the bulge of Africa to central Asia, Johnson inexplicably excludes Southeast Asia, where half the world's Muslims live and where no such equivalent "threat" is apparent.

Johnson writes that in this vast arc, "Western style concepts" such as "democracy, personal freedoms, and the rule of law . . . are denied"—his use of the passive voice disguises who does the denying. Amos Perlmutter (1992) argued that "Islam, fundamentalist or otherwise," is incompatible with "liberal, human rights-oriented, Western-style, representative democracy," so that Islamic religious movements "should be stifled at birth." Those unsympathetic to Islam and Muslims are not the only ones to objectify Islam. Muslim leaders and intellectuals, such as Tunisia's exiled Rachid al-Ghannouchi (1992), also do so. In an essay entitled "Islam and Freedom Can Be Friends," he invoked such concepts as the role of "government in Islam," as if "Islam" prescribed a clear and timeless point of view.

Such objectifications of Islam as a religion and as a civilization permeate U.S. policy and public discourse. Huntington (1993b: 24–25) argues that "non-Western civilizations" have increasingly become political actors. Updating Arnold Toynbee's notion of civilizational traditions, Huntington sees "Islam" and "Confucianism" as antithetical to the West and suggests that the West develop strategies to pit one against the other. Toynbee, upon whom Huntington relies, identified twenty-one distinct civilizations, of which six survive today. A closer look at Toynbee might have cautioned Huntington against invoking the moralizing and stereotyped historicism of an earlier generation. Toynbee writes, for instance, that the Ottomans (Osmanlis) failed as a civilization because "they achieved their astonishing triumphs by . . . assuming an animal nature [and] limiting their minds to the 'single-track' action of instinct." Consequently he relegated them to the category of "arrested" civilizations, which also included Polynesians, Eskimos, Nomads [*sic*], and Spartans (Toynbee 1947: 566–67).

The apparent simplicity of formulations such as Toynbee's and Huntington's encourages representations of "other" religions and civilizations as timeless essences, much as did the Orientalism of an earlier generation. In this respect, Huntington's crisp "West versus Rest" formula is as deceptive in its Manichean simplicity as Daniel Lerner's "Mecca or mechanization" (Lerner 1964: 405). This "essentializing" of civilizational traditions deflects attention from their internal and historical variations and from the vigorous internal debate among their carriers.

Nonetheless, Huntington's formulation reintroduces the concept of culture—albeit a dated and deeply flawed one—to the study of foreign policy and international relations and underscores that nation-states are no longer the sole pole of identity in politics. Civilizations, however, do not act on the human stage. The actors are the carriers of civilizational traditions, and among them, even in societies labeled as "traditional"—or alternatively as populist—there is diversity and internal debate over the identification of key civilizational values, who is "authorized" to articulate them, and how they are implemented. As a result, civilizations, like cultures, are "contested, temporal, and emergent" (Clifford and Marcus 1986: 18).

The issue of contested cultures and civilizations is especially important in assessing the prospects for democracy in the Arab world. Essentializing formulations such as Huntington's are pernicious because they take attention away from the cultural dynamics of political change. Few people maintain that being Arab is incompatible with being democratic, but some readily impute antidemocratic sentiments to those who are Muslim. Sometimes this occurs because the measure of "democracy" is narrowly defined in a manner which privileges parts of the West. Seymour Martin Lipset (1994: 1) approvingly cites Schumpeter, defining democracy as "that institutional arrangement for arriving at political decisions in which individuals acquire the power to decide by means of a competitive struggle for the people's vote."[2] In this view, democracy is either present or absent. In contrast, Michael Hudson, a political scientist concerned primarily with the Middle East, stresses the transition to participatory rule more than formal institutional arrangements. Democracy, he writes, is not an "ideal condition but . . . a process through which the exercise of political power by regime and state becomes less arbitrary, exclusive, and authoritarian" (Hudson 1988: 157).

There is a middle ground between these two approaches to democracy, and it involves paying more attention to cultural understandings of authority and "just" rule than do either Hudson or Lipset. Rather than looking primarily at what have become the standard indicators of democratization—elections, the growing significance of private voluntary associations, and political pluralism—it focuses on the growth of democratic attitudes and popular understandings of "just" rule and governance. By this measure, bureaucracies and the military might continue to conduct themselves arbitrarily, but even the most arbitrary rule must legitimate itself in the language of democracy. To use a judicial analogy, there are many cases in which countries go through a halfway house on their way from the iron cage of unremitting authoritarianism to the freedom of democracy, which is the case in many Middle Eastern states today. But it is when a regime retains ultimate political control but allows some degree of press and political freedom that the demand for greater political freedom can and does rise up. In discussing Muslim—"particularly Arab"—notions of political authority, Lipset unfortunately confines himself to a string of authorities who assert that Islamic doctrines are "alien" to political freedom (Lipset 1994: 6). The result is to assume that Muslims, more than the followers of other religions, are guided by religious doctrines that inhibit their participation in democratic rule. But he does recognize the significance of organizational norms, including those inculcated by some former colonial regimes, in influencing the prospects for democratic rule (Lipset, Seong, and Torres 1993). Hudson (see Schumpeter 1950: 251) concentrates more on how to bring about democracy than on a formal definition; but he is likewise principally concerned with institutional arrangements rather than with changing cultural assumptions. It is for this reason that I focus on what we mean by "Muslim politics" and thus challenge the assumption that "Islam" is a principal factor inhibiting the growth of democracy.

In this essay I suggest how (1) "Muslim politics" can be defined without resorting to the "essentialist" definitions of an earlier era and without imputing to them a prescriptive content; (2) mass communication and mass higher education are reshaping the political imagination in the Middle East (which I will show with examples from Morocco, Jordan, and the Arabian peninsula); and (3) an alternative to the paradigmatic and intellectual shortcomings of a "West versus Rest" approach to U.S. understanding of "other" people's politics can be devised.

Muslim Politics

It is not necessary to claim that Muslims are more driven by dogma and belief to delineate a specifically "Muslim" politics than adherents of other world religious traditions. Politics are "Muslim" when they relate to a widely shared, although not doctrinally defined, tradition of ideas and practice. The awareness of participating in a world-wide religious movement empowers Muslims in France, Egypt, and elsewhere, encouraging them to call for social and political reforms. The November 1979 attack on the Great Mosque in Mecca and the 1981 assassination of Egypt's President Sadat show how some Islamic groups use violence to confront political authority; but the 1989 head scarf controversy in Creil, France, which was resolved temporarily by the state's remanding of the issue to local authorities in order to avoid provoking a major political crises, is also an example of Muslim politics. One French commentator (Kepel, cited in Tinco 1994) has gone so far as to say that the 1989 head scarf dispute in Creil was in retrospect a "Copernican revolution," signaling a shift among French Muslim militants from regarding France as a land of work opportunities (*terre de contrat*) in which they temporarily reside, to regarding it as a land of mission (*terre de mission*) in which they are permanently settled. Muslim groups calling for democratization in such countries as Jordan, Egypt, Tunisia, and Morocco indicate how Muslims as self-conscious religious actors use the instruments of existing political systems to magnify their political voice and intensify pressure for reform. State authorities inevitably see both forms of assertiveness as a challenge to official ideologies and control over policy.

Even when asserting universality, Muslim politics assume distinctly national and local forms, and these reflect considerable internal debate. The statements of the leaders of the Algerian Islamic Salvation Front (Front

Islamique du Salut, FIS), like those of political movements elsewhere, range from moderate to radical populism (see Al-Ahnaf, Botiveau, and Frégosi 1991), but this divergence is not unique to Islamic movements. Before the FIS was outlawed in March 1992, this internal debate was publicly sustained within and without the movement, although the FIS equated its political voice with Islam and legitimacy ("another form of democracy") and opposition to Western-dominated "democrats" (Difraoui 1994: 123–24).

A useful way of looking at politics, including Muslim politics, is to perceive it as the setting of boundaries between decisionmaking units in society and the enforceable rules for resolving jurisdictional disputes among them. Even when Muslim groups accept the existing political hierarchy, however, they do not necessarily acquiesce in existing boundaries. For instance, the religious authorities (*ulama*) in Egypt vigorously protested President Sadat's 1979 effort to liberalize family law—specifically, women's rights in marriage. They saw Sadat's efforts as an intrusion on their authority. Muslim politics, like politics elsewhere, involves a contest over the extent of state control—locating the boundaries of legitimate state and nonstate activity.

The idea of politics as "a struggle about people's imaginations" (Pekonen 1989: 132) is a corrective to some conventional thinking. The notion of politics as centered on power relations and "interests" does not take account of relations among individuals within a society or between societies that are based on what they think is right, just, or religiously ordained (Cerny 1990: 17–18). More broadly, politics can be conceived as cooperation in and contest over symbolic production (see, e.g., Geertz 1973: 193–233) and control of the institutions—formal and informal—which serve as the symbolic arbiters of society. Politics as Leviathan is thus decisively abandoned in favor of politics as symbol maker. Of course, this perspective involves understanding culture as contested, temporal, and emergent.[3]

Despite the fascination of Western commentators with "fundamentalist" Muslim discourse, there has been less attention paid to the rising tide of Muslim moderates responding to what they see as the bankruptcy of traditionalist religious discourse. A case in point is the unanticipated popularity of Muhammad Shahrur's 800-page *al-Kitab wa-l-Koran* [The Book and the Koran], which booksellers in Kuwait and Morocco claim is "worse than Rushdie" because the author (a Muslim) attacks the "classical" religious authorities whom they approve. Banned in Saudi Arabia and initially in Egypt—but with at least 10,000 clandestine photocopies in each of those countries and on the open market in Egypt since late 1993—and personally approved for circulation by Sultan Qabus of Oman, Shahrur's book and others like it can be seen, in opposition to populist street slogans that assert the "true" meaning of Islam, as experiments in capturing a new readership and in defining Islam as involving dialogue and interpretation (see Eickelman 1993).

Mass Higher Education and the
Political Imagination in the Arab World

An exclusive focus on religious activism deflects attention from the more profound changes taking place throughout Morocco, Egypt, Jordan, and other places in the Arab world. These changes are correlated with mass higher education and mass communication, factors which have begun to affect profoundly how people think about authority and responsibility in the domains of religion and politics.

Throughout the Arab world, mass higher education has expanded significantly since the 1960s. As elsewhere in Muslim majority states, it is reshaping conceptions of self, religion, nation, and politics. It is as significant as the introduction of printed books in sixteenth-century rural France. Ironically, however, we know more about literacy in medieval and premodern Europe than in the contemporary Muslim and Arab worlds. Many scholars have noted links between advanced education and religious activism, but the focus on extremism deflects attention from conceptual innovations and emerging networks for communication and action (see Eickelman 1992).

Religious activism in the political sphere, the claims of its adherents notwithstanding, is a distinctively modern phenomenon, and its supporters are principally the beneficiaries of mass higher education. Such education may be important in itself, but it also suggests basic transformations in ideas of what people accept as legitimate political authority.

For the most part, mass higher education is a recent development in the Middle East and North Africa. It began in earnest only in the 1950s, with Egypt's commitment to universal schooling following the 1952 revolution. By the 1970s, after large numbers of students began to complete the advanced educational cycles, its consequences could be more clearly discerned. The timing of educational expansion varies for other parts of the Middle East. Major educational expansion in Morocco began after independence in 1956, accelerated in the 1960s, and today almost matches the rate of population growth. From 1957 to 1992, university enrollment grew from 1,819 to 230,000 students (see fig. 2.1). Fifty times as many women are being educated today as in the early 1960s.

A complementary measure of change is the circulation of books and magazines. The Moroccan writer Mohammed Bennis recalls his student days in Fez in the 1970s, when the first "little" intellectual journals began to flourish in Arabic rather than in French, which had been the dominant language of the educated elite. In lectures and public meetings, students began to insist that teachers and their classmates express themselves in Arabic and not use French words in Arabic syntax when Arabic words and phrases were available.[4] The shift from French to Arabic and the growing enrollments

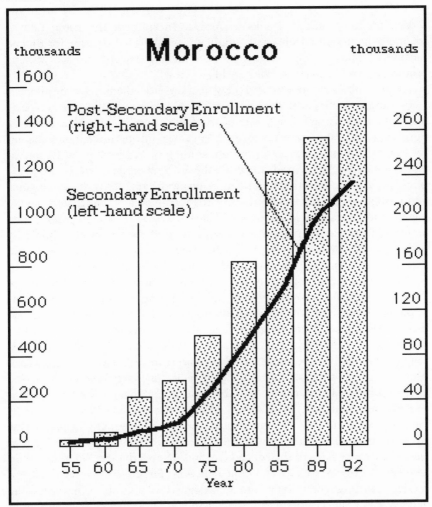

Fig. 2.1. Since mid-century, Moroccan secondary and post-secondary schooling, as in other Arab and Muslim countries, has become mass education. *Source*: Bennani 1992; World Bank 1981–92.

in higher education significantly increased participation in debates about politics, culture, and society. The intellectual effervescence of the 1970s that Bennis describes saw the emergence of the first cohort of Moroccans to acquire their pervasive "habits of thought" in Arabic, the country's national language (Bourdieu 1988). As elsewhere, pressure from this cohort created a demand for "re-imagining" Islam and politics and produced a significant readership for "quality" books in Arabic. In spite of the rising rate of unemployment among university graduates, reading has become for them a means of "appropriating," organizing, and making objective ideas of society, politics, and self (Chartier 1987: 6–11).

As a result, new books and new markets for them have developed, suggesting a sea change in the images and vocabulary that affect the prospects for political thinking. Egypt, one of the few countries for which there are figures on readership, provides an excellent case study of the changing market for books and magazines. Although studies of readership in Egypt, as elsewhere in the Arab world, are weak, the few that are available suggest that only 1 to 2 percent of the population reads books regularly. But discussions about books—by word of mouth, the broadcast media, or widely read news-papers and magazines (Gonzalez-Quijano 1994: 398–408)—reach much larger segments of the population. Even censors draw attention to books by banning them or attempting to restrict their circulation. The most rapid growth is occurring in publications with religious content, and the growth of secular mass education has thus increased attachment to Islamic culture. As Gonzalez-Quijano (1994: 159–60) explains, during the Nasser era in Egypt, religious books were of marginal importance, at least in terms of official production figures. With the opening of the book market in the 1970s, the relaxation of censorship controls, and subsidies from the oil-rich states, religious books became much more common. In recent years, books have become a part of mass culture in Egypt, and "products" intended for the consumption of a literary elite have become an endangered species.

Although "Mickey-Jîb" (Mickey Mouse) remains the best-seller, what Gonzalez-Quijano calls "Islamic books" are growing rapidly in popularity. These are inexpensive, attractively printed texts, accessible to a readership that lacks the literary skills of the educated cadres of an earlier era. They are often a breezy mix of oral style and colloquial diction. The covers take advantage of modern printing technologies and are designed to be both readily accessible and eye-catching. Unfortunately, the vivid colors of Shaykh Abd al-Hamid Kishk's *Ayyuha l-Muslimun, Ufiqu* (O Muslims, Awake, 1989) cannot be reproduced in figure 2.2. A Muslim with a bright blue beard is seated in front of a red-covered Koran on a table, shielding his eyes, as an orange and blue serpent above him is poised to strike. Other covers are reminiscent of pamphlets distributed by the Jehovah's Witnesses. Layla Mabruk's *Rihla ila alam al-khulud: adalat yawm al-qiyama* (A Trip to Eternity: Justice on Judgment Day, 1989) shows a weakened hand sticking out of a bright red pool, while above the title, encircled by a green garland and oblivious to the scene below, two Muslims pray. A Saudi pamphlet with a curious cover showing a bright red ball plunging into a well in an otherwise parched desert (fig. 2.3) explains that democracy, which is "creeping" (*tatasarrub*) into the

Muslim world, is incompatible with Islam—because while Islam offers governance by the Creator (*al-khaliq*), as understood by a properly instructed religious elite, democracy, a non-Arabic term, necessarily implies rule by the created (*al-makhluqin*), in which unbelievers and the ignorant have an equal say in governance and usurp God's rule (Sharif 1992: 16–18). In many parts of the Muslim world, including North Africa, this style of argument—in some respects a mirror image of Huntington's—is regarded with amusement by many; but it also offers a style of argument more accessible than that sustained by Muslim moderates such as Binsaid (1993), who argue for political pluralism in mainstream Arab print media.

Fig. 2.2. With its eye-catching cover, breezy, colloquial style, and focus on themes that concern many of the newly educated, Kishk's *O Muslims, Awake!* (1989) represents a new form of religious best-seller.

Fig. 2.3. Sharif's book, *The Truth about Democracy* (1992), although weak in argument and design, nonetheless addresses a theme that concerns many religiously minded Muslims. Its low price and wide distribution give it a significant audience.

Some authors experiment with the comic-book format, including stories from the Koran (e.g., Seddik 1989), published in the month of Ramadan and intended principally for French-speaking European Muslims. A citation from Surat Yusif (12:3), "Thanks to the Koran, we will relate to you the most beautiful of stories," appears in Arabic and French on the back cover as a means of legitimating the enterprise, as does the claim that the book is based on the established authorities in the Koranic sciences (Seddik 1989: 3). The price of such a work, together with the North European physiognomies of heroes and villains (drawn by European artists), suggests the technical and representational tensions implicit in what Douglas and Malti–Douglas (1994: 109) call the "stripification" of Islamic themes and the Arab world. Tunisia's Higher Council of Ulama banned the book and subsequently banned a book by prominent Tunisian historian Muhammad al-Talbi that ridiculed their decision (Talbi 1992: 120–21). The ban on Talbi's book, which contains a strong appeal against religious censorship, was later reversed.

If comic books such as Seddik's are experiments geared to an affluent audience, "Islamic" books seek to capture the religious—and with increasing explicitness, the political—imagination of a new generation. In them, readers find echoes of what they already know, and they find answers to their questions about religion and conduct. Conventional intellectuals may accord no legitimacy to the commercial entrepreneurs who benefit from a market that allows Shaykh Sharawi to sell 250,000 copies of a book when the sale of 10,000 books is regarded as a success and 50,000 as a best-seller. However, few can fail to recognize the significance of an emerging and distinctive "popular culture" in which the "Islamic" book has become a mass commodity (Gonzalez-Quijano 1994: 270, 412).

In retrospect, the 1952 Egyptian revolution appears less a break with the past than an intensification of the existing monarchical vision of directing change from above. This notion is visualized by King Farouk's personal bookplate (in Gonzalez-Quijano 1994: 96b), which shows a printing press directly under his name and a crown, and a city with minarets in the background. A learned man in front of the press passes a book to a peasant kneeling next to his plow and oxen. This self-image of the distribution of knowledge was not significantly challenged in the years of the military junta and Nasser's presidency. The real revolution came later, as mass education created a new public for the printed word. In retrospect, the economic reforms set in motion in the 1970s unintentionally created the space for a cultural and intellectual reorientation through "market forces" that favored "Islamization from below"—uncontrolled and uncontrollable by state forces. Figure 2.4 shows the shifting forces of book production and readership in Egypt, a trend that is more pronounced in regions where book circulation is not hindered by state control.

In a general sense, the implications of mass higher education and mass communication include (1) a changed sense of authoritative discourse, (2) the emergence of a sense of religion and politics as system and object, and (3) altered conceptions of language and community.[5] First, mass education fosters a sharp break with earlier traditions of authority, by means of direct, albeit selective, access to the printed word. Belief and practice are now expressed publicly without reference to the authority of traditionally edu-

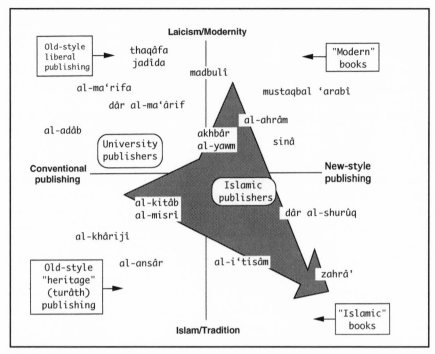

Fig. 2.4. The rise of mass higher education facilitated the emergence of cultural entrepreneurs such as the publishers of "Islamic books" in Egypt. During the "opening" (*infitah*) that followed the Nasser era, they developed new markets and audiences that overshadowed those of traditional publishers and their audiences, as shown by the shaded arrow on this chart. Adapted from Gonzalez-Quijano 1994, figure 15; used by permission.

cated religious elites and are more directly related to political action than was the case earlier. The rise of this new dominant discourse affects both the expressive forms of the state and its religious and secular opposition. Secondly, mass education and mass communication encourage the conception of religion and politics as self-contained systems that can incorporate features from other systems. Mass education encourages this by treating Islam as one subject among many in the curriculum, even as students are told that "Islam is one" and all-encompassing. The successive editions of Sayyid Qutb's *Social Justice in Islam* (1st ed., 1949; 7th ed., 1974) show how he refined his view of Islam as "an inwardly consistent and harmonious 'system,' . . . making it possible for it to be at once flexible, comprehensive, and distinctive" (Shepard 1992: 200, 211). Even radical Islam "accepts much that is borrowed from the West" (Shepard 1987: 315; see also Shepard 1989), with the borrowing facilitated by the fact that religion is seen as a "system" (*nizam*), although such borrowings are often denied or unrecognized. "Moderates," as opposed to radicals, are more likely to acknowledge these borrowings, arguing that while Islamic principles are eternal, the ways in which they are implemented can be adjusted to historical context. This point was brought home by a religious activist in the Arab Gulf. In 1978, he explained that democracy would never take hold in the Muslim world because it was a concept alien to *shura* (consultation), which was Koranic and Islamic. In 1990, he asserted that *al-dimuqratiyya* (democracy) was compatible with Islam. When this author later reminded him of what he had said a decade earlier, he replied: "Now we know better. Shura is not a major concept in the Koran and its few usages there are ambiguous. Democracy can be adapted to Islamic ideals" (interview, Rabat, June 11, 1992). Likewise, when Islamic activists in Morocco declare that they are engaged in the "Islamization" of their society, they make explicit their sense of one system of ideas and practices—theirs—acting against the system of beliefs and practices held by other members of society. Among the Ibadiyya of Algeria and Oman, modern education and intensified contact with other Muslims have encouraged such phenomena as catechisms (Ausht 1982), videos, and pamphlets to help Ibadi students explain their doctrines to Muslims liable to misunderstand them (Khalili 1988).

Finally, the standardized language of mass higher education encourages a new sense of community and affinity. In India, the temple-mosque dispute at Ayodhya in December 1992 went from a local matter to a national crisis in Hindu-Muslim relations because of "a massive expansion in the availability of television and the ending of the Indian government's carefully managed news monopoly." The narrative of the BBC World Television reports of the incident, widely followed by English-speakers in India, was a model of balance, but the pictures acted "as recruiting banners for the militants on both sides" ("Feeding Fundamentalism" 1993). The video clips fed to Oman television by an American network at the time of the massacres in the Sabra/ Shatila refugee camps in Beirut in 1982 had a similar effect, as did footage of the Hebron/al-Khalil killings and their aftermath in February 1994. Benedict Anderson (1983) argues that the rise of written vernacular languages in Europe and the spread of print technology have created language communities wider than those of face-to-face interactions yet narrower than the communities created by shared sacred languages. With modifications, this premise can be transposed to the Arab world in which there has been intensified access to the printed word as well as a transition to a more standardized Arabic in terms of the spoken word. In Arab countries where other languages such as Berber or Kurdish are spoken, there is an increased use of Arabic as the principal language of education and formal communication.

One indication of shifts in the religious and political imagination of a younger, educated generation in many parts of the Middle East is the effort of the state to co-opt religious discourse. In Morocco in the 1960s and early 1970s, both the monarchy and its political opposition employed a "developmentalist" idiom in which "religious" issues were separated from "political" ones. By the late 1970s, the public language of the monarchy's supporters was much more religiously oriented. The king himself asserted that he was developing a cadre of Ministry of the Interior officials trained in administration and Islamic thought, claiming that his actions were modeled on those of the Prophet Muhammad (Hassan II 1984: 162).

The state has learned to talk back through the media to popularize the "official" political story, as illustrated in a comic book history of Morocco, available in Arabic and French, which tackles even the attempted overthrows of the monarchy in 1971 and 1972 (Saint-Michel 1979). Conversely, mass education empowers citizens to talk back to state authority by making the state one actor among many, and thus changing how the state can represent itself.

Is Democracy Likely?

Although mass education and mass communication are profoundly changing political expectations and ideas of legitimate rule throughout the Middle East, the prospects for democracy vary with the political institutions specific to each country. This is not to say that developments in one country do not have significant repercussions in another. The specter of intolerant religious radicalism and equally violent state responses in neighboring Algeria are reported daily in the press and television. In Egypt, assassinations and violent clashes between radical Muslim and state-sponsored hit squads became commonplace.

Such violence, especially the radicalization of Algerian politics since 1989, led directly to Morocco's October 1992 municipal elections and the June 1993 parliamentary elections. Although there were reported instances of fraud in both elections, they were generally perceived as more fair than preceding ones (International Foundation for Electoral Systems [IFES] 1993: 3).[6] Until the January 1992 military takeover, Algeria followed the "big bang" model of democratization—rapid and direct implementation of decisionmaking on the basis of a popular vote. In contrast, Morocco's approach has been incremental (see fig. 2.5). As was the case for the 1992 municipal elections, the June 1993 parliamentary elections for 222 of the 333 parliamentary seats did not result in a clear victory for any party. Elections for the remaining 111 indirectly elected parliamentary representatives took place on September 17, 1993.[7] On April 26, 1994, "partial" municipal and

Activity	Date	Turnout	Results
Constitutional Referendum	September 4, 1992 11,804,038 votes	97.29%	99.96% 'Yes'
Communal Elections	October 16, 1992	75%	5,724 elected
Parliamentary Elections—Direct	June 25, 1993	63% 13% voided	222 elected
Parliamentary Elections—Indirect	September 17, 1993	—	111 elected
"Partial" Elections—Direct	April 26, 1994	53%	14 elected to parliament others to municipal councils
"Partial" Elections—Direct	September 16, 1994	—	3 elected to parliament

Fig. 2.5. Critics have noted flaws in Morocco's 1992–1994 elections, but the country's incremental approach has had the advantage of allowing time for political activists and government officials at all levels to adjust to new political forms. *Source: Al Bayane* (Casablanca). Official election results.

parliamentary elections—for fourteen seats—were held in the electoral districts where earlier results had been invalidated.

The reasons for the large number of invalid votes in the June 1992 elections—13 percent of the 7,153,211 votes cast nationally (with up to 50 percent in some towns, such as Tangiers)—vary with region, but a high rate of invalid votes can be read as a sign of greater willingness to use the tools of the "system," flawed as it is, and an awareness that the system can be manipulated to the voters' purposes. As with the October 1992 municipal elections, some candidates reportedly sought to purchase votes. In some towns, including Casablanca and Khouribga, the "market value" for votes varied between 50 and 100 Moroccan dirhams, roughly the same as for the October 1992 municipal elections. Unfortunately, polling station reports (*taqrir an amaliyat ihsa al-aswat*) do not distinguish between empty envelopes and votes invalidated for other causes. However, interviews which the author conducted with polling station officials and party observers in one locality on the day after the elections suggest that the majority of invalidated votes was due to blank envelopes; a survey of election results in one area where detailed results were accessible suggested a correlation between a high incidence of null votes and votes for a losing candidate who was reputed to have purchased votes (see also IFES 1993). In some areas, such activities were limited because candidates engaged attorneys to monitor the practices of rivals and because opponents actively sought to secure the support of local officials. Threats by rival parties to report illegal practices to local electoral commissions and to other authorities indicate a greater confidence in the "rule of law" and the electors' growing sophistication and awareness of the gap between the rhetoric of the state and its practices.

There is no way of knowing the degree of abstention or of empty envelope voting for religious reasons, although Islamists in some areas encouraged abstention. Likewise, the drop in participation in the elections suggests less official coercion and compares favorably with the results of Tunisia's March 20, 1994, presidential and parliamentary elections, in which Zine el-Abidine Ben Ali was reelected by 99.81 percent of the voters, with a 99.96 percent turnout.[8] Parliamentary results were less spectacular, but Ben Ali's party captured 144 of the 163 parliamentary seats, with the remaining 19 divided among four opposition parties (*Al Bayane,* March 22, 1994).

An exclusive focus on election results deflects attention from major changes taking place beneath the surface. The procedures involved in preparing for the elections and in convincing the voting population and political parties to participate suggest that the "rule of law" could work. They suggest that a transition can be made to a less arbitrary, exclusive, and authoritarian rule, notwithstanding the conditions of rapid population growth, stagnating economies, rising unemployment, and a young citizenry which—thanks to mass education and mass communication—is more articulate than preceding generations and more susceptible to radical religious alternatives.

What the formal results failed to indicate were the complex arrangements needed to set the elections in motion and to convince Morocco's political parties that the elections would be fair. The behind-the-scenes negotiations were not secret—the fact that they were taking place was widely known and reported in the national press. Among the issues involved were (1) the creation of national and regional electoral commissions, including rules of procedure on how to handle instances of fraud and abuse; (2) computerized election registration to reduce the possibility of electoral fraud; (3) lowering the voting age from twenty-one to twenty;[9] and (4) granting political parties access to television for the first time.

Other changes were more subtle. By mid-1992, the activities of human rights groups began to be reported regularly in the national press. Even when newspapers refrained from publishing details of human rights abuses because of censorship rules, some national newspapers referred to banned books and to the continued concerns of foreign human rights groups. Another innovation followed Hassan II's August 20, 1992, speech from the throne in which he called for a major reexamination of the rights of women and a revision of the *mudawwana*, the *sharia*-based legal code governing family law administration in Morocco. Even if its results were modest, it set up conferences and drafting sessions that gave the appearance of movement, especially when coupled with the election of two women to parliament. Finally, press laws were liberalized. The relaxed restrictions culminated in a major scandal in mid-February and March 1993, when Moroccans were treated to daily accounts—a morality play for Ramadan, as it were—of the trial of a senior Casablanca police official for sex crimes involving an estimated 1,500 female victims, all of whom he videotaped. Although the broadcast media remained silent, the print media covered the trial extensively. For the month of Ramadan, the circulation of Moroccan newspapers soared, as journalists honed their investigative (and tabloid) skills, and newspapers regularly sold out.[10]

There are flaws in Morocco's electoral process; but in contrast with past elections, these flaws cannot be imputed exclusively to a grand design from the center. Despite their claims to the contrary, Moroccan political parties cover the country unevenly. Unlike the situation that existed immediately after independence in 1956, no party has deep roots in all the rural areas, where local candidates with no committed party affiliation other than cooperation with the government, usually in the form of local officials, still prevail. Even the defeated parties acknowledge a "transparency" (*shafafiyya*) in the 1992 and 1993 elections. The poor showing in many areas suggested that Morocco's political parties have only begun to master the techniques needed to secure mass support.

Politically active Moroccans ask why these apparently significant political changes are occurring now. One reason is the long-term cultural transformation in religious and political sensibilities suggested in this essay. A more immediate element of timing specific to Morocco is suggested by an opposition political leader:

> We are seeing the first stage in the break-up of the system of power in Morocco. In the 1970s and 1980s we asked the question, 'What is the role which political parties can play in the monarchy?' Now the question has changed to 'What is the role of a monarchy in a modern society?' Technically this is a forbidden question, but Hassan knows that this is the issue on everyone's minds. (Interview, Rabat, June 11, 1992)

Rémy Leveau (1993a: 13; 1993b), perhaps the most astute long-term French observer of Moroccan politics, goes so far as to say that the Morocco of the 1990s is as different from the Morocco of 1960 as present-day Spain is from 1975, the year Franco died. The comparison initially gives reason for hope, but it also gives reason for caution. Spain's transition to democracy after Franco was not without major threats. The Spanish economy had already developed major international ties not directly dependent on the government, and the middle class had grown significantly; differences between life in the city and in the countryside had narrowed. In spite of reasonably positive economic indicators from Morocco in recent years, the role of the government—and the palace—continues to predominate, and the rising population continues to threaten the modest economic advances of recent years. Nonetheless, most Moroccans are convinced that the conduct of the current elections breaks with past practices, allowing "democracy" to begin to acquire a specific substance and the "rule of law" to become more than a slogan.

An examination of elections elsewhere in the Middle East suggests ways that the social institution of parliamentary elections, "implanted from the West, is being shaped, interpreted, and experienced in terms of indigenous cultural meanings and practices," while providing a framework to challenge and reshape them (Layne 1994: 108). Linda L. Layne writes that one underlying issue in Jordan's March 1984 by-elections was whether tribespeople would vote along tribal lines. Although traditional tribal leaders still retained considerable moral authority, voters in general cast ballots for those considered best able to represent them, and the choices did not necessarily follow tribal lines or support the existing tribal leadership. As in the West, voting is a ritual intended to instill an aura of legitimacy. Whereas Morocco uses color-coded ballots to facilitate participation by literate and illiterate voters, in Jordan illiterates were required to declare their vote verbally to election officials; at polling stations, even those who were literate insisted on declaring their preferred candidate. Layne says that in this practice, the Arab value of personal autonomy and the ideology of democratic elections complemented and reinforced one another. Secret votes equate with a lack of distinction between persons. In the Jordanian tribal context, giving "voice" (*sawt*) to one's vote—the literal meaning of "vote"—was a means of refusing to separate the role of voter from that of person (Layne 1994: 112–23). A more recent study of Jordan's 1993 elections, which took place without any major charges of irregularities, suggests further success in institutionalizing elections and developing civil society—including the participation of Islamist groups—within the framework of the monarchy (Brand 1995).

On the Arabian Peninsula, where opposition in many countries is expressed only in a "politics of silence" (Waterdrinker 1993: 52–61) rather than openly, elections have occurred in Kuwait and Yemen. Even the most conservative governments have begun to emulate the language of moderates, enhancing or establishing consultative councils. These steps may be hesitant and in some cases cynical, but they acknowledge the need to demonstrate a semblance of popular participation to sustain legitimacy. Understanding these steps also means going beyond the formal, statist language of some political activists and making sense of local political forms and issues (Eickelman 1984). For example, in Yemen, poetry is a major vehicle for political contests, and poems are often a means of conveying political ideas and relating them to local interests and identities (Caton 1990). Moreover, rather than belong to just one political party, most people belong to several. The shifting weight which they give to these identities has the effect of sustaining civil society (Dresch and Haykel 1995). Dresch argues that understanding the prospects for democracy in the Yemeni context requires a "local knowledge" which recognizes the specific forms which political participation take in Yemen and which cannot be subsumed by any single, culturally universal, instrument such as elections. Elections acquire an importance only when interpreted in context of political understandings derived neither from an overly determined metatheory—"elections are the only means to determine the people's will"— nor from directly "observing the flow of Yemeni social life without the benefit of dialogue with informed Yemenis" (Dresch and Haykel 1995). Moreover, in Yemen, as elsewhere, the limits to what is considered "political" are in flux.

Interim governmental restraints on individual and group voices that are articulating their claims do not negate the trend toward popular participation in governance associated with rising educational levels and access to information about alternative systems of governance. Part of the political contest over boundaries involves timing. In just over two years, democracy in Morocco— accelerated and given focus by events in neighboring Algeria—has begun to acquire a substance beyond governmental decrees and party slogans. The same is true elsewhere, for instance, in Turkey and Jordan.

Clash of Civilizations or Crashed Paradigm?

In terms of the prospects for democracy in the Muslim Middle East, the clash is not the "West versus Rest"—a point to which it is necessary to return because of the strong economic and political influence that states external to the region can lend to developments within it. Progress toward representative government has been slow in the Arab world, but this is in part due to the preferences of some Western states to sustain known elites at the expense of expanding the political arena. During the Cold War years, the United States— to contain the presumed Soviet threat, secure the free flow of oil to the West, and defend Israel's security—systematically opposed popular nationalist leaders and regimes that were "willing to experiment with political freedom" or that were moving too quickly to replace the old order (Cottam 1993: 20, 32– 33). In some cases, these concerns continued after the end of the Cold War—

in the case of some oil-rich states, the United States speaks softly about human rights abuses, and U.S. concern about promoting democracy was far from prominent when the Algerian military canceled the December 1991 elections. In some parts of the Arab world, the debate over the meaning of democracy and its implementation is often vigorous; elsewhere, as in the Gulf states, it is only beginning. The voices of Muslim moderates, although threatened, are likely to increase in volume.

Perhaps what is needed at this stage is a new way of thinking about politics and policy that goes beyond the Western conventional wisdom of the Cold War years. Responding to critics of his proposal to replace the Cold War foreign policy paradigm with one based on the clash of civilizations, Huntington (1993b: 36) argues that people think "abstractly" when they think "seriously." Although the Cold War paradigm "could not account for everything that went on in world politics," it accounted for "more important phenomena than any of its rivals" and "shaped thinking about world politics for two generations." Huntington invokes Thomas Kuhn's *The Structure of Scientific Revolutions* (1962) to assert that scientific advances consist "of the displacement of one paradigm by another." By analogy he claims that we need an equivalent "simple map of the post–Cold War world" (Huntington 1993b: 36–37).

Just as he invoked Toynbee's 1930s-era notions of "civilization," Huntington also invoked a notion of scientific advance from the 1960s; it privileged the role of theoretical traditions over other, equally important factors which historians of science now recognize as such. Since Huntington saw fit to advance his argument on foreign policy thinking by drawing on Kuhn's arguments about physics from the 1950s and 1960s (Fuller 1992), it is useful to explore how historians of science currently think about scientific advances and to assess whether these ideas offer, by analogy, more satisfactory ways of thinking about foreign policy and issues such as the prospects for democracy in the Middle East.

Historians of science no longer focus almost exclusively on "theory," as Kuhn did, invoking specific cases only to "confirm, refute, or generate theory" (Galison 1988: 208). Alongside theoretical traditions, with all their breaks and continuities, they afford equal weight to experimental traditions with an equally complex set of internal dynamics, and to the design and refinement of the devices and measures through which the world of physics is perceived and represented. Galison, for example, proposes that those who seek to understand developments in science should avoid assuming that there is a fixed, hierarchical relation between theory, the instruments of perception, and experiment. There is no reason to assume that any one of these factors is privileged over the others:

> In individual instances, it is frequently the case that one may impose structure on the other. But this is exactly the task at hand: to discover and articulate the

mediative processes by which experiments and theories each constrain the other's activity. (Galison 1988: 208)

Discarding the idea of a universal, hierarchical relationship between theory, the design and use of instruments through which the world of physics is perceived, and practice allows "the subcultures of physics to follow whatever dynamical process exists in different historical epochs." There is a wide variety of possible relationships "between the categories of instrumentation, experimentation, and theorizing" (Galison 1988: 210); recognizing this diversity allows for a more effective understanding of how theory, instruments, and experimentation interact.

Kuhn's model, explicitly designed to keep "'pure science' in the good favor of the American public," had the apparent benefit of providing a blueprint for constituting any academic or policy-making practice as a science (Fuller 1992: 241). Perhaps Huntington's paradigm can best be seen as inadvertently keeping established policymakers from envisioning alternative ways of thinking about policy and the future of democracy in the post–Cold War era and neutralizing radical challenges to the conventional way of looking at other people's politics.

Perhaps what is needed at this stage is a Muslim (and Arab) Alexis de Tocqueville, capable of suggesting an ethnographic analysis of the myths of Western foreign policy and of Western perceptions of Muslim politics (cf. Beeman 1990: 167–68). Deprivileging "theory" allows one to avoid creating a new, equally "simple" model of post–Cold War politics that would serve more as a block to creating effective foreign policy than as an aid to it. Perhaps George F. Kennan (1994) best expresses how this alternative view can be transposed to thinking about the future of governance and foreign policy options:

> Our statesmen and our public are unaccustomed to reacting to a world situation that offers so many great and all-absorbing focal points for American policy. And it is not surprising that we should now be hearing demands for some sort of a single grand strategy of foreign policy, to replace our fixation on the Soviet Union.

With the collapse of Cold War great power politics, it is time to discard the search for a universal paradigm and replace it with a different way of posing questions and seeking answers. Kennan suggests that we re-imagine how the world looked to U.S. statesmen in the early years of independence and toward the end of the nineteenth century as a means of looking at the challenges we will face in the years ahead. In the specific terms of the Middle East and North Africa, it entails listening to voices other than those of a Westernized elite. The first step is to learn to elicit the cultural notions of legitimate authority and justice and to recognize the multiple voices of the Muslim and Arab world attuned to these issues. Ideas of just rule, religious or otherwise, are not fixed, even if some radicals claim that they are. Such notions are debated, argued, often fought about, and re-formed in practice. The issue is not whether such debates are occurring but how to recognize their contours, as well as the obstacles and the false starts, both internal and external, to making governance less arbitrary and authoritarian.

Notes

1. Rimington (1994), in the first public speech by the head of MI5, Britain's domestic intelligence service, offers a considerably more nuanced view. She states that three-fourths of the work of MI5 concerns terrorism and that half of the service's resources are devoted to combat Irish terrorism. The threats of Islamic terrorist groups are mentioned alongside those posed by groups from the Indian subcontinent, the former Yugoslavia, Kurds, and Middle East state security services seeking to eliminate regime opponents.

2. Lipset's citation is incorrect. In the original, Schumpeter writes that the "democratic method" is "*that institutional arrangement for arriving at political decisions* which realizes the common good by making the people itself decide issues through the election of individuals who are to assemble in order to carry out its will" (Schumpeter 1950: 250 [italics mine]). Only the italicized words are Schumpeter's. In "streamlining" Schumpeter's original, Lipset has removed the phrasing that ties Schumpeter's idea more directly to institutional arrangements culturally and historically specific to the West.

3. This discussion is based on Eickelman and Piscatori (1996), where this argument is further developed.

4. Interview, Mohammed Bennis, Mohammediya, July 16, 1992.

5. See Eickelman (1992) for an elaboration of these points as they affect religious practices and expressions.

6. For details of Morocco's recent electoral experience, much of which I observed in 1992–93, see Eickelman (1994).

7. The 111 indirectly elected members of parliament include 69 provincial delegates, chosen from among the various elected municipal counselors: 7 from the Chambers of Artisans, 10 from the Chambers of Commerce and Industry, 10 from the Chamber of Salaried Workers, and 15 from the Chamber of Agriculture.

8. Ben Ali (1994) responded to a French journalist's comment that the election results were "a bit too good" by accusing him of a "European perspective" in which a 99 percent victory was abnormal. Ben Ali invoked a "cultural" argument: Had the interviewer better understood the "profound realities of the Arab-Muslim world," he would have recognized that the vote was a "massive adhesion to a project of national salvation." Moroccans greeted this invocation of "tradition" to explain Ben Ali's success at the polls with amusement.

9. The "opposition" parties first argued that the voting age should be lowered to eighteen to reflect Morocco's population demographics; the king publicly argued against any change. With continued resistance from the opposition parties, which threatened not to participate in the elections, the electoral age was lowered to twenty without further comment in June 1992.

10. The police official, Hajj Muhammad Mustafa Tabit, was arrested on February 18 and condemned to death on March 15. For an English summary of the trial and

its implications, see Rocco (1993). The Ministry of Justice announced his execution eight hours after it occurred on July 9, 1993, indicating that the monarch had rejected a prior appeal for clemency. See also Mayer (1993: 93–105), who links the management of the Tabit case to the issue of women's rights in the Moroccan constitution and in public life.

References

Ahnaf, M. Al-, Bernard Botiveau, and Franck Frégosi. 1991. *L'Algérie par ses islamistes.* Paris: Karthala.

Anderson, Benedict. 1983. *Imagined Communities: Reflections on the Origin and Spread of Nationalism.* London: Verso.

Ausht, Bakr bin Said. Circa 1982. *Dirasat islamiyya fi-l-usul al-ibadiyya.* Algiers: n.p.

Bayane, Al (Casablanca). 1994. "Le Double Electoral de Dimanche en Tunisie." March 22, p. 1.

Beeman, William O. 1990. "Double Demons: Cultural Impedance in U.S. Iranian Understanding." In Miron Rezun, ed., *Iran at the Crossroads: Global Relations in a Turbulent Decade,* pp. 165–79. Boulder, CO: Westview.

Ben Ali, Zine el-Abidine. 1994. "L'intégrisme, c'est maintenant votre problème." Interview with Jacques Jacquet-Françillon, *Figaro,* August 2, p. 5.

Bennani, Aziza. 1992. "L'université marocaine: evolution et adaptation." *Al Bayane* (Casablanca), September 28.

Binsaid, Said. 1993. "Al-hiwar wa-l-fahm la al-qafliyya wal-jahl" [Dialogue and understanding, not alienation and ignorance]. *Al-Sharq al-Awsat* (London), July 7, p. 10.

Bourdieu, Pierre. 1988. *Homo Academicus.* London: Polity.

Brand, Laurie A. 1995. "'In the Beginning Was the State . . .': The Quest for Civil Society in Jordan." In *Civil Society in the Middle East,* vol. 1, ed. Augustus Richard Norton, pp. 148–85. Leiden: E. J. Brill.

Caton, Steven C. 1990. *"Peaks of Yemen I Summon": Poetry as Cultural Practice in a North Yemeni Village.* Berkeley: University of California Press.

Cerny, Philip G. 1990. *The Changing Architecture of Politics: Structure, Agency, and the Future of the State.* London: Sage.

Chartier, Roger. 1987. *The Cultural Uses of Print in Early Modern France,* trans. L. G. Cochrane. Princeton: Princeton University Press.

Clifford, James, and George E. Marcus. 1986. *Writing Culture: The Poetics and Politics of Ethnography.* Berkeley: University of California Press.

Cottam, Richard W. 1993. "United States Middle East Policy in the Cold War Era." In Dale F. Eickelman, ed., *Russia's Muslim Frontiers: New Directions in Cross-Cultural Analysis,* pp. 19–37. Bloomington: Indiana University Press.

Difraoui, Abdelasiem el-. 1994. "La critique du système démocratique par le Front Islamique du Salut." In Gilles Kepel, ed., *Exils et royaumes: les appartenances au monde arabo-musulman aujourd'hui,* pp. 105–24. Paris: Presses de la Fondation Nationale des Sciences Politiques.

Douglas, Allen, and Fedwa Malti-Douglas. 1994. *Arabic Comic Strips: Politics of an Emerging Mass Culture.* Bloomington: Indiana University Press.

Dresch, Paul, and Bernard Haykel. 1995. "Stereotypes and Political Styles: Islamists and Tribesfolk in Yemen." *International Journal of Middle East Studies* 27, no. 4 (November): 405–31.

Eickelman, Dale F. 1984. "Kings and People: Oman's State Consultative Council." *Middle East Journal* 38, no. 1 (Winter): 51–71.

———. 1992. "Mass Higher Education and the Religious Imagination in Contemporary Arab Societies." *American Ethnologist* 19, no. 4 (November): 643–55.

———. 1993. "Islamic Liberalism Strikes Back." *Middle East Studies Association Bulletin* 27, no. 2 (December 1993): 163–68.

———. 1994. "Re-Imagining Religion and Politics: Moroccan Elections in the 1990s." In John Ruedy, ed., *Islamism and Secularism in North Africa*, pp. 253–73. New York: St. Martin's.

Eickelman, Dale F., and James Piscatori. 1996. *Muslim Politics.* Princeton: Princeton University Press.

"Feeding Fundamentalism." 1993. *The Economist* (London). August 21, p. 36.

Fuller, Steve. 1992. "Being There with Thomas Kuhn: A Parable for Postmodern Times." *History and Theory* 31, no. 3 (October): 241–75.

Galison, Peter. 1988. "History, Philosophy, and the Central Metaphor." *Science in Context* 2, no. 1: 197–212.

Geertz, Clifford. 1973. *The Interpretation of Cultures.* New York: Basic.

Ghannouchi, Rachid al-. 1992. "Islam and Freedom Can Be Friends." *The Observer* (London), January 19.

Gonzalez-Quijano, Yves. 1994. *Les gens du livre. Champ intellectuel et édition dans l'Egypte Republicaine (1952–1993).* Thèse de doctorat de l'Institut d'Études Politiques de Paris, Mention Sciences Politiques.

Hassan II. 1984. *Discours et interviews.* Rabat: Ministry of Information.

Hudson, Michael C. 1988. "Democratization and the Problem of Legitimacy in Middle East Politics." *Middle East Studies Association Bulletin* 22, no. 2 (December): 157–71.

Huntington, Samuel P. 1993a. "The Coming Clash of Civilizations or, the West against the Rest." *New York Times,* June 6, p. 19.

———. 1993b. "The Clash of Civilizations?" *Foreign Affairs* 72, no. 3 (Summer): 22–49.

International Foundation for Electoral Systems. 1993. "Morocco: Direct Legislative Elections." Washington: International Foundation for Electoral Systems.

Johnson, Paul. 1991. "Another Moslem Invasion of Europe." *Los Angeles Times,* December 20.

Kennan, George F. 1994. "The Failure in Our Success." *New York Times,* March 14, p. A17.

Khalili, Ahmad bin Hamad al-. 1988. *Who Are the Ibadhis?* Trans. A. H. al-Maamiry. Zanzibar: al-Khayirah Press.

Kishk, Abd al-Hamid. 1989. *Ayyuha l-Muslimun, Ufiqu* [O Muslims, Awake!]. Cairo: al-Mukhtar al-Islami.

Korniyenko, Georgy M. 1993. "Soviet Policy in the Middle East: A Practitioner's Interpretation." In Dale F. Eickelman, ed., *Russia's Muslim Frontiers: New Directions in Cross-Cultural Analysis,* pp. 38–46. Bloomington: Indiana University Press.

Kuhn, Thomas S. 1962. *The Structure of Scientific Revolutions*. Chicago: University of Chicago Press.

Layne, Linda L. 1994. *Home and Homeland: The Dialogics of Tribal and National Identities in Jordan*. Princeton: Princeton University Press.

Lerner, Daniel. 1958. *The Passing of Traditional Society: Modernizing the Middle East*. New York: Free Press.

Leveau, Rémy. 1993a. *Le sabre et le turban: L'avenir du Maghreb*. Paris: François Bourin.

———. 1993b. "Le pouvoir marocain entre la répression et le dialogue." *Le Monde Diplomatique*, October, p. 13.

Lipset, Seymour Martin. 1994. "The Social Requisites of Democracy Revisited." *American Sociological Review* 59, no. 1 (February): 1–22.

Lipset, Seymour Martin, Kyoung-Ryung Seong, and John Charles Torres. 1993. "A Comparative Analysis of the Social Requisites of Democracy." *International Social Science Journal*, no. 136 (May): 155–75.

Mabruk, Layla. 1989. *Rihla ila alam al-Khulud: Adalat Yawm al-Qiyama* [A Trip to Eternity: Justice on Judgment Day]. Cairo: al-Mukhtar al-Islami.

Mayer, Ann Elizabeth. 1993. "Moroccans—Citizens or Subjects? A People at the Crossroads." *Journal of International Law and Politics* 26, no. 1 (Fall): 63–105.

Pekonen, Kyösti. 1989. "Symbols and Politics as Culture in the Modern Situation: The Problem and Prospects of the 'New.'" In John R. Giggons, ed., *Contemporary Political Culture: Politics in a Postmodern World*, pp. 127–43. London: Sage.

Perlmutter, Amos. 1992. Islam and Democracy Simply Aren't Compatible." *International Herald Tribune*, January 21, p. 6.

Quayle, Dan. 1990. "Text of Remarks by the Vice-President, Commencement Address, Graduation and Commissioning Ceremony for the Class of 1990, U.S. Naval Academy, Annapolis, Maryland." Washington, D.C.: Office of the Vice-President, May 30 (photocopy).

Rimington, Stella. 1994. "Security and Democracy: Is There a Conflict?" The Richard Dimbleby Lecture, transmitted on BBC 1, June 12.

Rocco, Fiammetta. 1993. "The Shame of Casablanca." *Independent on Sunday* (London), May 9.

Saint-Michel, Serge. 1979. *Il était une fois . . . Hassan II*. Paris: Fayolle.

Schumpeter, Joseph A. 1950. *Capitalism, Socialism and Democracy*. 3rd ed. New York: Harper and Row.

Seddik, Youssef. 1989. *Si le Coran m'était conté: Les hommes de l'éléphant*. Geneva: Éditions Alef.

Sharif, Muhamad Shakir al-. A. D. 1992/A. H. 1412. *Haqiqat al-Dimuqratiya* [The Truth about Democracy]. Riyadh: Dar al-watan li-l-nashr.

Shepard, William E. 1987. "Islam and Ideology: Towards a Typology." *International Journal of Middle East Studies* 19, no. 3 (August): 307–36.

———. 1989. "Islam as a 'System' in the Later Writings of Sayyid Qutb." *Middle Eastern Studies* 25, no. 1 (January): 31–50.

———. 1992. "The Development of the Thought of Sayyid Qutb as Reflected in Earlier and Later Editions of 'Social Justice in Islam.'" *Die Welt des Islams* 32, no. 2: 196–236.

Smith, Wilfred Cantwell. 1963. *The Meaning and End of Religion.* New York: Macmillan.

Talbi, Muhammad al-. 1992. *Ayal Allah: Afkar Jadida fi alaqat al-Muslim bi-nafsihi wa-bil-akharayn* [Men of God: New Thinking on the Relation of the Muslim with the Self and with Others]. Tunis: Cérès.

Tinco, Henri. 1994. "L'Islam de France se radicalise." *Le Monde,* August 12, pp. 1, 3.

Toynbee, Arnold J. 1947. *A Study of History.* Abridgment of vols. 1–6 by D. C. Somervell. New York: Oxford University Press.

Waterdrinker, Brigitte. 1993. *Genèse et construction d'un état moderne: le cas du Sultanate d'Oman.* Mémoire de DEA Études Politiques, Institut d'Études Politiques de Paris.

World Bank. 1981–92. *World Development Reports.* New York: Oxford University Press.

3.

Political Islam in the Maghreb

The Nonviolent Dimension

JOHN P. ENTELIS

Introduction

Despite the publicity militant Islam has received, the principal Muslim opposition movements in the Maghreb subscribe to a nonviolent transfer of national power. The three most popular and influential movements—Abdessalam Yassine's Justice and Charity in Morocco, Rachid al-Ghannouchi's an-Nahdah (Renaissance) in Tunisia, and the Islamic Salvation Front (FIS or Front Islamique du Salut) in Algeria headed by Abassi Madani and Ali Benhadj—are in fact politically moderate, though all are banned.

Neither government coercion (in Tunisia), state crackdown (in Algeria), nor monarchical containment (in Morocco) has extinguished support for these groups, especially among people living on the margins, or among elites. Yet the situation is strained by extremist groups extant within movements as well as those created outside them. For their part, government hardliners have instituted their own solutions, ranging from intensified political repression in Tunisia, to expanded surveillance of suspected groups by Morocco's Interior Ministry, to the application of brute force in the form of state-sponsored terrorist squads ("Ninjas") in Algeria. Human rights abuses and civil rights violations have risen dramatically in recent years, as reports from Amnesty International (1993 and 1994) and Middle East Watch (1994) have confirmed. In Algeria alone, between 40,000 and 50,000 people have died in the violence that has raged since the January 1992 military coup.

Should incumbent governments succeed in eliminating nonviolent Islamist groups, they will face a serious vacuum that can only result in greater political instability and social uncertainty. In short, while popular support for nonviolent Islamists in North Africa is holding, it is challenged daily—from above by recalcitrant officials and from below by fringe groups prone to violence. Should nonviolent Islamists be forced under or radicalized into violence, stability and democracy in the Maghreb will be unlikely any time soon.

Context and Definitions

Nonviolent Islamic reformism and revivalism in Arab North Africa have a long history, dating back to the early days of colonial occupation and even before. *Salafiyya* (from *salaf*, forefather) movements emerged in all three countries of the Maghreb in response to external aggression and perceived threats to indigenous culture and belief. Inspired by the *salafiyya* movement in the Arab Middle East, North African Islamic reformers emphasized the importance of returning to the Koran and *hadith* (prophetic traditions) as the basic sources of faith and practice. The reformers were particularly concerned with social and economic issues, but they conceived of these in religious and moral terms. Their movements intended not only to define a new doctrine but also to create a social movement through which the new ideas could be passed on to the young. And behind the reforms was a political imperative: Achieve independence and reestablish the region's Arabo-Islamic identity (Lapidus 1988: 688–89).

Today's nonviolent, Islamic-based political movements are thus following a recognized tradition by defying authority that is demonstrably unjust, unresponsive, and undemocratic. They use the power of the mosques and the streets to challenge the authority of regimes viewed as illegitimate.

Such movements seek, through prayer and preaching, to mobilize popular support for a political program that promotes their ideas for the just and good society as defined for them by Islamic teaching. They further influence people through debates at youth centers, pamphlets distributed in poor neighborhoods, and work in the community. They sponsor mass rallies, large demonstrations, and public assemblies that are testament to their impressive organizational abilities. While such efforts may at times degenerate into violence, violent action is not a structural component either of the movements' strategic thinking or of their tactics. And if reformist movements have in both the distant and the recent past given rise to radical offshoots—especially when moderation has failed to achieve results quickly or broadly—the nonviolent reformers do not bear the responsibility.

Islamically based political opposition movements in North Africa (see fig. 3.1) can be broken down into three separate but at times overlapping categories:

• *Religious.* These individuals and groups reject the authority of official or state-sponsored Islam and instead promote nonpolitical action in education, culture, and social activities. They believe in "bottom-up" political change resulting from a strategy of acculturation, socialization, and education. At the core of their thinking is a reemphasis on religious training and education of the young so as to ensure a devoutly Muslim political future.

• *Reformist*. Equally committed to the goal of a more "authentic" Muslim society, this group calls instead for direct political action to attain it. Its members advocate the use of democratic and electoral means—political organization, mobilization, and participation—to bring about a nonviolent transfer of power. Reform of both state and society is at the heart of their political agenda.

• *Radicals*. In the third category are hardliners who want to transfer power quickly and by any means, political or military, including violence, terrorism, and assassination. Its members subscribe to a puritanical belief system, and most favor the imposition of Islamic law, strictly interpreted. It is to this group that the label "Islamic fundamentalism" best applies.

Different peoples and movements inhabit these three broad categories of Muslim activism directed against incumbent power. And while some individuals may undergo political transformation causing them to move from one group to another, the distinguishing characteristic of each movement is its commitment to certain core beliefs of action: nonpolitical (religious), political (reform), and militant (radical).

Figure 3.1. Islamist Groups in North Africa (1996)

	Religious	Reformist	Radical
Algeria			
Organization	HAMAS; an-Nahdah	Islamic Salvation Front	Armed Islamic Group
Leadership	Mahfoud Nahnah; Abdallah Djaballah	Abassi Madani; Ali Benhadj	Antar Zoubri ("Abou Talha")
Membership	10,000; 15,000	500,000–1 million	500–1,000
Tunisia			
Organization	The Dawa	An-Nahdah	Islamic Salvation Front
Leadership	Collective	Rachid al-Ghannouchi	Mohamed Ali al-Horani
Membership	1,000–5,000	20,000–50,000	NA
Morocco			
Organization	Sunni Movement	Justice and Charity	Islamic Youth
Leadership	Al-Fiqh al-Zamzami (d. 1989); son, al-Siddiq	Abdessalam al-Yassine	Abdelkrim Mottei
Membership	10,000–20,000	35,000–50,000	1,000–2,000

Tunisia

Meetings with Tunisian government officials, independent journalists, human rights activists, university professors, and supporters of an-Nahdah provide a stark portrayal of the current political situation in the country. Yet, despite the adversity facing the movement, its leaders (Rachid al-Ghannouchi, Salah Karkar, and Habib Mokni) continue to espouse a nonviolent transfer of political power. This position is supported by an-Nahdah followers in Tunisia, Europe, and the United States. Attacks such as those directed against the central office of the RCD (Rassemblement Constitutionelle Démocratique, the government party) in Bab Souika (Tunis) in February 1991, which caused the death of one security guard and seriously wounded others, have not been repeated. To date, no militant group dedicated to a violent overthrow of the regime has emerged within an-Nahdah, although such groups exist outside it—for instance, the obscure "Front Islamique du Salut" (Islamic Salvation Front), formed in August 1994. Advocating armed struggle, this radical Islamist party is led by Mohamed Ali al-Horani, who has attacked al-Ghannouchi in the pages of the organization's Vienna-based newspaper, *El-Rajaa* (The Convulsion) for his policy of "peaceful confrontation."

An-Nahdah

Founded as the Islamic Tendency Movement (Mouvement de la Tendance Islamique, MTI) in 1979, an-Nahdah (Renaissance) is Tunisia's principal movement of political opposition. Although never officially recognized, it remains the most popular Islamic organization committed to challenging the incumbent regime, with the ultimate goal of assuming political power to establish a more "authentic" Arabo-Islamic society. Talks with an-Nahdah leaders abroad and its supporters in Tunisia, along with observations of the party's political behavior and evaluation of its leader's writings, confirm the view that this movement is the Maghreb's premier, politically motivated, nonviolent Islamist organization. Its identity and orientation are the product of the thought of one man, Rachid al-Ghannouchi.

Following in the tradition of Islamic reformers before them, al-Ghannouchi and his an-Nahdah supporters have allowed the Islamic discourse to be transformed into a political discourse. For them, both Bourguibism—as an ideology of transformation through secular modernism—and its imitative successor ideology, promoted by Ben Ali, have proven inadequate. They consider official Islam and the imams of the state-run mosques to be invalid. The alternative political-religious discourse provided by an-Nahdah, however, does not advocate either a complete political turnover or a popular uprising. While an-Nahdah's leaders may offer a counter-culture, or perhaps even a counter-society, they are not suggesting a counter-state. And despite the severe repression that they have suffered under Ben Ali since 1989, an-Nahdah spokespeople believe they can attain political power through legal means. They also are optimistic that the present state apparatus, once in more skillful hands, will be capable of transforming the country (Vatin 1987: 170).

An-Nahdah continues to promote reformist political programs that compete with those of the state, as opposed to advocating a program of total rupture with the established order. The question of rupture recalls the archetypal distinctions between legalism and violence, as well as between liberalism and authoritarianism, that have run the length of historical Islam. In the most current phase of Islamist expression under conditions of authoritarian control and state repression, an-Nahdah continues to disavow the use of violence and repeatedly expresses its support for democracy (see Gasiorowski 1992: 90).

For its part, the government of Tunisia is determined to extinguish completely all vestiges of political Islam in the country. Through a combination of coercion, imprisonment, torture, administrative detention, surveillance, and cooptation, the Ben Ali regime is pursuing a policy of total eradication that leaves no possibility for compromise. Such policies are being supplemented with a strategy of cultural transformation, political socialization, and national education intended to produce "new" Tunisian men and women who will be committed to Western, secular values. The ultimate goal is the creation of a "modern" (i.e., Western-type) state. For fifty years (1936–1986) Habib Bourguiba pursued exactly such a strategy. The result was the emergence of an-Nahdah. There is no reason to believe that the less charismatic Ben Ali, heading a government that lacks a "national project," can be any more successful.

In its latest report on Tunisia's human rights situation (January 1994), Amnesty International severely criticized the treatment of Islamist political prisoners. Field interviews with numerous distinguished Tunisian political activists essentially confirm Amnesty's harsh assessment. Despite differing political perspectives, each activist verified the use of torture, incommunicado detention far beyond that allowed by law, and administrative harassment of released political prisoners.

In response to such criticisms, the Tunisian authorities argue that the tough policies have ensured economic growth, improved living standards, and protected social advances such as the integration of women into public and economic life. The crisis in Algeria has reaffirmed the view of Ben Ali's admirers abroad that only a cautious and firm approach can help Tunisia contain the challenge of populist Islam and deliver economic development. Radical Islam has been driven underground, with the results of the March 20,

1994, parliamentary and presidential elections offering a cautious opening to the mainstream opposition. However, had Moncef Marzouki, the former president of the LTDH (Ligue Tunisienne des Droits de l'Homme, or Tunisian League for Human Rights), been allowed by the authorities to stand against Ben Ali in the presidential elections, the test of the government's sincerity about opening up the political process would have been more valid. In any case, the government argues that if the economic gains can be sustained, Tunisia may one day boast of success in a region more often associated with stunted growth and disappointed popular aspirations.

But independent observers of the Tunisian political scene are more pessimistic, especially in light of the sweeping electoral victories—by overwhelming margins—achieved by Ben Ali and his ruling RCD in the March 1994 (legislative-presidential) and May 1995 (local) elections. The RCD now controls 144 of the of the 163 seats in the newly enlarged parliament and all of the country's 257 municipal councils. By a 99.91 percent vote, Ben Ali was reelected for another five-year term as president. But rather than providing a renewed sense of political confidence in the country's unique brand of Ben Ali democracy, the election results have created a deep political vacuum. Such transparently manipulated exercises have also made a mockery of the so-called legitimate opposition in parliament, which finds itself demoralized and discredited in the eyes of most Tunisians. Both the political and socioeconomic terrains still seem receptive to the influence of reformist Islamism in Tunisia today, notwithstanding (or because of) the country's current favorable economic performance and the maintenance of a tight, and at times brutal, security apparatus.

Prospects

All evidence points to the continuation, in the near and intermediate future, of current regime policies toward Islamist and all other political opposition deemed "threatening" to state security interests. Chronic unrest in neighboring Algeria will provide Ben Ali and his ruling RCD with further justification for maintaining a strict law and order regime. This goal will be achieved through a combination of coercion (draconian security measures), incentives (market-oriented policies to spur economic growth), populism (fostering social policies protective of the poor—e.g., food subsidies—and supportive of women's rights), and external aid (economic, security, and military from Europe and the United States).

An-Nahdah's status as the principal movement of political opposition to the current regime remains unchanged. What has changed, however, is that the party has been effectively silenced at home and its activities abroad seriously contained. In recent years, for example, Paris and Washington have collaborated in excluding from their territories an-Nahdah spokesmen. Al-Ghannouchi, for one, has repeatedly been denied a visa to enter the United States to lecture to American university and other audiences, despite the fact that he has committed no act nor made any statement threatening to American national or security interests. Indeed, not too many years ago, the Nahdah leader completed a very successful lecture tour of the United States.

Encouraged by such external support for its efforts to eradicate the Islamic "threat," Ben Ali's government will continue a policy of repression extending far beyond the Islamists to include secular opposition parties, human rights groups, and even outspoken feminists who don't necessarily share the regime's peculiar vision of Ben Ali democracy. Such actions will defer into the indefinite future the country's transition to democracy, however much the regime may publicly declare its commitment to political reform.

One political implication of current and future government policies will be the further alienation of the so-called legitimate opposition. A serious rift has already developed between the government and the five legal opposition parties, following the arrest in October 1995 and the sentencing to an eleven-year jail term in March 1996 of Mohamed Mouada, the leader of the MDS (Mouvement des Démocrates Socialistes), the main opposition group which holds ten of the nineteen seats designated for the opposition in the parliament. This is the first time that a senior member of the legal opposition has been treated in this manner, reflecting the regime's growing authoritarianism and increasing intolerance of any criticism, despite its already strong grip on power. The government will continue its hardline policy of cracking down on all forms of political dissent, muzzling the domestic press, intimidating human rights activists, and restricting the foreign media. It seems to have been lost on government decisionmakers that the failure to develop and nurture a credible secular opposition will only breed radicalism—Islamist or otherwise. Such actions have already increased public cynicism about Ben Ali's repeated claims that Tunisia has developed a fully democratic pluralist political system.

The government feels confident that it has tacit public support for its policies, especially among the expanding but still insecure urban middle class which seems to be willing to forego democratic reform in return for employment, housing, rising living standards, and immunity from the kind of chaos and political turmoil affecting Algeria. Surprisingly—and sadly—many of the country's leading intellectuals, journalists, and writers have collaborated (either actively or by their silence) in this governmental effort, despite the severe limitations this has had on basic civil and human rights, including the freedom of expression. While the often suffocating security presence is resented by many Tunisians, the government will continue to justify such oppression in order to avoid the kinds of "terrorist" acts which would damage tourism, scare off foreign investors, and encourage capital flight.

Tunisia's important overseas allies have thus far accepted Tunis's interpretation of the Islamist challenge and the solutions needed to remedy it— however much the government's authoritarianism and human rights failings have offended their sensibilities. Both France and the United States seem determined to buttress Ben Ali's rule in order to insure Tunisia's role as a useful ally on NATO's southern flank, a supporter of peace with Israel, a star "pupil" of market reform and economic restructuring, and an enclave of political moderation in a volatile region. It is unlikely that either Paris or Washington will apply any pressure on Tunis to alter its harsh domestic security programs as long as Libya remains threatening and Algeria chaotic. Indeed, in his most recent visit to the country in December 1995, the U.S. assistant secretary of state for Middle Eastern affairs, Bob Pelletreau, promised further "cooperation between our armed forces," and declared that the United States "would view with concern any threat or aggression against Tunisia" (press conference, December 1995, Washington, D.C.).

Narrowly defined and politically insensitive security concerns seem to have moved to the very top of the foreign policy agendas of all the parties involved—Tunis, Paris, Washington, Algiers, and Cairo. All share in the belief that "Islamic fundamentalism" constitutes the basic danger to regional security interests—not poverty, authoritarianism, political oppression, or cultural contempt. In this regard, Ben Ali has welcomed Liamine Zeroual's November 1995 presidential victory and both have been joined by Egypt's Hosni Mubarak in an Arab League-led effort to identify Islamist extremism as the principal threat to all incumbent governments in the region. They are being strongly supported in this effort by the West.

Morocco

The Islamist challenge in Morocco remains real. Major support comes from two categories of young people situated at the opposite ends of the socioeconomic ladder: university students and unemployed urban youth. Unlike the situation in Tunisia, however, the debate about political Islam is public, open, and vigorous, even though no Islamist party is legal and the leader of the most influential Islamist movement—Abdessalam Yassine of Justice and Charity (*Al-Adl wal Ihsan*)—was under house arrest in Salé from December 1989 until early 1996 when he was permitted limited public freedom.

Interviews with a broad range of student Islamist activists, government officials, intellectuals, university professors, journalists, and businesspeople reveal a relatively similar assessment of the current political situation—King Hassan II's personal stature and monarchical standing among most of his people remain high and beyond serious challenge. His religious authority as "commander of the faithful" is equally secure, albeit somewhat less so among sophisticated urban elites and educated youth. However, the political credibility and public policy effectiveness of all of the legal political parties both within and without parliament (*Majlis an-Nuwwab*)—those supporting the government as well as those in opposition—remain in serious doubt among the majority of the politically conscious electorate, as well as among otherwise politically passive or indifferent citizens.

Political Islam and Its Socioeconomic Context

Fueling the existing political disenchantment are ongoing social and economic problems that continue to exacerbate political tensions. These in turn are at the root of Islamist appeals. The most crucial challenge facing the regime are the questions of how to overcome pervasive unemployment and low living standards. Despite an upturn in the national economy fostered by the country's market-oriented reforms, urban unemployment remains officially at 20 percent but is probably closer to 40 percent. Underemployment is endemic in rural areas, and millions are dependent on the huge, informal economy for their income. The country also suffers from an exceedingly high illiteracy rate of more than 50 percent for adult males (closer to 80 percent for adult females), which effectively excludes large numbers of people from basic semiskilled work.

Unemployment and low wages have led many of those who could work in the formal economy into the informal sector and underground economy, a phenomenon richly detailed for the city of Fez in the perceptive work of the late Moroccan economist, Mohamed Salahdine (1988). While not a traditional source of Islamic recruitment, this category of semicriminal labor is quickly reaching the outer limits of consensual political behavior.

A parallel process of deculturalization is taking place as a consequence of the ongoing rural exodus to the cities. In 1993, for the first time, the urban population exceeded the number of those living in the countryside. Should current trends continue, it is expected that by the year 2000 the rural population will fall to 25 percent of the total (from nearly 50 percent in 1993), even though agriculture remains crucial to the economy. This has created new social pressures as traditional networks break down and urban slums become filled with peasants. Unless prompt action is taken to anchor peasants in the poor north and other depressed rural areas, significant segments of the urban poor will turn to radical action to overcome their condition of hopelessness and despair.

Another area of concern is the increasing number of labor disputes and the general labor unrest that have resulted from feelings of uncertainty about living standards as people begin to feel the pressure of Morocco's integration into the global economy. The lower middle classes and professionals are also being affected by these trends. With the lowest wages of any Mediterranean country with privileged access to the European Union, a broad swath of the lower and middle classes in Morocco is reacting with increased strike activity and labor protest.

In the political realm, traditional party politics have once again become moribund as a result of the inability of the opposition Kutla (Bloc) to follow up on its electoral victory in the June 1993 parliamentary elections. The Istiqlal (Independence)-USFP (Socialist Union of Popular Forces) alliance lost out in the controversial round of indirect voting held in September 1993. As a result, the established opposition must now be convinced that it is worth continuing with conventional party politics and the voting system, and right-wing parties must be reformed to make the system credible to voters.

Finally, the Sahara issue, while not yet resolved, can no longer serve as a symbolic substitute for real political and economic change. Its political capital as a popular symbol of national pride has virtually run out. As the so-called Saharan consensus comes to an end, Morocco's political leadership needs to reinvigorate local politics so that tensions bubbling below the surface can be channeled into legitimate politics rather than help to fuel an Islamist backlash.

Islamist Currents

All three currents of political Islam have found expression in modern Morocco. Al-Fiqh al-Zamzami (d. 1989) and his traditional Sunni movement is the least ideological and most authentically traditional of Morocco's Islamist movements. Zamzami himself underwent a transformation from Sufi to puritanical reformist in the 1950s. His sons and followers call themselves Sunni which, in the Moroccan context, is widely used to refer to Muslims who advocate a strictly Islamic way of life but are not directly involved in political activities (Munson 1993: 154).

The Sunni movement with which al-Zamzami is identified is a diffuse religious and cultural tendency rather than an organized political group. As such it resembles the apolitical movements described earlier, in which preaching and prayer predominate over political discourse and revolutionary action. Support comes from an indeterminate grouping of shopkeepers and blue collar workers in Morocco and in Europe.

If al-Zamzami represents the most traditional wing of the Islamic opposition faced by King Hassan in the late twentieth century, Abdelkrim Mottei (Muti) and his Islamic Youth (*al-Shabiba al-Islamiyya*) represent its most radical one (Munson 1993: 159). Founded in 1969 by Mottei, a former inspector in the Education Ministry and ex-USFP activist, al-Shabiba al-Islamiyya encompassed five factions and cultivated links with underground Algerian movements. Under Mottei's leadership, al-Shabiba al-Islamiyya began to attract supporters in Morocco's high schools and universities in the early 1970s. Mottei fled Morocco in 1975 for refuge in Teheran following the assassination of leftist journalist and Marxist intellectual Omar Ben Jelloun, whom the government alleged was the target of al-Shabiba murderers.

Mottei subsequently moved to Belgium. In 1984 he was sentenced to death in absentia for his alleged role in January 1984 rioting, during which more than 2,000 arrests were made after the distribution of tracts at outdoor religious meetings. In September of 1985, following the discovery of arms caches in July at border points with Algeria, twenty-six Islamists were sentenced (fourteen to death) in Casablanca for plotting to overthrow the monarchy. Three of these admitted to membership in al-Shabiba. Islamic Youth cells continue to operate, especially in the migrant community. For all intents and purposes, however, this most radical Islamic organization has been effectively shut down as a result of government repression and co-optation.

By the mid-1980s other groups were carrying the banner of radical religious protest. A Mottei colleague from 1976 to 1981, Abdellah Benkirane formed the Islamic Association. In 1986, he renounced violence and attempted open opposition politics. By 1992, the Islamic Association had become the Renewal and Reform movement—unofficially recognized and tolerated by Hassan. In interviews with this writer and others, Benkirane has repeatedly stressed his acceptance of the monarchy and his willingness "to work peacefully and through persuasion." Although his efforts to move into conventional politics have been thwarted, other Islamists accuse him of complicity with the regime. In either case, Renewal and Reform is of limited significance as an opposition movement and is ignored by mainstream politics. The ease with which outsiders can visit and interview Benkirane in Rabat suggests monarchical complicity. Some go so far as to contend that Benkirane receives a regular stipend from the government so that he may continue to spread his message of nonrevolutionary revivalism.

As elsewhere in the Maghreb, nonviolent Islamism dominates the political discourse of Islamic opposition in Morocco. Abdessalam Yassine's Justice and Charity organization is the largest and most popular of such movements. The government has cracked down on the movement, placing Yassine under house arrest in December 1989 and banning his group altogether in 1990.

The man who leads Justice and Charity is a respected albeit frail religious leader approaching seventy. Like his counterparts in Tunisia and Algeria, Yassine exudes a "spiritual aura" as well as a gentleness that comes as a shock to anyone familiar with the stridency of some of his published polemics. Like Madani in Algeria and al-Ghannouchi in Tunisia, Yassine's "scraggly beard" and the "twinkle in his eyes" suggest grandfatherly benevolence rather than religious fanaticism (Munson 1993: 162).

Yassine made himself known as early as 1974 with an open letter to King Hassan entitled "Islam or Deluge?" in which he warned Hassan that he will incur the wrath of God if he does not repent and return to the path of righteousness. In 1981, Yassine published, in French, *La Révolution à l'Heure de l'Islam,* which he described as a "book of appeal" as well as a "book of combat" (see Vatin 1987: 162). The issue, he wrote in the preface, was to "Islamicize modernity not to modernize Islam." The "great challenge" was to overcome *jahiliyya,* "a world governed by ignorance, violence, and selfishness; a world with no spiritual principles whatsoever." In this context, jahil societies are non-Muslim, Western societies whose undue influence on Islamic peoples explains their suffering, backwardness, and oppression (see Vatin 1987: 162–63).

He contended that these jahil societies have to be replaced by Islamic regimes that would establish "Islamic democracy." Such a democracy would introduce a system governed "by the wise, not the sly." The new rules would rest on three elements: the restoration of justice through law, the reestablishment of morals through education, and the revival of *hisba* (the power to control). Islamic democracy means representation (i.e., elections at each stage), responsibility, control and thus the power to sanction. Political participation and majority governance are the rule (Vatin 1987: 164–65).

Like all Islamic reform movements, Yassine identifies the "jahiliyya syndrome" as the central source of Islamic backwardness and suffering. The only weapon that can be successfully used to fight jahiliyya is *jihad,* but jihad as action, not as violence. It is less a battling with the enemy than an active supporting of "education and political action until jahiliyyan ideas and habits have been completely defeated" (Vatin 1987: 164–65).

Based upon strict observance of the *sharia,* the quarterly periodical *Al Jamaa* has advocated a nationwide, nonviolent drive toward social justice. Yassine's *Révolution* drew upon the segment of the population living in absolute poverty (then at least 25 percent of the total and around 35 percent when those living marginally above were included) as much as it did on Hassan's quasi-secular reign for inspiration.

There are no reliable statistics on the membership in Yassine's movement, although the 500,000 put forth by the group itself seems highly inflated. On the other hand, the 5,000 to 10,000 figure provided by Benkirane seems too low. Based on the number who went out to demonstrate in 1990 and 1991 in the streets of Rabat, 50,000 does not seem an unreasonable figure.

While we may never know the exact number of people who are members of al-Adl wal-Ihsan, it is safe to say that large numbers of people—mostly educated youth but also unemployed youth (educated or otherwise)—respond favorably to Yassine's message of justice, democracy, opportunity, integrity, and pride. Deprived of local mosques to spread their message, Yassine's followers depend on word-of-mouth, radio cassettes, small circulation magazines and newspapers, and overseas Muslim communities to propagate their ideas.

Current Trends

One reliable Moroccan source identifies the existence of twenty-nine so-called Islamic tendency movements (*Maroc Hebdo,* January 21–27, 1994, p. 9). But only a handful have national popular support, and Yassine's group is far in the lead (Abdallah Benkirane's Renewal and Reform is a very distant second). For the most part, Islamist political activity in Morocco is nonviolent, despite numerous incidents on university campuses in which Islamists and leftists have fought one another. In an outburst on February 2, 1994, government security forces had to be called in and classes suspended indefinitely at the university in Fez because of clashes between Islamist and leftist students. Similar incidents have been repeated on other campuses as recently as mid-1996.

Where political support is relatively equally divided between Islamists and leftists (as is the case on the campuses in Fez, Oujda, Rabat, and Kenitra), the number of violent incidents between these groups tends to increase. Where Islamist student support is dominant, however, such as at the university centers in Casablanca, Marrakesh, El Jadida, and Mohammedia, tensions rarely overflow into overt conflict, whether directed at university and government authorities or at opposing student groups. Baath-oriented leftist university students have an established record of aggressive behavior. As their support has dwindled on campuses such as Fez where they were once dominant, they have been quick to engage the more popular Islamist groups in physical assaults. A pattern of such assaults has been evident in recent years.

The degree to which the questions of the who, what, when, where, how, and why of Islamism are raised and debated is revealed by the treatment of the subject in the print media. *Maroc Hebdo,* an independent weekly newspaper published and edited by Mohamed Selhami in Casablanca, is one excellent example. In its issue of January 21–27, 1994 (no. 113), for example, a fifteen-page section was devoted to the subject: "Le Casse-Tête Integriste: La Mouvance Islamiste Chez Nous" [The Fundamentalist Riddle: The Islamist Current among Us]. Every critical aspect of political Islam—its socioeconomic origins, organizations and leaders, support on university campuses, relationship to women's issues, status in France, the roles of extremism and violence—were treated in both a nonideological and nonpropagandistic tone. Similarly, an interview with Saïd Naoui (an Islamist student leader at the law faculty of Hassan II University in Casablanca) appeared in the January 13, 1994, issue of *Libération,* the USFP's French-language daily newspaper. This article was candid and forthright as well.

These are but two of the numerous examples one can cite to demonstrate how both Islamists and the government seek to engage and debate the question of political Islam in the country. To be sure, this has not led to formal political recognition of any Islamist movement. Nor does such recognition seem likely any time soon. But given the degree of violence occurring in Algeria and the oppressive political environment being created in Tunisia, it is clear that Moroccan government officials, Islamist activists, and independent-minded intellectuals, journalists, and academicians have chosen a more moderate path that emphasizes public dialogue and discourse rather than confrontation and violence.

Nevertheless, this does not guarantee that political violence will not erupt in the near future. The conditions that tend to motivate people to take violent action are still present: an enormity of economic problems, a deep malaise extant among unemployed youth living in squalid conditions in the country's large cities, and bleak prospects for high school and university students for finding rewarding and appropriate employment when they graduate. Further, the cultural and moral challenges posed by the pervasiveness of Western tourism, entertainment, films, television, music, and literature also raise disturbing questions for Moroccan conservatives, traditionalists, and believers. But in all of these instances, populist Islam—whose message is just as much political and moral-cultural as it is religious—provides many with hope for change. It will continue to influence the thinking and attitudes of the young and the urban poor through religious discourse and delivery of services—jobs, housing, emergency medical treatment, subsidized food, and tutoring.

For its part and with an eye to what is going on in other parts of the Maghreb, the government of Morocco continues to pursue an incremental approach to democracy by releasing political prisoners, improving its human rights situation, promoting elections, televising parliamentary debates, and permitting open public discussion to appear in the country's press. Should this accommodationist environment be maintained, there is little likelihood that Islamic radicalism will substitute for peaceful reformism in the near future.

Algeria

More than five years after the military coup d'état of January 11, 1992, and in the aftermath of General Liamine Zeroual's election to the presidency on November 16, 1995, the Islamic Salvation Front (FIS) remains the premier movement of political opposition in Algeria today. Should elections be held in the near future, a relegalized FIS would win, as it was about to when the military halted the December 1991 legislative elections. The group's "mainstream" political leadership—Abassi Madani, Abdelkader Hachani, Rabah Kébir, Anwar Haddam—continues to remain committed to a political solution to the country's current crises. These so-called *jazairis*—those committed to a distinctly "Algerian" solution to Algerian problems, and whose intellectual inspiration comes from the writings of Malek Bennabi (d. 1973)—reject all models of a pan-Islamic society, advocate an electoral strategy for assuming power, and support the gradual application of the *sharia* (Islamic law) in Algeria. However, the more radical positions of FIS leaders Ali Benhadj, Kamareddine Kherbane, and other so-called internationalists committed to an Islamic holy war (*jihad*)—and inspired by Iran and other "foreign" models—are still considered part of the spectrum incorporated within the Islamist "front."

Context

Islamic revivalism emerged in Algeria as part of the awakening of Arab-Muslim consciousness in the Middle East and North Africa during the period between the world wars. Both locally derived forces and external influences were involved. Most important among the internal factors was the psychological impact of World War I on the Algerian masses. Although the majority of the population remained indifferent to the social and economic appeals of the Francophone assimilationist elites (*évolués*), this was not the case with the inherent appeal of Islam, with which all Algerians could identify as a religio-cultural as well as a political symbol. More important, perhaps, was the influence of the pan-Islamic salafiyya reform movement on the thinking of certain Algerian religious figures. Calling for a return to the puritanical ways of the Muslim past in order to mount a more effective challenge to European technological and organizational superiority, the salafiyya movement was aimed at reasserting the Islamic identity and Arab-Muslim heritage of individual Arabs. The leading Algerian Muslim figure of this Islamic reformism was Shaykh Abdelhamid Ben Badis. Along with other Muslim reformers, Ben Badis created in 1931 the Association of Algerian Ulema, whose motto was to be "Islam is my Religion, Arabic is my Language, Algeria is my Country," reflecting the group's nationalist character and its emphasis on the dual Arab and Islamic nature of Algeria (see Entelis 1986: 42).

Official or State Islam

After gaining independence from France in 1962, the Algerian state officially incorporated Islam. The new ruling military-party hierarchy integrated Islam's religious institutions, coopted its clerical class by requiring state-approved certification, and screened (and sometimes even composed) Friday mosque sermons. All of this was administered by the Ministry of Religious Affairs, through which the state supervised and controlled the expression of Islamist thought. Respected religious thinkers who were identified with salafiyya reformism were allowed to voice their ideas within a narrow Islamic religio-jurisprudential framework. To ensure ideological compliance, these thinkers were often named to posts as government functionaries responsible to the Ministry.

Alternative or Populist Islam

Yet official Islam in independent Algeria was challenged from the very beginning. Only a year after independence, the Qiyam al-Islamiyya (Islamic Values) association, founded by Malek Bennabi and Tidjani al-Hachani, opposed the secular and socialist policies of Ahmed Ben Bella (1962–1965) and, later, of Houari Boumedienne (1965–1978). Bennabi himself was a serious scholar but his followers often used violence; this led to suspension of the organization in 1966 following demonstrations protesting the execution in Egypt of the popular Islamist thinker and activist Sayyid Qutb. It was banned altogether in 1970.

Yet state Islam failed to satisfy the many deep aspirations of disoriented Algerians. Into this vacuum stepped Mustafa Bouyali, who came to represent the most violent expression of that disaffection. In the 1980s, his small group of militant followers in the Armed Islamic Movement (Mouvement Islamique Armé, MIA) initiated attacks against the government in the Larbaa region south of Algiers. In 1987, he was hunted down and killed by security forces; his remaining followers were imprisoned.

A more rational and nonviolent discourse of anti-state Islamism was being promoted by other less flamboyant but more scholarly figures during the same period. Shaykh Abd al-Latif Soltani and Shaykh Ahmad Sahnoun, respected Islamic legal scholars who had long opposed the secularist policies of both Boumedienne and Chadli Benjedid (1979–1992), were thrust into the spotlight by a series of clashes between Islamists and government forces in 1981 and 1982. Of particular significance were the mass arrests at a November 1982 religious rally at the University of Algiers; these in turn led to a protest gathering of 100,000 demonstrators in support of Islamist youth at the university. Among those arrested were Soltani, Sahnoun, and Abassi

Madani, then a little-known university educator. When Soltani died under house arrest in March 1984 at the age of 82, his funeral procession drew over 25,000 mourners in what was the largest Islamic demonstration since the one in 1982 (see Noakes 1993).

With Soltani's death, Sahnoun became the most prominent Muslim leader in Algeria. He founded the Islamic Dawa (Preaching) League known as the Rabita (League) in an attempt to bring together different strands of Islamic thought. Among those also involved in the Rabita were Abassi Madani, Shaykh Mahfoud Nahnah, and Abdellah Djaballah. Sahnoun strove to keep the movement from splintering while at the same time encouraging open debate and free expression of the often contrasting yet equally legitimate viewpoints among Islamist thinkers and activists. The Rabita sought to remain apolitical and concentrated instead on social, cultural, educational, and religious questions. Likewise, Sahnoun sought to distance himself from any overt political role, even though the Rabita's activities have had and continue to have considerable political impact (see Noakes 1993).

The bloody riots of October 1988, in which thousands of young people took to the streets to protest against the state's chronic failure to satisfy socioeconomic needs—basic education, adequate health care, employment opportunities, available housing, sufficient food supplies—transformed Islamism in Algeria into a political movement. A new breed of politically active Islamists—bent on reforming state and society not just by social action and education but through direct involvement in the political process—came to the forefront. In quick fashion, the preachers and Islamic thinkers trained in the philosophical school of Ben Badis's reformism were displaced as the voice of alternative Islam. Islamists did not spearhead the October riots but acted as a stabilizing force, with people like Ali Benhadj (at the time an activist preacher of the Sunna mosque in the capital's Kouba district) helping to restrain the rioters' anger.

It is Benhadj's fellow FIS leader, Abassi Madani, who probably best exemplifies the philosophical as well as generational link between the preachers (religious Islamists) and politicians (reformist Islamists) of oppositional Islam. Born in 1931, Madani was a youthful member of the pre-independence nationalist PPA-MTLD (Parti du Peuple Algérien-Mouvement pour le Triomphe des Libertés Démocratiques) of Messali Hadj. He became associated with FLN (Front de Libération Nationale) founders Mustafa Ben Boulaïd and Rabat Bitat, and joined the party upon its creation in 1954. Arrested for his participation in the outbreak of the insurrection in November of the same year, he spent the duration of the war of independence in prison. During Ben Bella's presidency he was associated with al-Qiyam. He emerged as a leader of the Islamic movement after the November 1982 demonstrations at the University of Algiers, at which time he cosigned (with Islamic legal scholars

Shaykh Abd al-Latif Soltani and Shaykh Ahmad Sahnoun) a list of fourteen demands aimed at the regime. That act earned him more than a year in prison (see Kapil 1990: 34).

With the move toward more political openness that followed the 1988 riots, the Islamic Salvation Front was formed in March 1989 and legally accredited as a party in September 1989. From its outset the FIS was an amalgam of different currents of political thought within the Islamist movement (see fig. 3.2), and although its members agree on the ultimate goal of an Islamic state based on sharia, there are disagreements over both strategy and tactics. Moderate and radical wings look to Madani and Benhadj, respectively.

Straddling both wings is a young generation of FIS "technocrats" who

Figure 3.2. Three Strands of FIS

Preachers/Reformers
Preaching as means to moralizing public life
Adaptive, evolutionary, social
Outside of official or state Islam, including its religious hierarchy
Representatives:
•Tijani al-Hachemi • Abd al-Latif Soltani (1902–1984)
• Omar Arbaouri (b. 1912)
• Mesbah Houidek • Malek Bennabi • Abassi Madani

Radicals/Revolutionaries
Frontal assault on "impious" state
Arabophone, petty bourgeoisie, radicalized in prison
Influenced by writings/sayings/actions of Sayyid Qutb
Born out of confrontation with socialist system, radical Islam
feeds on a repression that it sees as intrinsic to the mukhabarat state
Representatives:
• Mustafa Bouyali (d. 1987) (MIA) • Ali Benhadj (FIS)
• Abdelkader Chebouti (AIS)
• Said Mekhloufi (AIS) • Mohamed Said (d. 1995) (GIA)
• Abderrazak Rajjam (d. 1995) (GIA)

Technocrats
First generation of university graduates since independence (1962)
Scientific and Western (U.S./France/U.K.) education
Upwardly mobile toward modern technocratic elite
Socialized into Islamism on campus, not in mosque
Professions: educators, professors, scientists, engineers, physicans
Representatives:
• Abdelkader Hachani • Said Guechi • Benazzoz Zebda • Rabah Kébir
• Mohamed Boukabache • Said Mouley • Hani Haddare

have had extensive educational and scientific training in the West (France, the United States, and the United Kingdom), where they have received advanced degrees in technical, scientific, engineering, or computer fields. Modern in outlook and in professional training, this first generation of university graduates since independence has been socialized into Islamism on the university campus rather than in the mosque. Rabah Kébir and Abdelkader Hachani are two noted examples of such technocrats.

Despite their different personalities and tactics, Madani and Benhadj have come to symbolize the basically cooperative character of political Islam. They did not allow their differences to impede the FIS in organizing and mobilizing support. After the party's legalization, the leadership quickly began to prepare for local and regional elections set for June 1990. While the ruling FLN enjoyed a considerable edge in funding and organization, the FIS surprised many with its rapid formation of a party infrastructure. This was attributed to its use of a preexisting network of mosques throughout the country, its ability to organize cadres already involved in Islamist activities, and the considerable skill and charisma of Madani and Benhadj. The results were overwhelming FIS victories in the June elections and then in legislative elections in 1991—despite the incarceration of both leaders that June (see Noakes 1993).

Emboldened by the Front's success, Shaykh Mahfoud Nahnah and Abdallah Djaballah created their own Islamist movements, HAMAS (Movement for an Islamic Society [1990]) and an-Nahdah (Renaissance [1990]), respectively. Both represent a form of moderate Islamism less willing to challenge the state. In fact, it is uncertain whether the two are truly independent of government control, with some suggesting that they are being manipulated by the state in an effort to "divide and rule" political Islam. Nahnah's participation in the 1995 presidential election is cited as one recent example of HAMAS's "collaborationist" standing. It also seems likely that the authorities are attempting to revive the legitimacy of the preachers and clerics of "religious" Islam in order to undermine the popularity of the FIS.

This interpretation is confirmed in part by President Liamine Zeroual's creation on May 18, 1994, of the so-called National Transition Council (TNC in French), an unelected body intended to act as an interim legislature and forum for debate prior to the holding of postponed parliamentary elections. According to the Algerian head of state, the TNC is to be one of the three pillars of his regime, together with the National Economic and Social Council (installed on May 9, 1994) and the presidency. For their part, all of the main political parties have boycotted the new body, save for HAMAS, which has five seats in the 200-member assembly.

Following the arrest of Madani and Benhadj and the suspension of the 1991 election results following the 1992 coup, the FIS leadership split. Some advocated a hard line toward the government while others promoted dialogue. All, however, were ultimately displaced following the army's banning of the FIS in March 1992 and the arrest of many of the Front's leaders and followers, including pro-Madani moderates such as Abdelkader Hachani. Not surprisingly, the violent strand of Islamism has reemerged to spearhead the struggle against the government.

Radical Islam

Despite its belief in the primacy of politics over revolution to achieve power, the FIS has been increasingly radicalized by the circumstances in which it finds itself: The Front's leadership is imprisoned, dispersed, or in exile; thousands of FIS militants are holed up in desert camps; government-directed death squads are killing and intimidating Front supporters; and the regime is entirely under the control of a military determined to impose "law and order" at any cost. In response, the Front has pursued a dual strategy of politics and diplomacy on the one hand, armed action on the other. While unable to confirm the precise organizational links between the FIS and the plethora of radical groups that has emerged since early 1992, it is clear that whatever ties exist serve to apply pressure on the ruling military group.

Yet a fundamental historical and structural distinction separates more moderate reformers from radicals. While the former use violence as a tactic of last resort to pressure a recalcitrant, oppressive leadership, the latter consider violence central to the political "cleansing" necessary to establish a new social order. The emphasis on the cathartic value of violence as a psychopolitical experience recalls the theory of revolutionary struggle put forth by Frantz Fanon nearly four decades ago during the Algerian war of national liberation (see Fanon 1968).

Islamic radicalism in Algeria is associated with Mustafa Bouyali, a man who conducted a violent struggle against what he described as the "impious" state from 1981 to 1987, when he was killed by government security forces. His followers never laid down their arms, however, and continued to fight viciously against the hated secular nation-state.

Pacified during the FIS's domination of the political landscape between 1989 and 1992, radical Islam has resurfaced with a vengeance since the 1992 coup. The current crop of radicals is composed of former Bouyali followers opposed to the FIS's political strategy and a new breed of salafiyyist militant—the latter "re-Islamized" by the FIS and further radicalized following the interruption of the electoral process in 1991 (see Labat 1994a and Labat 1994b).

The Bouyalists were pardoned by President Benjedid in November 1989, and the last group still in jail reentered society when the FIS had been legalized and was operating openly. Encouraged by the FIS-organized strikes of May and June 1991 and, more decidedly, by the 1992 coup, they now form the core of those militants involved in the most violent acts against the state. Their goal is straightforward and unambiguous: total destruction of the "corrupt" nation-state, which they want to replace with a pure, "authentic" Muslim state (see Labat 1994a and Labat 1994b).

ISLAMIC SALVATION ARMY (AIS)

The newer generation of Islamic radicals has been intellectually inspired by FIS figures who have turned away from the Front following the suspension of the elections. The best-known among them is Said Mekhloufi, a forty-three-year-old former army officer who in early 1991 published a pamphlet on "Civil Disobedience: Foundations, Objectives, Means, and Methods of Action" that was distributed in mosques throughout the country until the government banned it.

In the pamphlet, Mekhloufi writes that "democracy is a method used by the state to bend people to its wishes" and that "the point of view of the majority cannot be taken into account when preparing for an Islamic state" (Labat 1994b: 54). Public contests of political power have no future as the sole tactic of resistance; those who desire change must instead pursue "a unique solution consisting of completely overturning the regime based on popular struggle using the principle of civil disobedience," which itself is an intermediary step between political action and armed military action (Labat 1994b: 54). This follows from the logic of "gradual dissuasion," which leads to "direct conflict" as a means by which to accomplish a complete rupture with the state. As a consequence of his writings and beliefs, Mekhloufi was removed from the *majlis ash-shura* (consultative council) of the FIS in July 1991 when it decided the Front would participate in December legislative elections. He went underground and continues to direct actions against the state in the *maquis* (countryside).

Another Muslim radical instrumental in creating an "Islamic armed struggle" is Abdelkader Chebouti, an officer in the guerrilla FLN, who served in the army after independence and was among the Bouyali followers granted amnesty in 1989. Never a member of the FIS or its supreme council, Chebouti had close ties to Ali Benhadj, who had flirted with the Bouyalists. Mekhloufi and Chebouti came to represent a fusion of the ideological puritanism of the salafiyyists with the armed militancy of hardened guerrillas—whose formative experience included combat time in Algeria's war of national liberation, the war in Afghanistan, and the fight in the maquis with Mustafa Bouyali. It was therefore no surprise when Mekhloufi and Chebouti teamed up in 1992 to create the Armed Islamic Movement (Mouvement Islamique Armé, MIA; later renamed Islamic Salvation Army [Armé Islamique du Salut, AIS]) whose name, intent, and spirit borrowed directly from the Bouyalist experience. In early 1992 the ruling military junta overturned the

December 1991 election results, forced the resignation of President Benjedid, installed a puppet regime of discredited ex-FLN politicians, and abolished the FIS as a legal political party. With the delegitimization of the Front, the AIS became the FIS's unofficial armed wing and so brought the Islamic radicals to political prominence in Algeria (see fig. 3.3).

If Abassi Madani represents the FIS's political and philosophical link between the preachers and the reformers, Ali Benhadj represents that between the reformers and the radicals. Born in 1956, Benhadj (known by his many admirers as "Alilou," an affectionate diminutive) is a former high school teacher who has been an Islamic militant since the 1970s; he has close ties to the Bouyali group. He was arrested in 1983 and sentenced in 1985 by a state security court. Benhadj represents the "mystical" tendency in Algerian political Islam. The many *fatwas* (Islamic decrees) that he has issued since his arrest in June 1991 reflect a form of mysticism meant to inspire followers to radical action. Arabophone-educated and intellectually nourished by the writings of Sayyid Qutb and Abdallah Azam, Benhadj approximates the thinking if not the actions of the radical Gamaa (Jamaa) movement in Egypt (see Labat 1994b). He is emblematic of the many radicals in the Middle East and North Africa who are Arabic-speaking teachers in primary and secondary schools and who act as independent imams, preaching their redemptive messages in mystical tones. Also in this group are petty arabophone functionaries who resent having a status subordinate to that of their French-educated superiors; men marginalized by their society who have experienced a romantic conversion to the "sacred" Islamic cause; and army deserters who are bitter because their officers, Western trained and educated, passed them over for promotion.

The radicalization of elements of the reformist group is a direct result of the regime's refusal to allow the FIS the fruits of its presumptive 1991 electoral victory. Nonetheless, these ex-FIS militants (who have formally separated themselves from the political wing of the movement or have

Figure 3.3. Islamic Salvation Army (AIS): Table of Organization (1995)

National Emir (Leader): Maddani Merzaq (aka Abou Haithem)
Eastern Region Emir: Madani Merzaq (successor yet to be named)
Western Region Emir: Ahmed Ben Aicha
Central Region Emir: Hussien Abd al-Latif (one of several commanders heading units in the central region; loyalty to Merzaq unconfirmed)

Source: François Burgat, "Algérie: l'AIS et le GIA, Itinéraires de Constitution et Relations," *Monde Arabe* 149 (July–September 1995): 113. Modified and updated by author.

joined/created another organization) still articulate an eminently political Islam that could find resonance in a more reformist and Islamic political environment.

But in the current climate of violence and terror, an even more militant and radicalized form of reform has emerged to challenge all three brands of Islamism: the Armed Islamic Group (Groupe Islamique Armé, GIA) (see Millet 1994).

THE GIA: ARMED ISLAMIC GROUP

Established in 1989, this diverse set of Islamic radicals challenges both the political leadership of the FIS and the military command of the AIS (see fig. 3.4). Its leaders are considered by members "scourges of God," dedicated to "purifying" Algeria by fire and steel. No one is immune from their attacks—nationalists, foreigners, journalists, writers, entertainers, even (or perhaps, especially) moderate Islamists such as Madani.

The GIA derives its notoriety from its attacks against foreigners, journalists, and military personnel, among others. Its strategy is to reject all forms of legal political action in order to establish "the Islamic caliphate in Algeria." Based on statements published in its Arabic-language daily newspaper *Al-*

Figure 3.4. GIA: Table of Organization (1995)

Successive Leaders (1992–1996)

- Mohamed Lavilley (d. 8/31/92)
- Abdelhaq al-Yiaida (d. 1994 in Serkadji prison massacre)
- Jaafar al-Afghani (Mourad Si Ahmed) (d. 2/94)
- Abou Abdallah Ahmed (Cherif Qawasmi) (d. 9/94)
- Abou Khalil Mahfoudh (interim)
- Abou Abderrahman Amin (Jamel Zitouni) (d. 7/16/96)

Commander-in-Chief (Supreme Emir): Antar Zoubri ("Abou Talha")
First Assistant: Abou Khalil Mahfoudh ("Abou Khalil")
Second Assistant (Head of Military Commission): "Khaled"
Head of Political Commission: Abderrazaq Rajjam*
Head of Information Commission: Mohamed Said*
Head of Judicial Commission (Sharia): "Abdelkrim"
[* = former FIS representatives reported to have
been assassinated in December 1995]

Source: François Burgat, "Algérie: l'AIS et le GIA, Itinéraires de Constitution et Relations," *Monde Arabe* 149 (July–September 1995): 113. Adapted, modified, and updated by the author.

Ansar (The Partisans), the group's head rejects the "religion of democracy," considering political pluralism to be "sedition": "We don't intend to participate in elections or enter into the parliament. It is only God who can legislate such things. . . . Our jihad consists of killing and getting rid of all those who fight against God and his Prophet" (Yared 1994a: 18). Intellectuals associated with the regime are specific targets of the group; but most of the GIA's energy is focused on the junta, with the "battle to continue until the complete destruction of the regime" (Yared 1994a: 18).

It is unclear how deeply anchored the GIA is among youth and others who might become supporters, if not activists, in the "armed struggle." What is less in doubt, however, is the impact of army enforcement measures on the otherwise indifferent and inert youth living in the slums of large Algerian cities. As the level of violence has escalated, government forces ("Ninjas"—ski-masked terror police) have conducted police sweeps (recalling the hated French practice in the war of independence) and tortured subjects; the result is that the inhabitants of poor neighborhoods look on the state as their enemy. In the squalor of places such as Eucalyptus, a rundown suburban city eight kilometers south of downtown Algiers, the arrest of teenagers whose only interests are sports and American movies and music reverberates throughout the city's other neighborhoods (Martinez 1994; see also Desjardins 1994). In the backlash, young people are becoming politicized, and the principal beneficiaries have been the GIA as well as the FIS. As a firsthand observer has reported, "the practice of torturing the young men of poor neighborhoods who are otherwise little politicized gives credibility to the Islamic discourse about the delegitimization of the state" (Martinez 1994: 96).

Rage against the authorities is widespread, and a broad range of political groups have lost legitimacy, including the FLN. For the poor and the hopeless, the FIS represents the armed struggle to provide justice to those who demanded it in the October 1988 riots (in which poorer Algerians played a central role), and whose rage was only stoked by the suspension of the elections three years later. The mobilization of youth behind the FIS is not a knee-jerk reaction to Islamism but instead reflects a respect for the concrete accomplishments of the FIS in areas of daily concern for the inhabitants of poorer neighborhoods: crime, jobs, housing, sanitation, health, and law and order.

Nonviolent Islamism Now or Never

While the armed struggle is waged among a triad of increasingly violent forces (the army, the AIS, and the GIA), the political wing of Islamism in Algeria, the FIS, is attempting to remain the premier political opposition movement. Its efforts to maintain a convincingly nonviolent posture, however, are ever more difficult—especially as events on the ground override restraints urged by any one individual, group, or movement.

Moderate FIS leaders have been forced underground or abroad (see fig. 3.5): Abdarraziq Rajjam is in hiding (with speculation that he had joined the ruling council of the GIA only to be assassinated along with Mohamed Said when he allegedly called for a "total unilateral truce" following Zeroual's presidential victory); Rabah Kébir is in Germany; and Anwar Haddam is in the United States. Activities in Algeria have been taken up by small groups of armed men operating under various and changing political labels, all of them dedicated to the violent overthrow of the state by any means possible. While these groups are not supported by the majority of the Front's adherents, they have impressed many of the disenfranchised youths holed up in the country's urban slums. These same young people are further radicalized by the government's hardline policy on violence. Thus while Kébir and Haddam give interviews in the West about the need for a peaceful transfer of power, Chebouti and his guerrillas—with the experience they acquired as *mujahidine* in Afghanistan—are conducting war in the countryside and in the cities.

Since late 1993, both the armed struggle and the political struggle in Algeria have intensified. While the political offensive has been maintained, the fighting and killing have also continued. Kébir and Haddam, the FIS's two leading spokesmen abroad, have increasingly stressed the need for nonviolent opposition in press releases, news conferences, and public declarations. Kébir in particular has been especially active in presenting the Front's "human face," although his earlier political actions were anything but nonviolent.

The wave of killings has continued unabated despite claims to the contrary by the newly elected president. This has increased the pressure on moderates on both sides of the divide as they face hardliners in their own camps while trying to maintain the integrity of their positions in the larger struggle for control of the Algerian state and society.

Figure 3.5. FIS External Executive Committee (as of March 31, 1995)

• Rabah Kébir: President
• Kamar Eddine Kherbane: Vice President
• Abdallah Anas: Member
• Anwar Haddam: President, External Parliamentary Delegation

The Rome Platform

It was under such conditions that secular and Islamic reformers in the political opposition convened the first of several meetings to propose a nonviolent alternative to the continuing bloodshed. Meeting in Rome in November 1994 (Rome I) and then again in January 1995 (Rome II), eight opposition political groupings ranging from the Berberist FFS (Socialist Forces Front of Hocine Aït Ahmed) to the FLN and including the FIS (represented by Kébir and Haddam), signed the Rome Platform ("Platform for a Peaceful Solution of Algeria's Crisis") on January 13, 1995 (see fig. 3.6). It committed the parties to a peaceful resolution of the Algerian crisis. The platform's twelve points are a model of democratic governance and political reconciliation:

- Rejection of violence as a means of acceding to or maintaining power.
- Condemnation of, and a call for the cessation of, exactions from and attacks against civilians and foreigners and the destruction of public property.
- Rejection of dictatorship.
- Respect for human rights.
- Respect for transfer of power through elections based on universal suffrage.
- Respect for popular legitimacy.
- Supremacy of law.
- Guarantee of fundamental liberties, individual and collective, irrespective of race, sex, religion, or language.
- Consecration of a multiparty system.
- Separation of the military from the state.
- Reaffirmation of the constitutive elements of the Algerian personality: Islam, Arabism, Amazighism.
- Separation of legislative, executive, and judicial powers.

Figure 3.6. Signatories to Rome Platform (January 13, 1995)

Ligue Algérienne des Droits de l'Homme (LADH):	Abdennour Ali Yahia
Front des Forces Socialistes (FFS):	Hocine Aït Ahmed
Front de Libération Nationale (FLN):	Abdelhamid Mehri
Front Islamique du Salut (FIS):	Anwar Haddam
	Rabah Kébir
Mouvement pour la Démocratie en Algérie (MDA):	Ahmed Ben Bella
	Khalid Ben-Smaïn
Parti des Travailleurs (PT):	Louisa Hanoune
An-Nahdah:	Abdallah Jaballah
Jeunesse Musulmane Contemporaine (JMC):	Ahmed Ben-Mohammed

On the face of it, the Rome Platform was a significant advance on the part of Islamic and other reformers, all of whom committed themselves to important democratic principles in full view of the international community. What was particularly revealing was the FIS's disavowal of its theocratic ambitions and open acceptance of the democratic principles of the sovereignty of the people and freedom of religion. The Front joined the seven others in rejecting violence as a means of obtaining or retaining power and accepted that in any negotiation with the regime, all parties (including the army) would be entitled to guarantees, all the while tacitly reserving the right to rebellion for as long as the regime refused to negotiate (see Roberts 1995a, 1995b). By aligning itself with the rest of the democratic opposition which, taken together represented 82 percent of those Algerians who voted in 1991, the FIS was committing itself to a peaceful transition of political power. It was also seeking to steal the thunder from its radical challengers both within and outside the movement. Sadly for all Algerians, both the army and the GIA vehemently rejected and furiously denounced the Rome Platform, thereby further emboldening the radicals in Algeria to continue their hardline stands.

Presidential Election: Prelude to Dialogue or Reinforced Army Rule?

The presidential election of November 16, 1995 (see fig. 3.7), which saw Major-General Liamine Zeroual score a decisive victory over his carefully chosen and politically impotent opposition, has been viewed by some as a prelude to resuming publicly what had hitherto been a secret dialogue with

Figure 3.7. Presidential Election (November 16, 1995)

Name	Affiliation	Votes	% of valid votes
Major-Gen. Liamine Zeroual	Army	7,088,616	61.00
Shaykh Mahfoud Nahnah	HAMAS (Islamist)	2,971,974	25.58
Sad Saadi	RCD* (Berberist)	1,115,796	9.60
Noureddine Boukrouh	PRA** ("modern" Islamist)	443,144	3.81
Registered Voters	15,969,904		
Votes cast	12,087,281 [75.69% of registered voters]		
Valid votes	11,619,532 [96.13% of votes cast]		

* Rassemblement pour la Culture et la Démocratie
** Parti du Renouveau Algérien

Source: IFES, *Elections Today* 5, no. 4 (January 1996): 40.

the moderate FIS leadership—despite the continuing imprisonment of Madani, the banning of the party, and the boycott of the election itself by all the members of the Rome Platform.

This view sees Zeroual as having gained the upper hand in the struggle between "eradicators" and "conciliators" in the government and the army, which provided him with the necessary popular mandate to go forward on two fronts simultaneously: preparing the political groundwork for new municipal and legislative elections while continuing to pursue a ruthless campaign of extermination against the GIA and AIS. The election itself is thus interpreted as a victory for democracy as well since it represented the first-ever contested multiparty election for a head of state in the Arab world—a statement devoid of any real meaning given the retrograde status of Arab politics. With hardliners such as Chief of Staff Lt. Gen. Mohamed Lamari and his counterparts in the state apparatus now in temporary check, those who subscribe to this view believe that Zeroual will move quickly to exploit incipient divisions within the Rome group so as to broaden his otherwise narrow base of public support. Mehri's forced resignation as secretary-general of the FLN along with conciliatory statements being made by former premier Mouloud Hamrouche and the FIS's Rabah Kébir in the aftermath of Zeroual's victory are then seen as an indication that the Algerian political landscape is about to undergo some change.

An alternate interpretation is less generous or optimistic about the election result and its meaning. With no credible opposing candidate permitted to run (the FIS was banned from doing so), there was never any real doubt about the electoral outcome—only the size of the vote. The army's massive presence on election day prevented violence but also intimidated and coerced voters to go to the polls. Despite talk of dialogue, the FIS remains illegal and its leadership in prison. Civil society is being contained from every direction as opposing voices are brutally silenced. Press freedoms have been severely curbed, basic civil liberties ignored, and human rights violated daily. And although the government would like people to believe that the relatively large voter turnout reflected support for the incumbent and his policies, the reality is that Algeria's silent majority was simply fed up with the violence and chaos and hoping an elected authority could begin to reestablish law and order. Clearly what the populace was not expressing was support for the military—an institution which has yet to regain its former luster and legitimacy, lost during the deadly riots of October 1988.

All evidence seems to point toward less—not more—democracy, involving greater application of armed coercion, political manipulation, propaganda, and widespread use of secret police tactics as the means by which to reestablish the old authoritarian order. In this sense, we are witnessing the "Ben Alization" of Algeria in which a law-and-order authority tries to contain if not destroy all vestiges of populist Islam while promoting itself as a free market economy interested in encouraging foreign investment, privatizing state-run enterprises, enticing Western tourism, inviting greater outside participation in the hydrocarbon industry, and generally gaining or seeking to gain the favor of European, American, and Asian investors so as to overcome the massive economic problems that many believe are at the root of the country's political turmoil and social disarray. In its political dimension, this approach involves the suppression of all forms of autonomous civil society activity, justified in the name of fighting terrorism and Islamic fundamentalism—policies which find receptive audiences in the West.

Yet Algeria is not Tunisia. The country is too socially complex, too advanced in its level of political awareness, too sophisticated in its understanding of propaganda and dissimulation, and too close to its democratic experience to be bullied about by second-rate army officers. More importantly, the ills that first led Algerians to give overwhelming support to the Islamists remain—political authoritarianism, a centralized economy, bureaucratic mismanagement, rampant corruption, cultural insensitivity (such as a policy of "mindless" Westernization and secularization). Until these are rectified, any short-term political or military successes the army achieves may be rapidly overtaken by another round of extremism in which nonviolent Islamists such as those in the FIS could be the victims.

References

Al-Ahnaf, M. 1993. "Maroc: Force et Faiblesses des Acteurs Juridiques." *Monde Arabe: Maghreb-Machrek*, no. 142 (October–December): 16–23.

Al-Ahnaf, M., Bernard Botiveau, and Franck Frégosi. 1991. *L'Algérie par ses Islamistes*. Paris: Karthala.

"Algérie." 1991. *Les Cahiers de L'Orient*, no. 23 (entire issue).

"Algérie: Vers l'Etat Islamique?" 1990. *Peuples Méditerranéens*, nos. 52–53 (July–December).

"Algérie-Maghreb: La Stratégie des Islamistes." 1994. *Courrier International*, no. 169, January 27–February 2, pp. 9–12.

Amnesty International. 1993. *Algeria: Deteriorating Human Rights under the State of Emergency*. New York: Amnesty International USA.

———. 1994. *Tunisia—Rhetoric versus Reality: The Failure of a Human Rights Bureaucracy*. New York: Amnesty International USA.

Belbah, Mustapha. 1994. "A la Recherche des 'Musulmans de France.'" In Gilles Kepel, ed., *Exils et Royaumes: Les Appartenances au Monde Arabo-Musulman Aujourd'hui*, pp. 331–45. Paris: Presses de la Fondation Nationale des Sciences Politiques.

Burgat, François, and William Dowell. 1993. *The Islamic Movement in North Africa*. Austin: University of Texas–Center for Middle Eastern Studies.

Cesari, Jocelyne. 1993. "Algérie: Contexte et Acteurs du Combat Pour les Droits de l'Homme." *Monde Arabe: Maghreb-Machrek*, no. 142 (October–December): 24–31.

Desjardins, Thierry. 1994. "La République Islamique des Eucalyptus." *Le Figaro* (Paris), January 7, p. 4b.

El-Difraoui, Abdelasiem. 1994. "La Critique du Système Démocratique par le Front Islamique du Salut." In Gilles Kepel, ed., *Exils et Royaumes: Les Appartenances au Monde Arabo-Musulman Aujourd'hui*, pp. 105–24. Paris: Presses de la Fondation Nationale des Sciences Politiques.

El Gahs, Mohamed, and Saïd Ahid. 1994. "Un 'Barbu' Imberbe se Confie à *Libé*." *Libération*, no. 888, January 13, pp. 1, 3.

Entelis, John P. 1986. *Algeria: The Revolution Institutionalized*. Boulder, CO: Westview.

———. 1989. *Culture and Counterculture in Moroccan Politics*. Boulder, CO: Westview.

———. 1992. "Introduction: State and Society in Transition." In John P. Entelis and Phillip C. Naylor, eds., *State and Society in Algeria*, pp. 1–30. Boulder, CO: Westview.

———. 1994. "Islam, Democracy, and the State: The Reemergence of Authoritarian Politics in Algeria." In John Ruedy, ed., *Islamism and Secularism in North Africa*, pp. 219–51. New York: St. Martin's.

———. 1995. "Political Islam in Algeria: The Nonviolent Dimension." *Current History* 94, no. 588 (January): 13–17.

———. 1996. "Civil Society and the Authoritarian Temptation in Algerian Politics: Islamic Democracy versus the Centralized State." In Augustus Richard Norton, ed., *Civil Society in the Middle East*, vol. 2, pp. 45–86. Leiden: Brill.

Fanon, Frantz. 1968. *The Wretched of the Earth*. New York: Grove.

Gasiorowski, Mark J. 1992. "The Islamist Challenge: The Failure of Reform in Tunisia." *Journal of Democracy* 3, no. 4 (October): 85–97.

Gellner, Ernest, and Jean-Claude Vatin, eds. 1981. *Islam et Politique au Maghreb*. Paris: Editions du CNRS.

Hedges, Chris. 1994. "Islamic Guerrillas in Algeria Gain against Military Rulers." *New York Times*, January 24, pp. A1, A6.

Hermassi, Elbaki. 1991. "The Islamicist Movement and November 7." In I. William Zartman, ed., *Tunisia: The Political Economy of Reform*, pp. 193–204. Boulder, CO: Lynne Rienner.

Jourschi, Slah. 1994. Personal interview, January 13, Tunis, Tunisia.

Kapil, Arun. 1990. "Algeria's Elections Show Islamist Strength." *Middle East Report* 166 (September–October): 31–36.

Labat, Séverine. 1994a. "Islamism and Islamists: The Emergence of New Types of Politico-Religious Militants." In John Ruedy, ed., *Islamism and Secularism in North Africa*, pp. 103–21. New York: St. Martin's.

———. 1994b. "Islamismes et Islamistes en Algérie: Un Nouveau Militantisme." In Gilles Kepel, ed., *Exils et Royaumes: Les Appartenances au Monde Arabo-Musulman Aujourd'hui*, pp. 41–67. Paris: Presses de la Fondation Nationale des Sciences Politiques.

———. 1996. *Les Islamistes Algériens: Entre les Urnes et le Maquis*. Paris: Seuil.

Lamchichi, Abderrahim. 1992. *L'Islamisme en Algérie* Paris: Editions L'Harmattan.

Lapidus, Ira M. 1988. *A History of Islamic Societies.* Cambridge: Cambridge University Press.

"Le Casse-Tête Integriste: La Mouvance Islamiste Chez Nous." 1994. *Maroc Hebdo* (Casablanca), no. 113 (January).

Leveau, Rémy. 1993. *Le Sabre et le Turban: L'Avenir du Maghreb.* Paris: François Bourin.

Lowrie, Arthur L., ed. 1993. *Islam, Democracy, the State and the West: A Round Table with Dr. Hasan Turabi,* May 10, 1992. Tampa, FL: World & Islam Studies Enterprise.

Magnuson, Douglas K. 1991. "Islamic Reform in Contemporary Tunisia: Unity and Diversity." In I. William Zartman, ed., *Tunisia: The Political Economy of Reform,* pp. 169–92. Boulder, CO: Lynne Rienner.

Maroc Hebdo (Casablanca). 1994. January 21–27, p. 9.

Martinez, Luis. 1994. "Les Eucalyptus, Banlieu d'Alger, dans la Guerre Civile: Les Facteurs de la Mobilisation Islamiste." In Gilles Kepel, ed., *Exils et Royaumes: Les Appartenances au Monde Arabo-Musulman Aujourd'hui,* pp. 89–104. Paris: Presses de la Fondation Nationale des Sciences Politiques.

Middle East Watch. 1994. *Human Rights Abuses in Algeria: No One Is Spared.* New York: Human Rights Watch.

Millet, Gilles. 1994. "La Genèse de Groupes Armés qui ont Débordé le FIS." *Libération* (Paris), March 14, p. 21.

Munson, Henry, Jr. 1993. *Religion and Power in Morocco.* New Haven: Yale University Press.

Noakes, Greg. 1993. "Islamism vs. the State in Algeria." *Middle East Affairs Journal* 1, no. 3 (Spring–Summer): 14–28.

Roberts, Hugh. 1994. "Algeria between Eradicators and Conciliators." *Middle East Report* (July–August): 24–27.

———. 1995a. "Algeria's Ruinous Impasse and the Honourable Way Out." *International Affairs* (London), vol. 71, no. 2, pp. 247–67.

———. 1995b. "State and Army Repression Is at the Heart of Algerian Violence." *Irish Times* (Dublin), February 6.

Roth, Katherine. 1993. "Interview with Rabah Kébir." *Institute of Current World Affairs* (December 5): 8 pp.

Rouadjia, Ahmed. 1990a. "Doctrine et Discours du Cheikh Abbassi." *Peuples Méditerranéens,* nos. 52–53 (July–December): 167–80.

———. 1990b. *Les Frères et la Mosquée: Enquête sur le Mouvement Islamiste en Algérie.* Paris: Karthala.

Salahdine, Mohamed. 1988. *Les Petits Métiers Clandestins: 'Le Business Populaire.'* Casablanca: Eddif Maroc.

Simon, Catherine. 1994. "Algérie: Le Pouvoir Paraît Se Résigner au Dialogue avec les Islamistes." *Le Monde* (Paris), February 14.

Taarij, Hinde. 1992. *Les Voilées de L'Islam.* Casablanca: Eddif Maroc.

Vatin, Jean-Claude. 1987. "Seduction and Sedition: Islamic Polemical Discourses in the Maghreb." In William R. Roeff, ed., *Islam and the Political Economy of Meaning: Comparative Studies of Muslim Discourse.* Berkeley: University of California Press, pp. 160–79.

Vergès, Meriem. 1994. "La Casbah d'Alger: Chronique de Survie dans un Quartier en Sursis." In Gilles Kepel, ed., *Exils et Royaumes: Les Appartenances au Monde Arabo-Musulman Aujourd'hui*, pp. 69–88. Paris: Presses de la Fondation Nationale des Sciences Politiques.

Yared, Marc. 1994a. "Qui Derrière le GIA [Groupe Islamique Armé]." *Jeune Afrique*, no. 1725 (January 27–February 2), pp. 16–18.

———. 1994b. "Radioscopie de la Nébuleuse Islamiste." *Jeune Afrique*, nos. 1720–21 (December 23, 1993–January 4, 1994), pp. 20–23.

Zghal, Abdelkader. 1991. "The New Strategy of the Movement of the Islamic Way: Manipulation or Expression of Political Culture?" In I. William Zartman, ed., *Tunisia: The Political Economy of Reform*, pp. 205–17. Boulder, CO: Lynne Rienner.

4.

The Politics of Human Rights in the Maghreb

SUSAN WALTZ

Across the Maghreb, human rights issues have edged their way to the center of the political stage. Tunisian President Zine el-Abidine Ben Ali appointed a presidential adviser on human rights in 1990 and established a national commission to investigate claims of human rights abuse the following year. Tunisia hosted the African regional meeting preparatory to the 1993 World Conference on Human Rights and later that year established a national human rights prize. Morocco's King Hassan II created a royal Consultative Council on Human Rights (CCDH) in 1990 and in 1993 named a former human rights activist to head a newly created Ministry of Human Rights. Algerian President Chadli Benjedid had also named a human rights minister, and the High State Council that assumed power upon his resignation in January 1992 created an Observatory for Human Rights to serve as a national watchdog.

Governments have placed new emphasis on human rights, but the notion itself is not new to states in the region. Well before the contemporary period, Maghreb states joined the emergent international human rights regime and sought to exercise influence in international human rights bodies. Two multilateral treaties—the International Covenant for Civil and Political Rights (ICCPR) and the International Covenant for Economic, Social, and Cultural Rights (ICESCR)—form the backbone of the international human rights regime, and Tunisia and Algeria acceded to them shortly after they were opened for signature and ratification in 1965. The treaties entered in force in 1976, and Morocco ratified them in 1979. In 1981 the Moroccan delegate to the United Nations Commission on Human Rights served as rapporteur, and Tunisia was represented in the independent Human Rights Committee established by the ICCPR.

Endorsement of emergent international standards did not, however, automatically bring adjustments to domestic behavior. Practice has not kept pace with professed commitment, then or now. In all three countries torture has been widespread, facilitated by provisions for incommunicado detention known as *garde-à-vue*. Some political prisoners in the region have died as a result of torture while in police detention. Political trials have been common, and procedures have frequently made a mockery of fairness and justice. Prison conditions in some instances have been exceptionally harsh, and in Morocco, hundreds of individuals were "disappeared" and held incommunicado as officials denied they were in custody. For many years a climate of fear stifled political activity in Algeria, and a number of political dissidents there were assassinated.

The fact that both the idea of human rights and practices that abuse those rights have formed part of the North African political landscape for many years confuses efforts to analyze the politics of human rights in the contemporary period. But that history notwithstanding, since the late 1980s it has been evident that governments in the Maghreb are devoting substantial political energies to promoting their attachment to human rights, implementing rights-related reforms, and deflecting domestic and international criticism. How is the current concern to be explained? Further, how significant is it in terms of the enduring political features of the region? An answer to the first of these questions must take into account both the rise of a North African human rights movement after 1977 and the mounting criticism levied by international society, the press, and Western governments. Answering the second question leads us to weigh political rhetoric against political reality. To set the stage for both questions, attention is first directed away from the subjects of this study and toward its object, respect for human rights and the politics that surrounds it.

Human Rights and Political Practice

The international attention focused on human rights victims in recent years has been accompanied by a tendency to disassociate human rights practices from their political context. It is important to recognize, though, that political repression and the human rights violations that come in its wake are useful tools for those who govern. Critics and regime opponents are nearly always an irritant to rulers, and at times the expression of discontent may threaten to topple a government or its leaders. As Donnelly (1986: 617) notes, respecting human rights is irksome to those who govern. It likewise runs counter to Machiavelli's advice that rulers do well to cultivate fear (Adams 1992: 45–47). Yet as Migdal (1988: 226) writes, a politics of survival that turns on fear may very well involve the systemic weakening of the state's agencies and promote a kind of political deinstitutionalization that over the long run makes governance more difficult. Human rights problems are associated with authoritarianism and political systems that set rulers above the rules. They multiply in situations where arbitrary powers accrue to those charged with governance.

In North Africa, human rights abuses over the past four decades have strengthened the hand of personal rulers and accentuated arbitrariness in government. Broad-based nationalist movements helped oust French colonists, but at independence important questions about popular participation and power sharing remained unresolved in each country. To assist in the drive to assert political control, leaders in each state developed a security apparatus. But knowledge is power, and knowledge about dissidence is a special sort of power. To some degree, each agency developed a measure of autonomy and claimed for itself the privilege of power.

The transformation of colonial agencies into domestic intelligence and security forces followed quickly on the heels of independence. Even before 1960, Moroccan monarch Mohammed V made use of an impressive security apparatus, and his son and successor Hassan II continued the practice. Both the army and an internal security force known as the Sûreté Nationale (SN) were used to quell internal uprisings, but unrest in the 1960s and two successive coup attempts in the early 1970s (in which top generals and security chief General Mohammed Oufkir were implicated) resulted in reorganization to limit the accumulation of power within units beyond the immediate reach of the palace. Today the SN shares responsibility for internal security with a bureaucratic rival, the Auxiliary Forces; both agencies report to the Ministry of the Interior but are overseen by the Royal Gendarmerie, a division of the armed forces and as such commanded by the palace. In addition, two intelligence agencies are said to have direct access to the Interior Ministry and the palace. The SN remains the principal security agency, though it is itself subdivided into four separate units. The most prominent of these include the Urban Corps, which is generally responsible for assuring order in urban areas and which is also the first line of defense in times of unrest; and the Judicial Police, which has the power to make arrests and carry out interrogation of suspects in special detention centers (Nelson 1986: 362–69; Claisse 1992). Interior Minister Driss Basri is considered by many to be the second most powerful man in the kingdom as a consequence of his responsibility for the deliberately fragmented but formidable security apparatus.

Algerian heads of state beginning with Colonel Houari Boumedienne have relied on a multifaceted security apparatus, the most noteworthy element of which has been the intelligence branch of the military known as the Sécurité Militaire (SM). The SM was established at independence to conduct counterespionage activities, but after the 1965 coup its mandate was expanded to include surveillance of all political actors and activity, whether in support of the regime or in opposition to it. Its first two directors, Colonel Kasdi Merbah (1962–79) and General Lakhal Ayyat (1979–88), reported only to the president, who after 1965 was also Minister of Defense (*Jeune Afrique*, October 16, 1990). Broad powers facilitated arbitrary arrests, and many of those who fell into its hands were detained for extended periods and subjected to torture, beyond the reach of the judicial system (Redjala 1991: 170). Others were assassinated.

Frequently referred to as the "political police," the SM is alleged to have operated as freely in France as in Algeria, and even within its ranks coteries were formed to pursue particularistic agendas. Influential members of the SM were thought to be critical of Benjedid, and observers speculated that they had helped instigate each of the main incidents that troubled the Benjedid regime from 1980 to 1988 (Harbi 1989). After the events of October 1988, regime critics charged that the army, through the SM, had abused its powers and was responsible for the torture and ill-treatment of many taken into custody. Benjedid responded to those charges by initiating a series of reforms intended to limit the scope of the SM's activities. Its name was changed in 1990 to the General Office of Documentation and Security (DGDS), and it was relabeled again in 1994 as the Department of Information and Security (DRS). With the vicious civil war taking a dramatic and bloody toll on thousands of Algerians since the military coup d'état of January 11, 1992, the DRS's reputation as a ruthless instrument of human rights repression remains intact.

In Tunisia, the Neo-Destour Party created by Habib Bourguiba developed a coherent and well-planted political organization to incorporate most Tunisians into the republican political system established in 1957; but what could not be accomplished directly by decree or through the promise of an extensive patronage system was achieved by coercion. Two police units were created shortly after independence to maintain control over urban and rural areas, and in 1967 these were brought together under a single Office of National Security housed in the Ministry of the Interior. The National Guard (gendarmerie) continued to serve security purposes, particularly in relation to counterinsurgency, but its more prominent responsibilities included patrol of the country's highways and emergency response efforts.

Tunisia's Sûreté Nationale (SN), on the other hand, was primarily charged with maintaining public order. As it was originally configured, the SN was a decentralized organization and its units were responsible to the governorates to which they were assigned. By the mid–1980s the locus of control had shifted, and the chain of command led more directly back to the SN director—who at the time was General Ben Ali. Ben Ali oversaw not only the recognized national security police but also two auxiliary forces concerned with riot control and intelligence (Nelson 1986: 311). Both of these two specially trained forces, the Public Order Brigade and the plainclothes Office of Territorial Security, have participated in the arrest and detention of political opponents. Many detainees have claimed they were tortured while held in the SN cells in the Ministry of the Interior (Amnesty International 1990).

The targets of repression shifted over the decades, according to perceptions of political threat. In the early years after independence, nationalist rivals were targeted. Several of these were personal opponents of individual leaders; in some cases they were associated with a region or an ethnic group. Tunisia's first political trial, brought before a specially created High Court, opened even before the end of 1956; both the family of Lamine Bey, who had nominally ruled Tunisia in the final years of the French Protectorate, and Bourguiba's archrival Salah Ben Youssef were accused of political crimes (Bessis and Belhassen 1988). In Morocco, the army helped stamp out a rebellion in the North, and in 1965 the monarch's leftist critic and popular opponent, Mehdi Ben Barka, was abducted in France and presumably murdered by Moroccan security forces (Violet 1991). One leading Algerian nationalist, Abbane Ramdane, died under suspicious circumstances in Morocco in 1957; four others were executed in 1959 after a tribunal presided over by Boumedienne found them guilty of treason (Redjala 1991).

Opposition began to take shape in the 1960s, and security apparatuses across the region refocused their attention on an emergent political left. In June 1963, shortly after Morocco's first parliamentary elections, about one hundred leaders of the National Union of Popular Forces (UNFP)—including several newly elected members of parliament—were arrested (Waterbury 1970). In Algeria, a coup d'état ousted Ahmed Ben Bella. To no one's surprise, he was placed under house arrest, but leftist dissidents who organized an opposition movement were also arrested. Tunisian authorities followed closely the activities of the national student union, and the fall of socialist super minister Ahmed Ben Salah in 1969 brought collateral arrests of numerous student leaders (*Le Maghreb*, December 26, 1981). Over the next two decades, repression in Tunisia centered on Baathists, workers, and trade unionists, and after 1981, on Islamic activists. In Algeria, women's groups and ethnic Berbers were punished for challenging the state. Islamists arrested in the early 1980s were accused of violent crimes, but some were held for years without ever being brought to trial. Moroccan dissidents over the past two decades have included leftists, trade unionists, and Islamists, but the Western Saharan war provided the state with another rationale for repression. After 1975 hundreds disappeared from southern Morocco, and to advocate autonomy for the disputed territory was to write one's own prison sentence.

Political Interest in Human Rights

In the first decades after independence, security agencies exercised important discretionary powers; when reforms were implemented, they were intended only to reduce the potential threat they posed to state leaders. Leaders
in many instances sanctioned pursuit of their political enemies and allowed
rights to be violated with impunity. Some efforts were made to cloak political
maneuvers and machinations in the trappings of law, but often those at the
helm of state resorted to extralegal or minimally legal measures.

Such practices were well entrenched, and for the politics of human rights,
the late 1980s were therefore watershed years. The particulars varied from
country to country—but prison doors opened, laws regarding political detention were altered, and both press and political parties were granted more
liberties. The bloodless coup that replaced Tunisia's aging president Bourguiba with his prime minister, Ben Ali, was the pivotal event; it unleashed new
energies across the region. In Tunisia, measures of judicial clemency were extended to more than three thousand individuals jailed for politically related
crimes. Structural reforms included the imposition of limits on the presidential term of office, the abolition of the State Security Court, and the development of legal limits to incommunicado pretrial detention. Opposition forces
were allowed new freedoms, facilitating their legal recognition and the operation of an independent press (Zartman 1991; Waltz 1991a).

It was only a matter of time before a similar wave of reform swept Algeria.
Riots that wracked the city of Algiers in October 1988 accelerated a process
of political liberalization that had slowly been set in motion two years before.
In early 1987, Berber human rights activists arrested two years earlier were released from prison and a human rights organization that enjoyed government
support was permitted to issue reports on prison conditions, psychological
hospitals, and the status of children (Bababji 1989). Of even greater significance, the Algerian League of Human Rights celebrated its first anniversary,
in April 1988, with a national conference on censorship and self-censorship.
The conference was boycotted by the official press but the room in which it
was held was packed. The seal of silence was broken, and over the following
months an association of Algerian journalists was formed. Journalists and
activists alike openly denounced the torture that accompanied widespread arrests in October and secured government promises to curtail the practice. A
Ministry of Human Rights was created, and early in 1989 Chadli Benjedid
inaugurated an overhaul of the political system with a commitment to elections and a new constitution. The June 1990 municipal elections were opened
for contest, and Islamists behind the newly raised banner of the Islamic Salvation Front (FIS) scored a victory in all major municipalities. Legislative elections planned for December promised to install Algeria's first popularly chosen parliament—until the whole process was interrupted by a military coup.

In Morocco it was not so much the political system as the monarch himself that seemed to undergo transformation. Hassan II had on numerous public occasions denied that Morocco held more than a handful of political prisoners; accordingly, the first hint that important changes were in the offing came in May 1989, when fifty long-term and well-known leftist prisoners were released from Kenitra's Central Prison. Later in the year he would declare before European television audiences, "If I knew that even 1% of what Amnesty International says is true, I wouldn't be able to get a wink of sleep" (De Barrin 1990). In 1990, he created the CCDH to advise on human rights issues, and in 1991, other prison doors began to swing open. First, the wife and children of General Mohammed Oufkir were released to freedom. For most of nineteen years they had been held secretly, unable to communicate with the outside world, as apparent payment for Oufkir's orchestration of the attempted coup in 1972. In June 1991, some three hundred of the "disappeared" Saharans for whom Morocco had never acknowledged responsibility quietly reappeared. Most of the remaining Kenitra dossiers were closed two months later, and Abraham Serfaty, one of Morocco's most best-known dissidents, was released into exile. In September, a rumor circulated noisily in diplomatic and human rights circles: The notorious military prison at Tazmamart had been razed. Slowly, over the next several months and well into 1992, its thirty surviving inmates were returned to civilian life; and in December 1991, even the Boureqat dossier was dusted off. The three brothers of mixed French and North African parentage once known as dandies at court but long since fallen from favor emerged from underground cells at Tazmamart where, like the military prisoners, they had been hidden from view and from memory. Some of the world's longest held political prisoners had been set free.

The spate of releases and apparent reversals of longstanding policies returns us to the first of the two questions posed at the outset of this essay: What concerns or events underlie these developments? How are they to be explained? Socioeconomic change pervasive in the region created the context for a change in certain human rights practices; but I would argue that the impetus for the implemented policy changes came from two distinct but interacting sets of actors that had not previously exercised great influence on North African politics. Scholars are increasingly recognizing the interplay between domestic and international actors, as well as the growing influence of nonstate actors in international politics (Rosenau 1990; Huntington 1991; Camilleri and Falk 1993)—the politics of human rights in the Maghreb is illustrative of the dynamic.

The backdrop for liberalizing change in the late 1980s was constructed during the previous decade, when socioeconomic pressures mounted across the Maghreb. Political violence erupted more than once in all three countries. The cycle began in Tunisia with the 1978 Black Thursday labor protests that brought the army into politics and tanks into Tunis. In 1984, the announcement of a precipitous increase in bread prices (and a longer-range plan to reduce social subsidies) spawned another series of protests. Unrest spread from cities in the south to Tunis. Although the policy was ultimately revoked, the discontent cost Interior Minister Driss Guiga his job; and had he not had the foresight to flee, it also would have cost at least his liberty (Tessler 1985).

Likewise, Morocco saw economic protests in 1981, 1984, and 1990. Riots in 1981 that centered on the Casablanca squatter settlement of Ben MSik were sparked by a decision to reduce price subsidies on basic foodstuffs as recommended by the International Monetary Fund. Protests in 1984 began in the north and spread across the country; they were provoked by an announced increase in education-related fees. Labor unrest mounted steadily, so that in the first four months of 1987 alone, there were more than twenty separate strikes in progress (Diouri 1992: 75–78). The 1990 unrest that swept the city of Fez began as a labor strike to protest curtailed freedom to organize and continuing restrictions on those sanctioned after the 1981 Casablanca riots.

Finally, Algeria also saw several protests, though none of them appear to have had any organizational backing. Berbers protested restrictions on cultural expression at Tizi Ouzou in 1980; announced educational reforms caused Constantine to erupt in 1986; and a vague call for a general strike prompted five days of political violence in 1988 in Algiers (Duran 1989). The region as a whole suffered economic decline. Drought cut agricultural revenues, declining oil prices reduced available foreign exchange, and in Morocco, a costly war in the Western Sahara—combined with massive infrastructure investment in occupied territories—drained royal coffers (Aghrout and Sutton 1990).

Expressions of economic discontent were amplified by Islamic activists who found voice in the 1980s and presented themselves as social critics and champions of the politically disfranchised. Although no single factor may be isolated as driving this movement, it is clear that in addition to economic and political discontent, it has derived support from widespread popular disaffection with the cultural orientations of the government and ruling classes (Munson 1993; Zghal 1991; Mortimer 1993; Burgat 1993). Importantly, conservative elements in society were offering challenges that could not easily be dismissed; and those in power were forced to acknowledge that they faced opposition on the political right as well as the political left.

Governments generally responded to the unrest with their own waves of arrest and repression, frequently followed by some conciliatory measures. After the dust of the 1984 unrest had settled in Tunisia, for example, Prime Minister Mohammed Mzali made a tour of the provinces and promised job creation initiatives. In Morocco, the squatter settlement of Ben MSik was razed, and low-income high-rise apartments were constructed on the site; similar new programs are envisioned for Fez. These old and familiar tactics, and the old and familiar rhetoric that accompanied them, were, however, no longer persuasive, and protest movements did not dissolve.

It is clear that a pervasive mood of domestic discontent, occasionally erupting in political violence, disquieted Maghrebi statesmen; but concern for popular sentiment does not easily explain the loosening of the repressive grip. Unrest had more commonly elicited firm response. When Moroccans took to the streets in 1965, for example, King Hassan II reacted by suspending Morocco's constitution; and after the 1971 and 1972 attempted coups, gestures of conciliation were offset by increased harassment of prominent members of the political opposition (Zartman 1987; Perrault 1990). In Algeria, the Berber cultural movement was repressed, and after the 1986 protests in Constantine, the ruling Front de Libération Nationale (FLN) only battened down the hatches. In Tunisia, Bourguiba opened the decade with promises of political liberalization, but by 1987 he was firmly committed to a policy of political repression. After 1990, Ben Ali similarly imposed new measures of control. But that is to anticipate the story.

At the beginning of 1987, governments across the region were committed to hardline policies. Little foreshadowed the dramatic changes that would begin within the year, and the indications of change that were there were easily overlooked. One subtle change involved the slate of political actors. Across the Maghreb, small groups of individuals, most of them well educated and many drawn from elite backgrounds, had organized themselves as human rights groups. Their express purpose was to work toward liberalizing change and an end to abuses. While they had no control over either socioeconomic malaise or the precipitous change that brought an alteration in the leadership in Tunisia, they were in place to press their cause when opportune moments presented themselves (Waltz 1995).

The first of these groups to emerge was the Tunisian League of Human Rights (LTDH), founded in 1977. Individuals from across the full spectrum of Tunisian political life—including Islamists and other unrecognized political groupings—joined the organization; but at its core were former Destourians disaffected with that party's aborted efforts to liberalize in the early 1970s (Ben Youssef-Charfi 1987). From its inception and throughout the tumultuous final years of Bourguiba's rule, it showed remarkable independence; in fact, *Le Monde* called it the "only voice of sanity" (April 12, 1987). Algerian activists were not so unified, nor was the government in power so willing to tolerate a voice of independence. Two separate groups, the Algerian League of Human Rights (LADH) and the Algerian League for the Defense of Human Rights (LADDH), were recognized, but only after twenty-three members of the latter group had spent a year in prison for belonging to an unauthorized organization (Amnesty International 1986). After the October 1988 riots, these two Algerian human rights groups spearheaded public expression of the need for political change (Bababji 1989: 241). In Morocco several years earlier, both the Istiqlal ("Independence") Party and the Social-ist Union of Popular Forces (USFP) had created human rights groups, but neither had developed an audible voice. The birth of the politically indepen-dent Moroccan Organization of Human Rights (OMDH) in December 1988 dissociated human rights from partisan contest and in the process rejuvenated the two existing organizations (Waltz 1991b).

The human rights groups introduced a new element to North African political life and in important regards awakened civil society. Through quiet meetings with government officials, press releases, and public seminars, they persistently raised difficult questions about practices that contravened domes-tic and international law and that were morally embarrassing to those in power. The elite background they shared with political leaders helped guaran-tee an audience and provide some measure of protection against repression.

The degree of political independence was not identical in the three countries, but in each instance groups could, with considerable credibility, claim that what they sought was a change in the rules of the political game rather than a lining of their own political pockets. Their position gave them a moral edge, and it presented new challenges to those in power, who were accustomed to meeting the elite's political demands through privilege and patronage. In response to acts of political repression, human rights groups levied their own charges that governments of the Maghreb were breaking domestic law and the international covenants to which they were signatory. By and large, indigenous human rights groups restricted their own actions to those legally permissible; upon that foundation they built a claim that they were not opposing the legitimate interests of the state. The sparring in which they engaged the state was not about the legitimacy of human rights but about the state's commitment to honor national and international laws and agreements into which it had freely entered. The presence of human rights groups guaranteed at minimum that legal transgressions would not be overlooked, as they often had been in the past (Ben Othman 1990).

Tunisia was the first state in the Maghreb to champion the cause of human rights in domestic politics: Circumstances surrounding the removal of Bourguiba had predisposed the new government to adopt the discourse of human rights and had greatly enhanced the LTDH's influence. Ben Ali's takeover followed a chaotic and frightening period when thousands were arrested, Islamist leaders were put on trial for political—but capital—crimes, and no one seemed to be in clear control. The LTDH was Tunisia's only credible voice in politics, and Ben Ali was in need of support. He invited key LTDH leaders to join his cabinet and embarked on a series of legal and political reforms. The period of reform experienced by Tunisia in 1988 thus was born of a domestic marriage between Ben Ali's new government and the LTDH. Even so, several aspects of that dynamic as well as the spread of concern for human rights across the region require explanation at another level and the introduction of a second set of actors.

The Moroccan case, probably more extreme than that of Algeria or Tunisia, points up the issues. Not only did Hassan II repeatedly deny the existence of the jails he ultimately emptied and the political prisoners he pardoned, but as late as 1990 Interior Minister Driss Basri shrugged off the concerns as a pack of lies, citing a Moroccan proverb: "The bereavement is intense, but the deceased is a mouse" (De Barrin 1990). It is unlikely that domestic forces on their own could ever have broken through the many-tiered barriers within the Moroccan political system to introduce human rights as a legitimate concern. Indeed, cooptation of the Istiqlal League of Human Rights (LMDH) and repression of the USFP-affiliated Moroccan Association of Human Rights (AMDH) in an earlier period attest to the inherent difficulties in the undertaking and to changes that had transpired in the interim. Growing interest in human rights at home was undoubtedly troublesome to Moroccan authorities, primarily because a changing political climate both at home and abroad made it costly to respond with severe measures of repression.

The inadequacy of domestic factors to explain fully the openings of the late 1980s directs attention to outside forces. Beyond the dynamics of domestic politics, international human rights pressures on Maghreb states had increased significantly toward the end of the 1980s. In the previous decade, human rights covenants entered into force, and respect for the cause had increased when Amnesty International received the Nobel Prize for Peace in 1977. In the United States, Congress pressed for the implementation of laws it had passed linking aid to human rights performance (Schoultz 1981: 203–209; Forsythe 1988), and Jimmy Carter's creation of a Bureau for Human Rights and Humanitarian Affairs within the U.S. State Department established human rights as a legitimate foreign policy concern. As a product of all of these developments, the international press gradually began to feature stories about human rights and human rights activists more prominently.

Internationally, more attention was accorded human rights, and with the resolution of Cold War tensions, these issues came to play greater roles in foreign policy (Huntington 1991: 85–100). Power speaks to power, and it was when political partners in Europe and the United States began to make clear their own concerns that the process of rights-related liberalizations ultimately commenced. In Algeria, the imprisonment of Abdennour Ali Yahia and other members of a newly formed League for the Defense of Human Rights in 1985 brought strong criticism from France—and French leftists. Ultimately, the government sanctioned—and sponsored (Bababji 1989)—a League of Human Rights, and to show good faith abroad, it created a Ministry of Human Rights that in fact accomplished, and tried to accomplish, little.

Morocco, with greater links to the West and with a more extensively documented human rights portfolio, came under yet more serious attack. In 1990, it reeled from disaster to diplomatic disaster with France, its major partner for both trade and aid. Plans for a year-long celebration of Moroccan culture, intended to renew bonds of friendship and promote commerce, were scrapped after human rights groups in France sought to use the events to exercise pressure for human rights improvements. Then the Harmattan publishing house released the scathing exposé of Hassan II's regime written by well-known French journalist Gilles Perrault (1990). Finally, Danielle Mitterrand, as president of a rights group known as France Libertés, participated in a press conference on the Western Sahara and announced plans to visit Saharan refugee camps in Tindouf, Algeria. Simultaneously, concerns for the Moroccan human rights record were expressed in the United States and in the United Nations Human Rights Committee (U.S. State Department, *Country Reports on Human Rights Practices* 1990; United Nations 1990). Hassan II was becoming isolated diplomatically, and not even Morocco's participation in allied efforts in the Gulf War spared scrutiny of Morocco's rights record. U.S. Congressional committees held hearings on North Africa in June 1991, and it was between June and the king's state visit to the United States in September that the most dramatic steps were taken.

Insofar as Tunisian reforms were clearly linked to domestic concerns, Tunisia may appear to be the exception here; but it is an exception that illustrates rather than undermines the argument that international forces had much bearing on the openings in the Maghreb. The most far-reaching liberalizations in Tunisia were enacted immediately after Ben Ali's accession to the presidency, and they clearly served the domestic purpose of legitimizing his rule and increasing support for his own presidency. The reforms, however, were not enacted in ignorance of the international climate. Among the first reforms proposed by Ben Ali were those advocated by international human rights groups; they took precedence even over the creation of commissions to study electoral and press code reforms (Waltz 1991a). Ben Ali was openly commended for introducing reforms by Tunisia's western partners, and France went so far as to award him a prestigious human rights prize. The diplomatic success of Tunisian reforms had an impact not only on Tunisia but on other actors in the region as well. It was in the context of acclaim for Tunisia that Colonel Muammar Qaddafi invited Amnesty International representatives to Libya, vowed to abolish the death penalty, and even climbed aboard a bulldozer to mow down an infamous prison (Coy 1989).

The human rights reforms and attention to individual dossiers that characterized the late 1980s and early 1990s were the product of several influencing factors, not one of which was sufficient alone to effect change. The efforts of domestic reformers, organized as effective voices of civil society, were reinforced by the support of influential actors abroad, ranging from the press and international society to powerful states and political allies. External support provided domestic pressure groups some measure of protection, and strong voices within both justified and amplified concerns from without. Indeed, outside actors relied on internal monitors to verify amnesties and evaluate the significance of reforms (see U.S. State Department, *Country Reports on Human Rights Practices*). For a time, converging pressures worked real and remarkable change in the region.

Evaluating Human Rights Reform

Questions about the long-term significance of human rights reform are problematic. The series of amnesties issued by Ben Ali in 1988 and 1989 and by Hassan II from 1989 to 1992 cannot be dismissed as empty gestures, inasmuch as they involved very real changes in literally thousands of individual lives. Likewise, the opening of the political system in Algeria was not simply pro forma, although the ultimate consequences were not those intended.

To what extent, though, have undergirding patterns been altered? Algeria is in the grip of social and political chaos, and within the system of formal politics the influence of the military remains paramount. For many Algerians, the right to life itself is threatened, as political assassinations are carried out by groups alternatively sympathetic or hostile to those nominally in power or to each other. In Tunisia, concerted repression of Islamists since late 1990 has entailed thousands of arrests, violations of pretrial detention laws expected to prevent torture, and even a number of well-documented cases of death in detention. During two trials of Islamists before military tribunals in July and August 1992, observers noted concerns about a broad range of issues bearing on the fairness of the trials, including widespread violations of Tunisian law concerning incommunicado detention, inadequate procedures to investigate claims of torture, and incidents of harassment and intimidation of defense lawyers (Lawyers Committee for Human Rights 1992). Perhaps more ominous in the long run was the dissolution in June 1992 of North Africa's oldest human rights group, the LTDH. Though its legal status was restored a year later, its former president was charged with spreading false information and imprisoned without bail in March 1994.[1]

In Morocco, King Hassan II created a new Ministry of Human Rights following legislative elections in 1993, and with a comprehensive amnesty in July 1994 emptied Moroccan prisons of all but about fifty political prisoners. Welcome as these measures have been to human rights groups in Morocco and abroad, insufficient time has passed to assess their full significance. The series of amnesties that raised similar hopes from 1989 to 1991 were followed by a series of political trials that resulted in long prison sentences for more than 120 individuals; labor leader Noubir Amaoui served more than half of a two-year sentence imposed in April 1992 for an interview in which he had strongly criticized Moroccan officials. The 1994 amnesty was to have definitively "turned the page," and it is noteworthy that it was accompanied by the abrogation of a 1935 law that for many years had provided the legal basis for the arrest of political dissidents engaged in peaceful protest. Questions about the Moroccans who "disappeared" remain, however, and the government has provided no account either of their fate or of the deaths of half of the military inmates at Tazmamart.

If the evaluation of significance must rest upon the cessation of abuse, or even the acknowledgment of and accountability for past violations, then the reforms and gestures of amnesty all across the Maghreb must be discounted. There have been some enduring legal reforms in all three countries, but they are greatly obscured by continuing patterns of abuse and by practices that violate even the reforms.

There are two other vantage points, however, from which the changes over the past decade appear more significant. The first angle is that of official rhetoric. In all three countries, the official line advanced by governments over the past few years has come to incorporate, even embrace, the notion of human rights. As noted, governments across the region have given new rhetorical emphasis to human rights and have created political bodies to reflect its new prominence.

Some dismiss the reforms and rhetoric as political gestures for public consumption, but therein lies much of the power they do have: They *are* for public consumption. By using human rights language and incorporating it into official discourse, North African officials imbue it with legitimacy. Talk alone has rarely engaged North African leaders fully, but official discourse helps frame political debate and in this case opens the door to accountability.

Evidence of the power of human rights rhetoric may be found in all three countries, but the Tunisian case is particularly instructive with regard to the potency of political discourse. Ben Ali rode into power on a human rights platform, and the regime's legitimacy was made to hinge on issues of human rights. When the new government failed to undermine the Islamists and again took up the tools of repression against them, it was faced with potential contradictions between word and deed. Torture was condemnable not only by universal standards but also in light of the regime's own publicly espoused position. Well-publicized deaths in detention in 1991 embarrassed the regime; the Driss Commission was appointed to investigate them—and to reduce public pressure. The following year, when trials of 269 Islamists commenced before military tribunals, the Ben Ali government was sensitive to concerns about human rights and thus met with human rights activists and opened the trials to outside observers. The trials themselves appeared in many regards to have been deficient, but at the same time there was substantially more candor surrounding these trials than similar ones in the past. Through 1993 "human rights" continued to serve as a byword for the Ben Ali regime; among UN members it sent the second largest delegation to the World Conference on Human Rights in 1993.

If the regular appearance of "human rights" within official Maghrebi discourse is one vantage point from which changes over the past few years take on significance in terms of long-range structural development, popular appreciation of the term is the second angle from which recent changes appear to be of more than passing interest. Several Maghrebi human rights activists have noted that the most impressive developments have been those that have transpired in society itself (*Jeune Afrique,* June 5, 1990; *Réalités,* August 10, 1990). *Huquq al-insan* ("human rights") is now a term to which meaning attaches across the region, and as a frame for political discourse it is readily adopted by nearly all active social movements. Intellectuals consider the concept more carefully, and critically, but they, too, have entered into a discourse on rights (Arkoun 1994: 106–13; Dwyer 1991; Ferjani 1991). Concerns have been voiced most ardently within the rather small nexus of committed activists who have led rights groups in each of the three countries; but interest in human rights extends well beyond inner circles. After the temporary suspension of its activities in 1992, the Tunisian League set about reviving not only its central leadership but also the forty-one branches scattered across the country. In Morocco, both the AMDH and the OMDH have multiplied their membership and have affiliate groups in most urban communities. Even in the midst of Algeria's civil unrest, the voice of human rights activists can occasionally be heard.

Human rights activism and the prominence of human rights in political discourse notwithstanding, it would be both naive and premature to claim that the notion of human rights inserted into Maghrebi politics in the late 1980s has left an indelible mark on the practice of governance in the region. Certainly the announced resolve of Morocco's semi-official CCDH to clear up questions about the "disappeared" (*Le Monde,* December 6, 1993) would have been unimaginable only a few short years ago; but the Tunisian government's imprisonment of LTDH leader Mohammed Marzouki for crimes of opinion would likewise have been unthinkable. Power is seductive, and those who hold extensive powers are rarely motivated to cede them. On their own, states and government leaders with a solid base of power may perceive little incentive to promote and uphold human rights, and the ability of interest groups to press for change can be limited. While the political commitments of those in power may wane, to the extent that human rights become embedded in discourse and in political structures, and to the extent that human rights ideals are supported by influential actors at home and abroad, human rights at least will remain on the Maghreb's political agenda.

Notes

1. See the following reports from Amnesty International: "Rhetoric Versus Reality: The Failure of a Human Rights Bureaucracy" (1994), and "Tunisia: Repression Thrives on Impunity" (1995). Marzouki was released without trial in July 1994, but that has not signaled political opening. From 1990 to 1992 the government was primarily concerned with curtailing Islamist activity, but in the 1994–96 period repressive measures were increasingly targeted at human rights activists—including prominant defense attorneys—and members of the legal opposition. In 1996, the leader of the movement of Social Democrats (MDS) was imprisoned, as was a member of parliament representing the MDS.

References

Adams, Robert, trans. 1992. Niccolò Machiavelli. *The Prince: A Revised Translation, Backgrounds, Interpretation, Marginalia.* 2nd ed. New York: Norton.

Aghrout, Ahmed, and Keith Sutton. 1990. "Regional Economic Union in the Maghreb." *Journal of Modern African Studies* 28: 115–30.

Amnesty International. 1986. "The Imprisonment of Prisoners of Conscience in Algeria."

———. 1990. "Tunisia: Summary of Amnesty International's Concerns." September.

———. 1994. "Rhetoric Versus Reality: The Failure of a Human Rights Bureaucracy."

———. 1995. "Tunisia: Repression Thrives on Impunity."

Arkoun, Mohammed. 1994. In Robert D. Lee, trans. and ed., *Rethinking Islam.* Boulder, CO: Westview.

Bababji, Ramdane. 1989. "Le phenomène associatif en Algérie: génèse et perspectives." *Annuaire de l'Afrique du Nord* 28: 229–42.

Ben Othman, Ahmed. 1990. "Les organisations non-gouvernementales." *Les Cahiers de l'Orient* 20: 231–35.

Ben Youssef-Charfi, Saloua. 1987. *La Ligue Tunisienne pour la Defense des Droits de l'Homme, Memoire pour le Diplôme d'Etudes Approfondies de Sciences Politiques.* Tunis: Université de Tunis.

Bessis, Sophie, and Souhayr Belhassen. 1988. *Bourguiba.* Vol. 1: *A la conquète d'un destin (1901–1957).* Paris: Groupe Jeune Afrique.

Binder, Leonard. 1989. *Islamic Liberalism.* Chicago: University of Chicago Press.

Burgat, François. 1993. In William Dowell, trans., *The Islamic Movement in North Africa.* Austin: University of Texas Press.

Camilleri, Joseph A., and Jim Falk. 1993. *The End of Sovereignty?* Australia: Edward Elgar.

Claisse, Alain. 1992. "Le Makhzen aujourd'hui." In Jean-Claude Santucci, ed., *Le Maroc actuel: Une modernisation au miroir de la tradition?* Paris: Editions du CNRS.

Coy, Patrick G. 1989. "Qaddafi's Revolution: Probing the Paradoxes." *Commonweal* 20 (October): 552–53.

De Barrin, Jacques. 1990. "Royal Privilege and Human Rights." *Manchester Guardian,* December 18.

Diouri, Moumen. 1992. *A qui apartient le Maroc?* Paris: L'Harmattan.

Donnelly, Jack. 1986. "International Human Rights: A Regime Analysis." *International Organization* 40: 599–642.

Duran, Khalid. 1989. "The Second Battle of Algiers." *Orbis* 33 (Summer): 403–27.

Dwyer, Kevin. 1991. *Arab Voices: The Human Rights Debate in the Middle East.* Berkeley: University of California Press.

Ferjani, Mohamed-Chérif. 1991. *Islamisme, Laïcité, et Droits de l'Homme.* Paris: L'Harmattan.

Forsythe, David P. 1988. *Human Rights and U.S. Foreign Policy, Congress Reconsidered.* Gainesville: University Press of Florida.

Harbi, Mohammed. 1989. "Sur les processus de relégitimation du pouvoir en Algérie." *Annuaire de l'Afrique du Nord* 28: 131–40.

Huntington, Samuel. 1991. *The Third Wave: Democratization in the Late Twentieth Century.* Norman: University of Oklahoma Press.

Lawyers Committee for Human Rights. 1992. "The Mass Trial of Islamists before Military Courts in Tunisia," August 21.

Migdal, Joel. 1988. *Strong Societies and Weak States.* Princeton: Princeton University Press.

Mortimer, Robert. 1993. "Algeria: The Clash between Islam, Democracy, and the Military." *Current History* 92 (January): 37–42.

Munson, Henry. 1993. *Power and Politics in Morocco.* New Haven: Yale University Press.

Nelson, Harold D., ed. 1986. *Morocco: A Country Study.* Washington, D.C.: U.S. Government Printing Office [Area Handbook Series].

———. 1987. *Tunisia: A Country Study.* Washington, D.C.: U.S. Government Printing Office [Area Handbook Series].

Perrault, Gilles. 1990. *Nôtre Ami le Roi.* Paris: Gallimard.

Redjala, Ramdane. 1991. *L'Opposition en Algèrie depuis 1962.* Paris: L'Harmattan.

Rosenau, James N. 1990. *Turbulence in World Politics: A Theory of Change and Community.* Princeton: Princeton University Press.

Schoultz, Lars. 1981. *Human Rights and United States Policy toward Latin America.* Princeton: Princeton University Press.

Tessler, Mark. 1985. "Tunisia at the Crossroads." *Current History* 84 (May): 217–23.

United Nations. 1990. "Human Rights Committee Begins Consideration of Report from Morocco." UN Press Release HR/2673 (November 7).

U.S. State Department. Annually. *Country Reports on Human Rights Practices.* Washington, D.C.: Government Printing Office.

Violet, Bernard. 1991. *L'Affaire Ben Barka.* Paris: Editions Fayard.

Waltz, Susan. 1991a. "Clientelism and Reform in Ben Ali's Tunisia." In I. William Zartman, ed., *Tunisia: The Political Economy of Reform,* pp. 29–44. Boulder, CO: Lynne Rienner.

———. 1991b. "Making Waves: The Political Impact of Human Rights Groups in North Africa." *Journal of Modern African Studies* 29: 481–504.

———. 1995. *Human Rights and Reform: Changing the Face of North African Politics.* Berkeley: University of California Press.

Waterbury, John. 1970. *The Commander of the Faithful.* New York: Columbia University Press.

Zartman, I. William. 1987. "King Hassan's New Morocco." In I. William Zartman, ed., *The Political Economy of Morocco*, pp. 1–33. New York: Praeger.

———. 1991. "The Conduct of Political Reform: The Path toward Democracy." In I. William Zartman, ed., *Tunisia: The Political Economy of Reform*, pp. 9–28. Boulder, CO: Lynne Rienner.

Zghal, Abdelkader. 1991. "The New Strategy of the Movement of the Islamic Way." In I. William Zartman, ed., *Tunisia: The Political Economy of Reform*, pp. 205–17. Boulder, CO: Lynne Rienner.

5.

The Origins of Popular Support for Islamist Movements

A Political Economy Analysis

MARK TESSLER

This chapter addresses the reasons there has been growing popular support for Islamist movements in many countries of the Middle East. It argues that the origins of this support are to be found primarily in the political and economic circumstances of these countries rather than in the religious and cultural traditions of their inhabitants. The analysis stands in opposition to the assessments offered by Islamist leaders themselves, who usually insist that popular support for their movements derives principally from the religious faith of the Arab masses.

The central thesis of this political economy analysis is reflected in the following statement of a young Algerian, who was asked in June 1990 why he had supported the Islamic Salvation Front (FIS) in the local and regional elections being held at that time: "In this country, if you are a young man . . . you have only four choices: you can remain unemployed and celibate because there are no jobs and no apartments to live in; you can work in the black market and risk being arrested; you can try to emigrate to France to sweep the streets of Paris or Marseilles; or you can join the FIS and vote for Islam" (Ibrahim 1990).

In developing the argument that support for Islamist movements derives primarily from economic and political circumstances, this chapter will devote most of its attention to Algeria, Tunisia, and Morocco, although some information about the other Arab countries will be presented as well. The chapter will also present original public opinion data from Egypt, and comparative data from Kuwait, in order to shed additional light on the nature and determinants of relevant popular attitudes. These data are presented in the text and discussed more fully in an appendix.

The Immediate Causes of Popular Discontent

As suggested by the young Algerian quoted above, the government in Algiers has for some time been unable to create jobs on the scale needed to accommodate the country's expanding population. While more than 300,000 young men and women seek entry into the labor force each year, job creation lags, having declined by one-third in 1991 alone, according to a report published the following year. As a result, according to the same study, "one of the few ways out for many is to eke out a living as a small-time black market entrepreneur." These *trabendistes,* as they are called, fly between Algiers and Spanish coastal cities, "loaded down with recorded tapes, jeans, auto parts, and anything else scarce and portable enough to make the trip worthwhile" (Abramson 1992: 20).

The situation is similar in other North African countries. In Morocco, for example, a household survey carried out in December 1984 by the semi-official *Le Matin du Sahara* reported that urban unemployment stood at 18.4 percent, with 44.9 percent of those having jobs working as unskilled or semiskilled laborers, and with many of these workers employed only on an irregular basis. These figures were also cited by an economic report published in 1987, which stated that they underline the severity of the urban employ-ment problem, particularly among the young, and concluded that "it is unlikely these proportions have altered much since 1984" (*Quarterly Eco-nomic Review of Morocco* 1 [1987]: 19). Further, the pattern has remained about the same, or if anything, worsened, since the mid-1980s (Parker 1984: 17; Marks 1994: 33). Urban unemployment is in the 20 to 25 percent range, and among urban young men under the age of thirty, especially those with limited schooling, estimates regularly range as high as 40 percent. Writing of Morocco in 1994, a knowledgeable analyst thus reports that "underemploy-ment is endemic and millions are dependent on the huge informal sector for their income" (Marks 1994: 33).

Well-educated North Africans are increasingly affected, too, as the situa-tion continues to deteriorate, or at least fails to improve. Indeed, unemployed Moroccan university graduates formed an association in 1992, the Associa-tion des Diplômés Chômeurs, in an effort to call attention to their plight. A recent doctoral thesis dealing with the attitudes of young Moroccans reports in this connection that "education increasingly leads to unemployment" and that many young men and women "attach little importance to their diplo-mas." Indicative of this view are the bitter comments of a number of informants, who insisted that "a diploma has absolutely no value in Morocco" and that "after graduation it will be a nightmare" (Bennani-Chraibi 1993: 213, 215, 241).

Education is a second area in which demands are unmet and expectations unfulfilled. Even though schooling no longer carries a guarantee of secure employment, millions of young North Africans seek an education in the hope of achieving a better life, and a large proportion of these are disappointed *before* completing their studies. Educational opportunities have expanded dramatically at the primary school level, but this has not been matched by comparable growth at higher levels, requiring many young men and women to drop out after only six or eight years. The previously mentioned *Matin du Sahara* investigation reported, for example, that 79.3 percent of the active urban population was either illiterate or had received only a primary school education. As late as 1986, only one-third of Moroccan youth between the ages of twelve and eighteen were attending school, and in Tunisia the figure was only 39 percent. With even high school and university graduates having difficulty finding suitable jobs, the prospects are particularly dim for those with only primary schooling.

Writing in 1988, an Algerian scholar reported in this connection that "in spite of democratization, the new educational system turned out to be highly selective" (Bennoune 1988: 227), and he presented statistics from the late 1970s to illustrate his point. He noted that for every one hundred pupils enrolled in primary school, twenty dropped out before the sixth year and another forty failed to pass the examination for a primary education certificate, which meant they were not allowed to stay in school. Of the remaining forty, only eighteen were admitted to high school, of whom sixteen were subsequently candidates for the *baccalaureate* examination. And with a pass rate of 25 percent for 1978–79, this meant that "only 4 pupils out of 100 would have a chance to go to the university."

Inadequate housing is yet another source of discontent. A study in Algiers in the mid-1980s documented the problem and offered striking illustrations (Jansen 1987: 18–20). For example, "colonial houses in the center of town have been converted into groups of dwellings of one or two rooms, each rented to a whole family and connected to a central court." An entire family may have as little as eighteen square meters, and five or more families may share a court with one water tap and one toilet. In addition:

> Shared houses are not found only in the colonial center of town. . . . The low income houses, planned for one family, had two rooms, a small kitchen, a toilet and a court. Most of them now have electricity but still no private water tap. The rural exodus filled them up quickly, however, and soon there were two families in each house, one in each room. More immigrants came, more children were born . . . the [two-room] houses now often contain four families.

A more recent study indicates that the situation has become even worse during the 1990s. The author concludes that the "housing problem in Algeria has become quasi-insoluble," adding that "in spite of ambitious plans, never achieved, the lack [of adequate housing] has not ceased to become more serious" (Lesbet 1994: 220).

The demographic pressures contributing to these problems are well known. The population of many Arab countries is growing by as much as 3 percent per year, in some cases even more. Moreover, this not only increases the aggregate demand for goods and services, it also gives rise to an increasingly skewed age distribution and makes it particularly difficult to meet the needs of young people. In the early and mid-1980s, for example, over 50 percent of North Africa's population was under the age of twenty, over 60 percent was under twenty-five, and almost 70 percent was under thirty. More recently, some decline in fertility has begun to reduce the proportion of the population under the age of fifteen. This is having little effect in the short run, however, as the fifteen to twenty-four age group, which includes most entrants into the labor force, continues to swell (Sabagh 1993: 31). In addition, a continuing exodus from the countryside has intensified the pressure in urban areas. In Morocco, for example, the urban population grew by 61 percent during the 1970s and early 1980s, in contrast to only 17 percent growth in rural areas. Two-thirds of all Moroccans now live in cities, whereas only one-fifth did so in 1965. In Tunisia, the rate of population growth in the capital was more than twice the national average from the mid-1960s to the mid-1980s, and the rate was higher still in many regional urban centers, such as Gafsa and Gabes.

All of this means, as noted, that the supply of jobs, education and housing has been unable to keep pace with demand and, as a result, that a steadily increasing number of individuals finds it impossible to fulfill aspirations for social mobility and a better life. According to an Algerian newspaper editor, quoted in 1991, "Out of the entire population of this country, there are barely one million persons with a civilized cycle of life, in the sense that they have good jobs, collect a reasonable salary, deal with banks and sometimes take vacations. The rest of the country lives at subsistence levels or below" (Ibrahim 1991).

While these problems and pressures affect huge numbers of individuals and almost all sectors of society, they are most pronounced among the young and in the cities. They also appear to be most intense among those who have received some but not extensive schooling, and particularly among men in this category (Tessler 1993). Unable to compete for the jobs that are available, often because their education is limited, legions of unemployed young men in the cities while away their days on street corners or in coffee houses, becoming ever more disillusioned and embittered. In Algeria, where the problem is presently most intense, they are sometimes called "homeboys" (*houmistes*), boys from the neighborhood, or "wall boys" (*hittistes*), unemployed youth who have nothing to do and so "hang out," leaning against the walls that line many city streets (Brown 1993: 11). Characterizing the situation more generally, a colloquium on cities and social movements in the

Maghreb and the Middle East held several years ago in Paris concluded that the urban areas of North Africa are "accumulating a mass whose transition is blocked" and which increasingly lives at a level "below that of normal city life" ("Etat, ville et mouvements sociaux" 1987: 58).

Expressions of Public Anger in the 1980s

The serious unrest that occurred in Tunisia, Algeria, and Morocco, as well as in a number of other Arab countries during the 1980s, may be understood against the background of the difficult living conditions affecting large segments of the population. A Moroccan economist referred in this context to the "population/jobs problem," which he characterized as a "time bomb that is ticking away" (Moffett 1989). Similarly, a series of *Jeune Afrique* articles on Algeria and Tunisia, written about the same time, described the situation as "explosive" (Digne 1989; Bourgi 1989; Soudan 1989).

And indeed there were explosions in North Africa during the 1980s. In June 1981, tensions associated with economic and political grievances exploded in violent riots in Casablanca, Morocco. The immediate cause of the disturbances was a reduction in food subsidies, which the government enacted in response to pressure from foreign creditors; but the scope and intensity of the rioting revealed the depth of public anger. As thousands of young men from the city's sprawling slums poured into the streets, roaming mobs attacked banks, auto dealerships, and other businesses and public buildings identified with elite privilege or government authority. In subduing the rioters, police sometimes fired into the crowd, and at least two hundred protesters were killed. Some estimates place the number much higher.

The rioting that broke out in Morocco in January 1984 made it clear that these disturbances were not an aberration. A rise in the price of basic commodities subsidized by the government was announced, and again the burden fell most heavily on the working class and the poor. In response, violent protests occurred in many parts of the country and rioting lasted for more than a week, leaving Morocco badly shaken when order was finally restored.

The first disturbances took place in Marrakesh, where students and unemployed youth from poorer neighborhoods took to the streets; these protests were then followed by demonstrations in Agadir, Safi, and Kasbah-Tadla in the south, and in Rabat and Meknès in the central part of the country. Disturbances of greater intensity thereafter developed in the north, the most neglected and underdeveloped region of Morocco. In Nador, for example, there were attacks on banks and the agency of the national airline, Royal Air Maroc, indicating anger at the government and special bitterness at institutions symbolizing elite privilege. In Al Hoceima, another northern city, protesting students were joined by fishermen, sailors, port workers, and many others, including women. Moroccan security forces used considerable violence in quelling the riots in these and other northern cities. Press reports spoke of 150 to 200 deaths, or in some cases even more, as well as hundreds injured and approximately nine thousand arrested (Tessler 1986).

January 1984 also was a time of unrest in Tunisia, and the country's experience was broadly similar to that of Morocco. Rioting actually began at the end of 1983, triggered by the government's December 29 announcement of a rise in the price of semolina. In response to this action, which served as a catalyst and released pent-up frustration produced by underlying economic and social problems, protests and demonstrations took place in the oases of the south, some of the nation's poorest and most neglected communities.

New Year's Day brought a new wave of rioting in Tunisia, with disturbances in major towns of the south, including Kasserine, Gafsa, Mitlaoui, and Gabes, and by January 3 there was also rioting in Tunis, Sfax (the country's second largest city), and other urban centers. In the capital, thousands of students, workers and unemployed young men from the city's slums roamed the streets, shouting antigovernment slogans and attacking symbols of authority and wealth. Thousands more shouted encouragement from open windows and rooftops. Protesters attacked cars and buses, tore up street signs, looted and set fire to shops and, in some areas, attacked public buildings. They also fought police and military units, which had brought in tanks, armored personnel carriers, and even helicopters to repulse the rioters. Order was not restored until January 5, by which time the country had witnessed a week of unrest and security forces had killed more than 150 persons (Paul 1984).

Algeria, too, experienced serious unrest during this period. In April 1985, for example, following rumors that homes being built for the poor would be allocated instead to government bureaucrats, there were riots in the Algiers casbah that brought police units into the streets. Disturbances continued for several days. There were also clashes between police and youthful members of militant Islamic groups, including a violent confrontation in October 1985 that resulted in the death of five policemen. Fall 1986 brought additional and more widespread disturbances. In November, student demonstrations in Constantine ignited three days of rioting, in which four protesters died and many more were wounded. Further, the Constantine riots were followed almost immediately by disturbances in other cities, including Setif, where the Air France office was attacked, as well as in Batna, Annaba, Skikda, and Oran.

In October 1988, Algeria was shaken by the most intense rioting since it became independent in 1962, experiencing its own equivalent of the January disturbances in Tunisia and Morocco (Vandewalle 1988a). In Algiers, Oran, Constantine, and several other cities, thousands of young people took to the streets to vent their anger over worsening economic and social conditions.

There was considerable property damage during the three days of rioting, with protesters setting fire to government buildings in several parts of Algiers. There were also lethal clashes between protesters and government security forces charged with putting an end to the disturbances. Estimates of the number of casualties varied widely, but it is generally agreed that at least five hundred of the protesters were killed and many more wounded. After order was restored, the government imposed a state of emergency on the capital and nearby areas.

People's Understanding of Their Predicament

To the extent one can judge, it does not appear that ordinary Arab men and women see their problems solely, or even primarily, as the unavoidable result of shortages created by population growth and other demographic pressures. Rather, many seem to regard their problems as grounded in existing patterns of political economy, and they accordingly attribute much of the responsibility for their plight to the political regimes by which they are governed. Complaints thus go beyond the fact that masses of people live in impoverished conditions and that for much of the population, especially the young, the prospects for an improved standard of living are not growing brighter and may even be declining.

Ordinary citizens in North Africa also complain about a large and growing gap between rich and poor. In their view, the burdens of underdevelopment are not shared equitably and, despite economic difficulties, there are islands of affluence and elite privilege that often involve luxury and excess. Moreover, these complaints are compounded by a widespread belief that membership in the country's elite is determined in most instances not by ability, dedication, or service to society, but by personal and political connections—the result being a system where patronage and clientelism predominate in decisions about public policy and resource allocation. Thus, while many live in conditions of distress, there is also a consumer class that is believed to support its privileged lifestyle with resources that should be used for national development.

Scholarly observers confirm the accuracy of at least some of these popular perceptions. For example, a 1988 study of economic reform in Morocco noted that the structural adjustment policies being pursued by the government were hurting the poorest categories of the population while benefiting others, and it then concluded that only "a very different kind of structural reform—involving a substantial redistribution of resources and a genuine democratization of Moroccan politics . . . [would] be sufficient to change the situation of the poorest social groups in Morocco" (Seddon 1989: 263). Moreover, and significantly, a study published in 1994 concluded that the situation had changed little: "Below the strata of the richest Moroccans, all social classes are [still] waiting to feel the benefits of reform" (Marks 1994: 33). Even the World Bank and the European Commission, the study adds, "readily concede the need for a more equitable distribution of resources."

As far as privileged access is concerned, a number of investigations report not only the limited magnitude but also the highly skewed distribution of opportunities for educational and professional advancement. A study conducted in Algeria, for example, reported that the chances for entering university are 30 times greater for the son of an agricultural manager than for the son of a farm laborer, and that those for the son of a technocrat or buinessman are 285 times greater (Dufour 1978). Noting that students at Algerian universities constitute a select group drawn from the most favored sectors of society, an American scholar described them as

> the 1 to 3 percent of Algerians who are destined, because of their family and personal connections, acquired wealth and influence, type and level of education, multilingual fluency, and technical-scientific accreditation, to assume the top- and secondary-level positions in each of the principal institutional components of the technocratic system: government, party, military, bureaucracy. (Entelis 1986: 92)

Other studies come to similar conclusions with respect to Tunisia and Morocco. Reporting on the Tunisian case, for example, one analyst observes that "university students and skilled cadres come predominantly from middle- and upper-middle-class social strata" (Stone 1982: 164). A recent account of the situation in Morocco notes that there is privilege not only in access to higher education but to postuniversity employment as well. "Morocco remains a very closed, very proprietary system," this analysis concludes, noting that "even college graduates without necessary family connections cannot get jobs" (Witter 1993).

In addition, there are also accounts of the indulgence and conspicuous consumption that characterize some segments of the elite. Describing the sources of popular discontent in Algeria, for example, a political scientist of Algerian origin writes that "in the midst of [the present] economic and managerial crisis, a few people succeeded in not only increasing their wealth but also displaying it in the form of late-model cars, new villa construction and new businesses," which in turn, understandably, "exacerbated the frustration of the masses" and "made them potentially rebellious against a state of affairs they neither liked nor understood" (Layachi 1992: 3).

Other observers also make these points, citing examples not only from North Africa but from elsewhere in the Arab world. In writing about the origins of popular discontent in Jordan, for example, one scholar notes that at the level of the masses, "many people were not willing to tighten their belts to pay for an economic crisis which they felt was the result of widespread corruption," and that among the elite, "a system of cronyism is pervasive," with opportunities for enrichment channeled by insiders to their friends and with top positions always going to the "same old faces, families and clans" (Amawi 1992: 27).

Indignation over the gap between rich and poor, over privileged access to opportunities for economic advancement, and over the perceived misuse of available national resources was readily apparent in the rioting that shook North Africa during the 1980s. In the Tunisian disturbances of January 1984, for example, knowledgeable local observers described the mood of demonstrators as one of "rage" or even "hatred." This was most apparent in the attacks on shops selling luxury goods and the incursions into fashionable elite neighborhoods. Also, in at least one instance, Mercedes and other luxury cars were set on fire by roaming bands, while less expensive models were damaged little if at all. Anger was thus directed not only at the government but also at the consumption-oriented middle and upper classes, population categories perceived to be prospering at a time when the circumstances of the masses were deteriorating and the regime was asking the poor to tighten their belts even more (Tessler 1991: 11–12). Similar sentiments were observed in Morocco during the disturbances of January 1984. In Nador, for example, some protesters carried pink parasols to express their disdain for royal pomp and their indignation at the excesses of the king and the elite.

The way that many understand their predicament is also illustrated by a conversation that took place during the Tunisian riots of January 1984 (Tessler 1991: 13). A Tunisian professional told of a discussion a few days earlier with several young men who worked in menial and low-paying jobs at the institution where he himself held a senior position. Upon learning that there had been riots in the residential quarter where he lived, the workers expressed the hope that he had not personally sustained any losses; for while he was indeed quite wealthy by their modest standards, they believed he was entitled to the rewards of his labors. He had gone to school for many years, and he now worked long hours in a position that contributed directly to the welfare of the nation.

The problem, the workers added, was that the same could not be said for most members of the nation's privileged classes. The young workers expressed their belief that the majority of Tunisia's elite prospered because of personal and political connections, gaining preferential access to, and then spending frivolously, resources that should be invested in the country's future. Moreover, most of these individuals were said to offer the country little in return, preferring to spend their wealth on imported luxury goods and only rarely investing in ventures that either created employment or increased economic productivity. In recalling this conversation, the Tunisian professional stated that he had told his interlocutors that their view of a corrupt and parasitic elite was exaggerated and oversimplified. In fact, however, he added privately that the analysis was not as wide of the mark as he would have wished.

There is clearly a political as well as a socioeconomic dimension to these complaints. As the frequent eruption of popular unrest makes evident, citizens throughout North Africa are deeply dissatisfied with the political systems by which they are governed. They are angered by an inability to hold their leaders accountable or to press for political change. Those who are more politically conscious complain that there are few legitimate mechanisms by which the populace can articulate grievances in a way that will have a meaningful impact on the political process, and none whatsoever by which it can remove senior political leaders whose performance is unsatisfactory. They note that the political openings of the late 1980s were timid and halting, with the partial exception of that in Algeria, and that progress toward democratization in Algeria ceased in the early 1990s.

More generally, political opposition is tolerated, if at all, only to the extent that it does not threaten the established political order. Dissident political activity is vigorously suppressed in this environment, with serious human rights violations in the treatment of radical opponents and strict limits imposed even on opposition movements that accept the rules of the game. As described in a 1988 study of political control in Morocco, "the government ensures that the behavior [of even loyal opposition parties] conforms to the major decisions taken by the Palace." The leaders of these parties are closely monitored by Moroccan authorities, who do not hesitate to limit their action or even to arrest them "if there is doubt about the nature of their activities" (Bendourou 1988: 39–40).

A number of analysts advance similar conclusions about the political judgments reflected in popular discontent. One observer writes of Algeria, for example, that people are no longer impressed by tales of their leaders' struggle for independence: "They want to know, as one student bitterly stated . . . why more than half of them are jobless 'while we earn billions per year from natural gas, and [the former head of the ruling party] lives like a king'" (Vandewalle 1988a: 2). Discussing the Constantine riots of 1986, another author makes the same point: The young protesters constitute a generation raised on "state corruption, social problems and political abuse." The overall cause of political alienation, he concludes, is a "system of power, patronage, and privilege that entrenched interests in the party, government, and the economy are unwilling to sacrifice in the name of some larger good" (Entelis 1988: 52–53). And again, writing more recently about the failure of Algeria's short-lived experiment in democratization, a scholarly analysis concludes that public anger has been fueled not only by an inadequate national development strategy but by the insistence of government and military hard-liners on total economic, political and ideological control (Layachi and Haireche 1992: 75; see also Entelis and Arone 1992).

A few public opinion surveys also document the depth and breadth of political alienation (Tessler 1993). In the case of Morocco, for example, a recent account summarizes four important survey research projects and reports that "while the state is feared, it is also often resented, if not hated . . . [and is] widely recognized as not representative of the people. This produces two main reactions, either complete apathy or at least passivity (sometimes viewed as acceptance), or alienation and activism in some anti-establishment form or medium" (Suleiman 1987: 113). Thus, in sum, evidence from a variety of sources supports the thesis that political discontent is widespread in North Africa and is in the first instance a response to systems of governance considered unresponsive at best and frequently exploitative.

Government officials often contend that complaints about regime performance are unreasonable and exaggerated. They assert that demands for rapid progress are unrealistic, with many citizens, and especially the young, failing to appreciate that development goals can only be achieved over the long haul. Many of these officials also insist that much has been accomplished, sometimes suggesting that complaints are the result not of government failures but, rather, of aspirations fostered by successful development efforts, most notably in the field of education. They sometimes argue as well that there has been progress toward the construction of democratic political systems, even though here, too, they call for patience.

Whatever the accuracy of these rebuttals, they rarely strike a responsive chord among the disillusioned and alienated segments of North Africa's citizenry, presumably because so many find confirmation in their own lives of the charge that something fundamental is amiss in the nation as a whole. They reason, logically though perhaps somewhat simplistically, that if the government were allocating resources wisely and in accordance with the true interests of the populace, they, their families, and so many of their friends would not be confronted with stagnation or even a decline in their modest standards of living. But their leaders do not give highest priority to the welfare of the masses, these critics continue. They instead preside over a political and economic system that is dedicated to the preservation of elite privilege and which accordingly distributes resources and opportunities on the basis of personal relationships.

This situation is often characterized as the problem of the "Arab regimes," or as the "crisis of leadership and legitimacy" in North Africa and other parts of the Arab world. As expressed by a scholar of Egyptian origin, there is a "severe, multi-dimensional, and protracted crisis faced by many regimes in the Muslim [and Arab] world. This crisis has been evidenced by a decline of state legitimacy and has resulted in 'state exhaustion'" (Karawan 1993: 162).

The same point is stressed by a Moroccan analyst, who describes the problem as one of "azmatology," from *azmah,* the Arabic word for crises (quoted in Karawan 1993; also in Dwyer 1991: 20).

Lessons from the Crisis in the Gulf

Students, professionals and other politically conscious Arabs frequently speak of a tacit alliance among domestic, regional, and even international political interests committed to maintaining the status quo. Those deemed responsible for their predicament, therefore, include not only the leaders and privileged elements within their own countries, but also both the political regimes and classes throughout the Middle East that stand in opposition to change and the foreign powers (including the United States) that are believed to be working to preserve existing patterns of political economy.

These sentiments were readily visible in North Africa during the Gulf crisis of 1990–91, confirming that the deep discontent felt by many ordinary citizens extends into the present decade and offering additional insights into the nature of popular attitudes. Iraq invaded Kuwait in August 1990, and shortly thereafter the United States took the lead in establishing an international military coalition that threatened to go to war against Iraq unless the country's leader, Saddam Hussein, withdrew his forces from Kuwait. The U.S.-led coalition attacked in January 1991 and quickly scored a decisive victory. Yet in many Arab countries, including all three states of the Maghreb, there was substantial popular sympathy for Saddam Hussein and broad opposition to the United States and its coalition partners (*La Guerre du Golfe* 1991; Zghal 1991: 161–62; Pollock 1992: 31, 35). Moreover, a number of analysts have pointed out that such sentiments were expressed most clearly and forcefully in Arab states characterized by a measure of political openness and by relative freedom of expression—in those states, in other words, where public opinion could be most readily discerned (Labib 1991: 195).

In Tunisia, for example, there were demonstrations in support of Iraq and expressions of militant opposition to the actions of the U.S.-led coalition. While public protests were for the most part limited in scope, both Tunisian and foreign observers agree that there was a very strong pro-Iraq and anti-U.S. undercurrent among the public at large (Riding 1990). Popular attitudes were similar in Algeria, where there were also massive public protests. Hundreds of thousands marched in Algiers and other cities following the attack on Iraqi forces in January 1991, and in Constantine there were attacks on the French consulate and the office of Air France. As a result, the governments of both Tunisia and Algeria, in response to this public pressure, condemned the Iraqi invasion of Kuwait but reserved their sharpest denunciations for the United States and its allies.

Pro-Saddam and anti-Western sentiments were no less present in Morocco, even though the country's leader, King Hassan II, had sent troops to Saudi Arabia as part of the international force put in place under UN auspices. Indeed, the expressions of support for Iraq coming from Morocco were among the most intense in the Arab world. In December 1990, street demonstrations and unrest in Fez, Tangiers, and several other cities, although only partly in response to developments in the Gulf, produced violent clashes with police. At least five protesters were killed and 127 injured, with opponents of the government putting the figures significantly higher. Much larger, although nonviolent, protests took place in February 1991, following the attack on Iraq by the U.S.-led coalition. A crowd that some observers estimated at 300,000 took to the streets of Rabat to demand the withdrawal from Saudi Arabia of all allied forces, including those from Morocco. Marchers burned American, British, French, and Israeli flags. Many carried copies of the Koran, and some displayed portraits of Saddam Hussein.

The Moroccan government responded by quietly distancing itself from the coalition and adopting a posture of undeclared but effective neutrality in the fighting in the Gulf. Moreover, the United States displayed an understanding of the situation facing the Moroccan king and did not complicate Hassan's position by pressing for active Moroccan participation in the anti-Iraq campaign. But while the monarch's action, and U.S. understanding, were sufficient to keep domestic protests from getting out of hand, it may be noted that support for Saddam Hussein among the Moroccan public remained strong almost three years after the crisis. A poll conducted late in 1993, for example, found that 55 percent of the urban respondents in a nationally representative sample had a very favorable view of the Iraqi leader, and another 25 percent had a favorable view (Huxley 1993).

It is doubtful that many North Africans actually approved of the Iraqi invasion of Kuwait. Most would probably agree that Iraq should have used political means to defend its interests, rather than attack a brother Arab country and divide the Arab world. It is also unlikely that many Tunisians, Algerians, or Moroccans would wish to live under Saddam's rule; the authoritarian and brutal character of the Baath regime in Iraq is well known, even in the Maghreb. Nor would most consider Saddam a credible champion of Arab independence, since he was for many years a willing client of the former Soviet Union. Finally, Saddam's use of Islamic symbols appeared cynical and hypocritical to many North Africans, particularly since the Iraqi leader is well known as a secular nationalist who in fact claimed to be defending the Arab world against militant Islam during his country's eight-year war with Iran.

The outpouring of public anger in North Africa in 1990 and 1991 thus was not produced by a high regard for Saddam Hussein or by support for his actions in Kuwait. Rather, as in a number of other Arab countries, the Gulf

crisis served as a proxy for a very different set of grievances and gave citizens
of the Maghreb an occasion to express once again the discontent that had
produced disturbances during the preceding decade. More specifically, there
is intense opposition to the economic and political status quo and a profound
desire for change; and Saddam Hussein, whether justified or not, was
regarded by many North Africans as a champion of the desired transformation.

Kuwait, the United States, and allied Arab regimes, by contrast, were seen
by many ordinary men and women as defenders of the established order, as
cynical political actors who claimed to want a new world order but in reality
were using force to ensure that change did not take place. In this popular view,
Saudi Arabia, Kuwait, and other oil-rich Gulf states constitute national islands
of privilege and represent a replication within the Middle Eastern regional
system of the very pattern of political economy that exists within their own
country and is at the root of their frustration and anger. A handful of
privileged Arab states, like the rulers and associated elites within most Arab
countries, are believed to be dedicated to the preservation of a political and
economic order that provides benefits for the few and is indifferent or even
hostile to the well-being of the majority.

These themes were repeatedly stressed at a colloquium on the Gulf crisis
held in Tunis in March 1991, shortly after the conclusion of the fighting in
Iraq. Academics and other intellectuals from Morocco, Algeria, Egypt, and
several other Arab countries joined Tunisian colleagues for two days of
discussion; and frequently articulated was the view that the war divided the
Arab world's rich and poor and at its core was a confrontation between
supporters and opponents of change (*La Guerre du Golfe* 1991). According
to one participant, while the Arab world suffers from poverty, inequality, and
social injustice, the war in the Gulf was fought and won by "les gros
consommateurs mondiaux"—that is to say, by a coalition of Western and
Arab governments with an interest in defending the established world order
(Ayari 1991: 14). Many others spoke of the imperialist alliance that defeated
Iraq, and while the United States, and to a lesser extent France, were frequent
targets of criticism, so also were privileged and indulgent Arab regimes who
were accused of defending the status quo and, consequently, of joining the
anti-Iraq coalition. Similar assessments of the coalition's motives, emphasiz-
ing a defense not of Kuwaiti sovereignty but of existing political and economic relationships, were advanced by analysts in other parts of the Arab
world as well (Yousif 1991; Telhami 1992; Karawan 1993).

Such judgments are relevant for an understanding of popular as well as
intellectual opinion, as demonstrated, for example, by a recent study of the
attitudes of young Moroccans, and also of the popular slogans and jokes that
circulated in Morocco during the crisis in the Gulf (Bennani-Chraibi 1993:
392–436). Saddam was represented as a man of action among those who saw

themselves as powerless and marginalized, whereas there was little sympathy for Kuwait, which was judged to be arrogant and selfish. "Unshared wealth was the central theme of discourse," the study reported (Bennani-Chraibi 1993: 413), although there was also concern for Palestinian rights and the removal of non-Muslim forces from the territory of Saudi Arabia. Thus, the members of the anti-Iraq coalition, which included Saudi Arabia and "bad Arabs" as well as foreign elements, were "associated with negative values" and were regarded as "the enemies of the people." In the view of many young Moroccans, "the sole motivation of the sultans of the Gulf, of Mubarak and even of Asad was to remain in power and protect their personal interests . . . to defend themselves against their own people, whom they fear" (Bennani-Chraibi 1993: 417–18).

A final indication of the continuing anger felt by many young North Africans is provided by the riots that broke out in Fez, Morocco, in February 1994. Protests by university students, many associated with Islamic movements, led to clashes with police, and these were followed by riots in which the students were joined by hundreds of young men from nearby Meknès and other towns. There were also violent clashes between Islamist and leftist students. At least seven people were killed as a result of the disturbances, with several dozen arrested and police anti-riot squads occupying the Fez campus before order was restored (Kokan 1994).

The Meaning of Support for Islamist Movements

In searching for an alternative to an unacceptable status quo, many North Africans and other Arabs are turning to Islamist political movements. The current Islamic revival actually began during the 1970s. New Muslim associations and study groups emerged, and there was also a sharp increase in such expressions of personal piety as mosque attendance and public prayer. Another indication of this development was a boom in the sale of cassettes dealing with Islamic themes, which, according to a journalistic investigation in Tunisia, were at the time estimated to be selling thousands of copies every month ("L'Islam contestataire en Tunisie," 1979). A study by a Tunisian scholar reported a few years later that militant Muslim groups were having particular success in attracting the young, including the relatively well educated, and that high schools and university campuses were accordingly serving as centers of activity and recruitment (Hermassi 1984).

The origins of this Islamic resurgence are diverse. They are rooted to a significant degree in the enduring religious attachments of ordinary Muslims, but they have been shaped to an equal or even greater extent by events that were transforming the political landscape of the Arab world. Of particular importance was the Arab-Israeli war of June 1967, which brought the Arabs a crushing defeat and thus cast doubt on the development ideologies of the states, particularly Egypt and Syria, that had led in the struggle against Israel. In the wake of the Arabs' defeat in the 1947–48 war for Israeli independence, traditional and feudalistic regimes had been swept away in Egypt, Syria, and elsewhere, to be replaced by governments which promised that a political formula based on socialism and some mix of pan-Arabism and secular nationalism would enable their countries to prosper.

Moreover, such revolutionary thinking assumed a dominant position in Arab political discourse during the late 1950s and early 1960s. It was championed by intellectuals and students, to the point that Islamic political movements were in fact having difficulty attracting followers among these categories of the population. To the extent one can judge, there was also broad popular support for the Arab world's revolutionary leaders, most prominently for Gamal Abdul Nasser but also, in North Africa, for the socialist regimes in Tunisia and later Algeria. These regimes enjoyed a high degree of legitimacy during the early and mid-1960s—despite their indifference or even hostility to political movements advocating greater respect for Islamic prescriptions in the formulation of public policy.

But this situation began to change after June 1967. With revolutionary regimes in Egypt and Syria defeated even more decisively than had been their feudalistic predecessors, there was suddenly a new logic and credibility to the Islamist argument that progress could be achieved only if the Arabs were guided by an indigenous political formula, namely that provided by Islam. Some Muslim thinkers asserted that the defeat was punishment for the Arabs' flirtation with foreign ideologies, for a turning away from the faith. More common, however, and almost certainly more persuasive to thoughtful Muslims, was the assertion, summarized in a major study of Arab political thought during this period, that Islam "could do what no imported doctrine could hope to do—mobilize the believers, instill discipline, and inspire people to make sacrifices and, if necessary, to die" (Ajami 1981: 52). Interestingly, both radical and conservative Islamic thinkers also placed emphasis on the importance of Israel's identification with Judaism, arguing that Israel was strong precisely because it accepted and embraced its association with an ancient religion. The implication, made explicit by Islamic theoreticians, was that Muslims should exhibit the same religious zeal and, as had the Israelis, reject the secularist fallacy of a contradiction between religion and modernity (Ajami 1981: 55, 69).

In addition to shedding light on the origins of the Islamic resurgence in the Arab world, including North Africa, the June war and its consequences call attention to the instrumental character of the case being advanced in the name of Islam. This remains the situation at present, with Muslim groups presenting themselves as vehicles for the expression of political discontent and campaigning for change under the banner, "Islam is the solution." Further, there is evidence that those who respond positively to this message desire not only that their political community be strong enough to meet external challenges, but also, and equally, that it be governed by a regime that is able and willing to deal effectively with domestic political and economic problems—hence the salience of a "solution." In Tunisia, for example, an empirical study based on surveys carried out in the late 1960s and early 1970s found that the Islamic revival in that country was being fueled, in substantial measure, by political and economic grievances and by a desire for political change (Tessler 1980: 13). Several studies carried out in Tunisia during the 1980s reached similar conclusions and in fact documented an acceleration of this trend (Waltz 1986; Vandewalle 1988b; Belhassen 1989).

Moving closer to the present, it thus appears that popular support for Islamist movements, including votes cast for candidates associated with these movements in Algeria (FIS) and Tunisia (an-Nahdah), does not necessarily reflect a desire for religious fulfillment, or mean that most North Africans genuinely favor governance in accordance with Islamic law in order to give existential meaning to their political community. Rather, many and perhaps most are motivated by more temporal considerations. As one knowledgeable analyst wrote of Tunisia in 1988, "the impact of the Islamist movement on Tunisia's political agenda in the years ahead will depend largely on how the country's political and economic problems are resolved. . . . [The growth of this movement is] only a symptom of a deeper malaise within Tunisian society" (Vandewalle 1988b: 617). Research carried out in Morocco offered a similar assessment, concluding that radical groups, particularly those with an Islamic ideology, will be able to attract support only so long as "the problems of social disadvantage and deprivation and of political marginalization" remain unaddressed and become increasingly severe (Seddon 1989: 263).

Writing of Algeria, where the Islamist movement has been strongest, many observers also emphasize the instrumental character of the FIS's appeal. According to a journalistic investigation carried out in 1992, for example, the Islamist movement has gained ground by winning converts "among victims of the corruption and inequality evidenced by the [gap between the] comfortable life of the old political leadership and the appalling housing and other conditions in which most other citizens live" (Abramson 1992: 20). And again, advancing a more generalized conclusion, two American scholars of Algerian origin argue that "economic deprivation, social exclusion, and political under-representation [have] encouraged the development of Islamist movements not only in Algeria but also in many other Muslim countries" (Layachi and Haireche 1992: 76).

Thus, what many North Africans and other Arabs appear to want is meaningful political change, and above all responsive and accountable government, rather than Islamic solutions per se. For a variety of reasons, Islamist movements have been well positioned to capitalize on discontent with the status quo. They offer effective vehicles for registering political dissatisfaction, and they have answers to the problems of their societies which, on the surface at least, appear coherent and plausible. But other mechanisms of political change and alternative visions of the future, to the extent they are available, might also be championed by those who have given their votes to Islamist candidates. Indeed, this is precisely the reason that Saddam Hussein received considerable support during the crisis in the Gulf, despite the Iraqi leader's history of opposition to radical Islam.

This underlying concern for an alternative to the political and economic status quo was forcefully articulated during the Gulf crisis by a journalist in Jordan, who wrote of an "essential message reverberating throughout the Arab world" and who castigated the United States and other Western powers for failing to understand the content of this message: There are everywhere "signs of a profound desire for change—for democracy and human rights, for social equity, for regional economic integration, for accountability of public officials, for morality in public life, for the fair application of international law and U.N. resolutions, and for a new regional order characterized by honesty, dignity, justice and stability" (Khouri 1990). The problem, he wrote in another article, is the pervasiveness of "autocratic rulers and non-accountable power elites [that] pursue whimsical, wasteful and regressive policies," and it is this situation that "will be challenged by the will of the Arab people" (Khouri 1991).

Describing the situation in the Arab world more generally, another analyst reports that the "demand for human rights, participation and democracy comes from across the political spectrum. . . . The call for democracy is the subject of meetings, conferences and academic studies" (Krämer 1992: 23). And still another scholar, a political scientist from the United Arab Emirates, makes explicit the relationship between these calls for political change and support for Islamist groups: "As long as Arab governments resist political participation and refuse to tolerate different political opinions, the strength of Islam as an alternative political ideology will continue to grow" (Al-Suwaidi 1995: 92).

Empirical evidence based on survey research in the Middle East also points to the conclusion that support for Islamist movements does not necessarily reflect a belief that existing political systems should be replaced by patterns of governance based on Muslim legal codes. In particular, this evidence indicates that considerations unrelated to the faith and religious attachments of ordinary Muslims are producing much of the support for contemporary Islamist groups. An original public opinion survey conducted in Egypt and Kuwait in 1988 found only a weak relationship between a scale measuring support for political Islam and contemporary Islamist groups on the one hand and, on the other, a scale measuring personal piety and attitudes toward the social salience of Islam. Surprisingly, perhaps, more than one-half of those with higher ratings on the scale measuring piety and social salience, and over 70 percent of the Egyptians with such ratings, expressed less favorable attitudes toward political aspects of Islam. Conversely, one-third of those who expressed greater support for Islamist political movements had lower ratings on the scale measuring religious piety and social salience. Moreover, this was the case in both Egypt and Kuwait, suggesting that the pattern may apply broadly throughout the Arab world. More information about the research on which these findings are based is presented in the appendix.

These findings are consistent with the conclusions of several other recent studies that have sought to explicate the relationship between Islamic attachments in general and support for political Islam in particular. For example, an American scholar who has conducted field work in Morocco insists upon distinguishing between traditional religious beliefs on the one hand and the ideology of Islamist political movements on the other, arguing that the latter "is not how most Muslims understand their religion" and that "a politicized conception of Islam differs radically from how Islam is normally understood by ordinary Muslims" (Munson 1992: 19). A similar point is made by a scholar from the United Arab Emirates, who conducted additional survey research in his own country and concluded that the "ideology and socio-political programs of religious groups are too political to appeal to traditional mainstream Muslims" (Al-Suwaidi 1995: 93).

Other findings from the 1988 survey in Egypt and Kuwait lend additional support to this thesis. For example, again in both Egypt and Kuwait, those expressing greater support for Islamist movements but having lower personal piety and social salience ratings are disproportionately likely to disagree with the statement that "Western values have led to moral erosion in my society." Further, in Egypt, younger individuals and men are overrepresented among those who support Islamist groups but are not personally pious. Younger men constitute the most volatile sector of society and the demographic category among which political and economic grievances appear to be most intense. All of this, again, suggests that it is the search for an alternative to the political and economic status quo, rather than an attraction to the specific content of Islamist slogans, that has produced much of the support that Muslim political groups currently enjoy.

Why Islamist Movements Are Filling the Void

Although non-Islamic challenges to the status quo would in theory find support among the discontented social classes of North Africa and other parts of the Arab world, it is in fact the case that large numbers of ordinary citizens are concluding that they can best work for political change by giving their support to militant Muslim movements. And in large part this is because of the organizational and ideological advantages such Islamic groups enjoy.

For one thing, in the undemocratic environment that until recently prevailed in most Arab countries, and that still prevails in many instances, mosques and other religious establishments offer opportunities to recruit and organize followers that are unavailable to more secular movements. Indeed, this is precisely the role that Islamic institutions played during the pre-independence period, when nationalist movements in North Africa and elsewhere were seeking to build mass organizations capable of challenging colonial domination. In Morocco, for example, the nationalist movement was built on a foundation established at the Qarawiyin Mosque University in Fez. In Tunisia, where the resistance movement was in fact led by men who had received a Western-style education and whose normative orientations were largely secular, nationalists held clandestine meetings in mosques and zawiyyas [religious lodges] and urged followers to pray five times a day for the martyrs of the revolution.

Analogous developments took place in the late 1960s and throughout the 1970s, a period marked by authoritarianism in North Africa and elsewhere in the Arab world. For example, a journalistic investigation conducted in Tunisia reported in 1979 on the crystallization of a political tendency that character-ized its platform as the "revival of Islam" ("L'Islam contestataire en Tunisie" 1979; Tessler 1980: 12). It had begun with formation of the Association for the Protection of the Koran, a group that in 1970 gained legal status as a "cul-tural" organization and then established an important center in the theology faculty of the University of Tunis. Over the course of the decade, however, while the political climate of the country was becoming more repressive (Tessler 1981), this tendency developed and organized itself into a "parallel society with its own laws and rules." French was not spoken, for example, and men and women did not shake hands. The "movement" held meetings de-voted to the study and discussion of religious themes, and it organized theater groups and operated a bookstore and publishing house.

The Islamic "underground" opposition continued to grow and gain fol-lowers in the 1980s, with developments in Tunisia paralleled by those in other Arab countries. According to a recent study of Algeria, for example, "at first, through a network of independent mosques, the Islamists preached educa-tional and mobilizational sermons. Later, they directly criticized governmen-tal policies and proposed their own remedies. . . . Their activities began to spread to different cities, where they challenged the secular authorities," and by 1985 there were signs of a well-structured political organization (Layachi and Haireche 1992: 76). It is against the background of these activities de-signed to build their movement during the first and middle part of the de-cade, when there was no legal political opposition, that the dramatic victories of the Islamic Salvation Front in the elections of 1990 and 1991 may be understood.

In some countries, Islamic groups have also built support through the provision of social services and through community assistance projects carried out under the banner of religion. The operation of clinics, schools, day care centers, and welfare distribution programs are among the most common of these activities. Also, in addition to these efforts aimed primarily at the urban poor, some Islamic groups have established publishing societies, investment companies, and even banks. Such efforts require a measure of organization that political authorities are usually required to tolerate, even though they may foster a belief that Islamic groups are more dedicated to helping ordinary men and women than are government officials.

The importance of these institutions and programs was stressed in a recent journalistic study of Jordan, which reported that the institutional network of the Muslim Brotherhood alone includes "some 20 Islamic clinics, one of Amman's largest hospitals, well over 40 Islamic schools, some 150 Koranic studies centers and other elements of what anti-fundamentalists call 'the infrastructure of an Islamic republic'" (Ibrahim 1992a). This is a very sizable operation in a country of only four million inhabitants.

A similar or even larger Islamist network exists in other countries, most notably in Egypt, but also in Algeria, Tunisia, among Palestinians, and elsewhere. As one scholar reports, groups associated with political Islam use socioeconomic institutions and programs, particularly those that target the poor, to "participate in the political process within the official parameters of permissible action while working to extract concessions from the state to allow the [Islamist] movement greater access to the masses and through them access to power" (Karawan 1992: 172). According to another scholarly analysis, focusing on Algeria, Islamists gained followers when they "quickly assumed certain social welfare functions, on such occasions as the earthquake of Tipaza, west of Algiers, and opened 'Islamic souks,' whose prices were well below those of the regular distribution circuits" (Layachi and Haireche 1992: 78).

Under such circumstances, Islamic groups have the additional advantage possessed by all opposition groups: They are free to criticize but have no statutory responsibility for delivering services, which means they can derive significant political advantage by making even modest contributions. This advantage would disappear should Islamists come to power, however. Indeed, after the FIS gained control of a number of Algerian municipalities in the elections of June 1990, the party began to be criticized for serious shortcomings in the operation of local government and for failing to deliver on a number of promised improvements (Ibrahim 1991; Layachi and Haireche 1992: 79). Similar complaints were heard in Jordan after leaders of the Muslim Brotherhood took control of several ministries following the November 1989 parliamentary elections.

Yet another factor working to the advantage of Islamist movements, and in some ways the most important, is the absence of alternative opposition parties with a credible platform. In particular, although Morocco is a partial exception, it is generally the case that North Africans and other Arabs no longer regard parties of the political left as suitable vehicles for the expression of opposition to existing regimes. This was evident in the Tunisian elections of April 1989, for example, where the leading socialist party received less than 4 percent of the vote and where the absence of any credible legal opposition contributed directly to the success of Islamist candidates who ran as independents.

This was also evident in Algeria, where leftist parties fared poorly in the election of June 1990, and about which one study concludes that gains made by the FIS reflect not only social and economic grievances but also, in combination, an "inability of the traditional secular opposition to channel popular demands" (Layachi and Haireche 1992: 76). Overall, the situation was summed up in summer 1991 by an Egyptian socialist, who told the author that his party was finding it increasingly difficult to counter the Islamists' appeal. "Islam may not be able to solve this country's problems," he stated, "but the Islamists at least have a credible slogan. They may be without a real solution, but we are without even the name of a solution."

Under these conditions, those who wish to register opposition to the government have little choice but to support Islamist movements; and it appears that in recent elections in Tunisia and Algeria, and presumably elsewhere, some voted for the candidates of these movements for precisely this reason. While it is impossible to determine the extent to which those who voted for the FIS or independents affiliated with an-Nahdah did so merely to express discontent, rather than because they genuinely consider Islam the solution to their country's problems, it is probable that the former explanation accounts for a significant proportion of the votes these parties' candidates received.

According to a recent scholarly account of the June 1990 elections in Algeria, for example, the results were much more of a defeat for the government than a victory for the FIS. The study reports that the "majority of the voters (between 55 and 82 percent depending on the parameters used) were not identifiable with the hard core of Islamist themes," and so concludes that "on evidence the 'rejection votes' very likely constituted a strong element in the old single party's defeat," rather than "sanction votes" indicating an identification with the FIS's ideology (Burgat and Dowell 1993: 281). This assessment is also supported by the investigation of an American journalist, who was told by one of his informants that "I voted for the FIS out of revenge" (Ibrahim 1990).

Another recent example, coming from outside the Maghreb, is provided by an account of the March 1992 election for the Chamber of Commerce in Ramallah in the Israeli-occupied West Bank. Candidates associated with the Islamist HAMAS movement handily defeated those identified with secular nationalism and the PLO. According to press reports, Palestinians complained of PLO officials who live lavishly and whose bank accounts contain funds that should be spent in the occupied territories; and it is for this reason, at least in part, that HAMAS was victorious in "a city with a large number of

Christian Palestinians who normally would never vote for an Islamic fundamentalist" (Ibrahim 1992b).

Although this analysis has stressed the instrumental considerations producing support for Islamist movements, the assertion that Islam is the solution strikes a responsive chord for other reasons as well. Islam is an indigenous belief system, familiar to almost all Arabs, even those who are Christian. It has shaped the Arabs' history, it helps to define their collective national identity, and it gives spiritual meaning to the lives of millions, even many who are not personally devout. Equally significant, by its very nature, as a culture and a legal system as well as a religion, Islam presents Muslims with a complete and coherent blueprint for the construction of a just political community. All of this makes it an attractive ideology to Arabs and other Muslims who are searching for an alternative political formula.

Nevertheless, growing popular support for activist Muslim movements cannot be explained exclusively, or even primarily, by Islam's familiarity and considerable normative appeal. On the one hand, as discussed earlier, available evidence suggests that there is only a weak association between the strength of personal religious attachments and the degree of support for Islamist groups and their political program. On the other, the salience of Islam as a religious faith and cultural system transcends historic swings in the strength of Islamist movements, suggesting once again that the present-day success of these groups is due primarily to recent political and economic developments rather than to the nature of Islam and its abiding importance in the lives of many ordinary Arabs. As one scholar argues in the case of Tunisia's an-Nahdah party, "feelings of dislocation and alienation among Tunisia's Muslims gradually turned the essentially apolitical group into an activist organization" (Vandewalle 1989/90: 5).

If this assessment is correct, if it is indeed political economy rather than religion and culture that holds the key to a proper understanding of the current Islamic resurgence, then the popular anger producing support for the FIS, an-Nahdah, and other Islamist movements will begin to dissipate if Arab governments display new vision and dedication in addressing the grievances of ordinary men and women. These regimes, with active encouragement and assistance from their external allies, will have to work with increased honesty and effectiveness on behalf of all of their citizens, and this in turn will require greater respect for human rights, a more equitable distribution of those burdens of underdevelopment that cannot be avoided, and, above all, progress toward democratization and genuine government accountability.

Appendix: Public Opinion Data from Egypt and Kuwait*

Public opinion surveys carried out in Egypt and Kuwait in mid-1988 deal with issues of religion and politics and may accordingly shed additional light on the origins of popular support for Islamist movements.

Data from Egypt may provide clues about attitudes in North Africa and other Arab countries where much of the population lives in impoverished conditions, where there has been some movement toward democratization in recent years, and where Islamic-tendency movements made major gains during the 1980s. Comparisons between Egypt and Kuwait will be helpful in determining whether particular attitudes emerge in this kind of environment or, alternatively, whether the normative patterns observed apply more generally throughout the Arab world and thus are not dependent on economic and political conditions.

Stratified samples of adults were selected in Cairo and Kuwait. Each sample includes both men and women and each is heterogeneous with respect to age, education, socioeconomic status, and neighborhood. Although better-educated individuals are somewhat overrepresented, the samples are generally representative of the active, adult, urban population. The distribution of each sample with respect to gender, age, and education is presented below.

	Total (N = 592)	Egyptians (N = 292)	Kuwaitis (N = 300)
Gender:			
Male	51%	52%	48%
Female	49	48	52
Age:			
Under 30	62	55	67
30–39	29	32	27
40 and over	9	13	6
Education:			
Intermediate or less	19	25	13
High school	28	27	28
Some post-secondary	22	17	28
University	31	31	31

*For additional analyses of these data, as well as additional methodological information about the surveys, see Tessler and Sanad (1994), Tessler and Grobschmidt (1995), and Tessler and Jesse (1996). These publications also present findings about Palestinian attitudes.

The surveys were carried out under the direction of Professor Jamal S. Al-Suwaidi of the United Arab Emirates University and the Emirates Center for Strategic Studies and Research. Interviews were conducted by teams of research assistants, or "intermediaries," who were selected on the basis of previous experience in survey research administration. Intermediaries were also given a four-day orientation, and the survey instrument was pretested in both countries.

The validity and reliability of survey items selected for subsequent analysis were evaluated through a technique known as factor analysis. Factor analysis identifies clusters of items that vary together and which thus may be analyzed in combination since they reliably measure the same concept. In the present instance, factor analysis has been used to measure two distinct dimensions of attitudes toward Islam, personal-social and political, as well as attitudes toward domestic politics, toward the United States and the West, and toward the local application of Western norms.

Nine items dealing with Islam were selected for subsequent analysis, and through the use of factor analysis it was determined that these items constitute two distinct attitudinal clusters. One deals with personal and social aspects of religion. The other deals with political aspects of Islam. All of the items and the strength of their association with each cluster are shown below.

1. Personal and Social Aspects of Islam

30. Would you support anyone in your family who wants to study in a religious institution?

32. How often do you refer to religious teachings when making important decisions about your life?

31. Do you support the application of Islamic law in social life?

15. Do you support the application of Islamic law to deal with civil and criminal matters?

36. How often do you read the Koran?

2. Political Aspects of Islam

38. Do you agree or disagree that religion and politics should be separate?

62. What do you think of the following statement: Religious practice must be kept private and must be separated from sociopolitical life?

72. Do you support current organized Islamic movements?

69. What do you think of the religious awakening now taking place in society?

Two attitudinal scales have been formed by combining the items in each cluster: a five-item scale measuring personal piety and social salience, and a four-item scale measuring support for political Islam and contemporary Islamist groups. Further, the strength of the association between the two dimensions of Islamic attachments has been examined and, as discussed in the text, attitudes toward personal-social and toward political aspects of Islam do not covary to the extent that might be expected. Specifically, more than half of the most pious respondents do not express strong support for political Islam, and more than one-third of those who do strongly support political Islam have lower levels of personal piety. These findings are shown in the table below, which crosstabulates dichotomized ratings on the two attitudinal scales.

Taken together, the two dichotomized dimensions of attitudes toward Islam produce a four-category typology of religious attachments. Respondents may be (a) higher both on measures of personal piety and social salience and on measures of support for political Islam and contemporary Islamic groups; (b) higher on the former set of measures but lower on the latter; (c) lower on the former set of measures but higher on the latter; or (d) lower on both sets of measures. The table shows that respondents are found in meaningful proportions in all four categories.

Item	Factor 1 (Personal-Social)	Factor 2 (Political)
30	.72945	.00153
32	.68098	.13009
31	.67403	.21164
15	.66808	.22825
36	.55939	.11639
38	.01436	.80070
62	.12740	.76350
72	.16159	.61355
69	.32806	.53887

Personal Piety and Social
Salience of Islam

Count Row Percent Col. Percent		Lower	Higher	Row Total
Support for Political Islam and Contemporary Islamic Groups	Higher	72 36.9% 24.0%	123 63.1% 47.3%	195 34.9%
	Lower	227 62.5% 76.0%	137 37.6% 52.7%	364 65.1%
	Column **Total**	299 53.4%	260 46.6%	559 100.0%

The four categories of religious attachments may be compared in order to determine whether any is more likely to be found in either Egypt or Kuwait, to determine whether any is associated with a particular set of demographic attributes, and to determine whether demographic correlates are similar or different among the two national samples.

As shown in the table below, there are significant national differences for three of the four categories. Specifically, (a) Egyptians are underrepresented among respondents with higher ratings on both the personal-social and the political dimensions of Islam, (b) Egyptians are also underrepresented among respondents with lower ratings on the personal-social dimension but higher ratings on the political dimension, and (c) Egyptians are overrepresented among respondents with higher ratings on the personal-social dimension but lower ratings on the political dimension.

The table also shows that support for political Islam and contemporary Islamic groups is lower in Egypt than in Kuwait. While it is possible that this is due to the differing cultural and religious traditions of the two countries, it is also possible that the difference is due, at least in part, to the more open and competitive political environment that existed in Egypt at the time the survey was conducted.

Count Row Percent Col. Percent		Egypt	Kuwait	Row Total
Personal-Social **Political**	Higher Higher	39 31.7% 14.3%	84 68.3% 29.4%	123 22.0%
Personal-Social **Political**	Higher Lower	98 71.5% 35.9%	39 28.5% 13.6%	137 24.5%
Personal-Social **Political**	Lower Higher	19 26.4% 7.0%	53 73.6% 18.5%	72 12.9%
Personal-Social **Political**	Lower Lower	117 51.5% 42.8%	110 48.5% 38.5%	227 40.6%
	Column Total	273 48.8%	286 51.2%	559 100.0%

The next table presents summary information about demographic correlates of the four categories of Islamic attachments. It indicates, for both the
Egyptian and Kuwaiti samples, whether any attributes associated with either
gender, age, or education are overrepresented in each category, thus presenting a partial demographic profile of the kinds of individuals who are disproportionately likely to possess particular attitudes toward Islam.

		Egypt	Kuwait
Personal-Social **Political**	Higher Higher	High school	
Personal-Social **Political**	Higher Lower	Male, older	Intermediate school
Personal-Social **Political**	Lower Higher	Male, younger	University
Personal-Social **Political**	Lower Lower	Female	

An interesting finding is that in Egypt those with higher ratings on the personal-social but not the political dimension of Islam are disproportionately likely to be older men, and that those with higher ratings on the political but not the personal-social dimension are disproportionately likely to be younger men. In Kuwait, neither gender nor age is associated with differing religious attitudes, whereas level of education helps to differentiate between those with higher ratings on one attitudinal dimension but not the other.

The data may also be used to examine normative correlates of differing Islamic attachments. Ten items dealing with attitudes toward (1) domestic politics, (2) the United States and the West, and (3) the local application of Western economic and cultural norms were selected for further analysis. The validity and reliability of these items were again established by means of factor analysis, which grouped the items into three unidimensional clusters. For purposes of parsimony, only two items from each cluster are examined at present. These are listed below, grouped in the manner established through factor analysis.

1. Domestic Politics

Do you agree or disagree that the government usually ignores the needs of the people? (Agree: Egypt, 68%; Kuwait, 39%)

Do you agree or disagree that public officials usually pursue their own interests first? (Agree: Egypt, 71%; Kuwait, 51%)

2. The United States and the West

Do you agree or disagree that your country should have a strong relationship with the United States? (Agree: Egypt, 57%; Kuwait, 47%)

Do you agree or disagree that Western development is an accomplishment worthy of great admiration? (Agree: Egypt, 59%; Kuwait, 43%)

3. Local Application of Western Norms

Do you agree or disagree that Western values have led to moral erosion in your society? (Agree: Egypt, 67%; Kuwait, 68%)

Do you agree or disagree that Western (capitalist) economic forms have been a major cause of inequalities and social problems in your country? (Agree: Egypt, 54%; Kuwait, 71%)

The table below presents summary information, for both the Egyptian and Kuwaiti samples, showing whether particular responses to any of the six items are overrepresented in any of the four categories based on attitudes toward Islam. Percentages, where shown, indicate the degree to which the proportion of respondents in that catagory exceeds the proportion of all respondents who answer a question about domestic politics, the West, or the local application of Western norms in the manner indicated. The table thus presents a partial normative profile of individuals who possess a given set of religious attachments. One interesting finding, discussed briefly in the text, concerns the differences between more religious and less religious supporters of political Islam. The former but not the latter appear to have negative views about Western values. Another interesting finding is that judgments about Western economic forms do not appear to be influenced by religious attachments.

		Egypt	Kuwait
Personal-Social **Political**	Higher Higher	Gov't ignores needs, 16% West values erode morals, 19%	Not strong relat. with U.S., 7% West values erode morals, 20%
Personal-Social **Political**	Higher Lower	Officials self-serving, 10% Strong relations with U.S., 8% West development not admirable, 12%	Not strong relat. with U.S., 8% West values erode morals, 11% West economics not cause prob., 18%
Personal-Social **Political**	Lower Higher	Officials not self-serving, 8% West development admirable, 7% West values not erode morals, 14%	West values not erode morals, 9%
Personal-Social **Political**	Lower Lower	Gov't cares, 11% West values not erode values, 17%	Officials self-serving, 9% Strong relations with U.S., 9% West values not erode morals, 25%

References

Abramson, Gary. 1992. "Rise of the Crescent." *Africa Report* (March–April).

Ajami, Fouad. 1981. *The Arab Predicament: Arab Political Thought and Practice since 1967.* Cambridge: Cambridge University Press.

Amawi, Abla. 1992. "Democracy Dilemmas in Jordan." *Middle East Report* 174 (January–February): 26–29.

Ayari, Chadly. 1991. "Le monde arabe et l'enjeu économique du nouvel ordre mondial." In *La Guerre du Golfe et l'avenir des Arabes: débats et réflexions.* Tunis: Cérès.

Belhassen, Souhayr. 1989. "Nous oeuvrons pour que l'islam occupe sa place en Algérie." *Jeune Afrique,* February 12.

Bendourou, Omar. 1988. "The Exercise of Political Freedoms in Morocco." *Review of the International Commission of Jurists* 40: 31–41.

Bennani-Chraibi, Mounia. 1993. *Les Représentations du Monde des Jeunes Marocains.* Paris: Thèse de doctorat de l'Institut d'Etudes Politiques.

Bennoune, Mahfoud. 1988. *The Making of Contemporary Algeria, 1830–1987: Colonial Upheavals and Post-independence Development.* Cambridge: Cambridge University Press.

Bourgi, Albert. 1989. "Etudiants: ou menera le désespoir?" *Jeune Afrique,* February 12.

Brown, Kenneth. 1993. "Lost in Algiers." *Mediterraneans* 4 (Summer): 8–18.

Burgat, François, and William Dowell. 1993. *The Islamic Movement in North Africa.* Austin: University of Texas Press.

Digne, Paul. 1989. "Algérie: un navire à la dérive." *Jeune Afrique,* February 12.

Dufour, Dany. 1978. "L'Enseignement en Algérie." *Maghreb-Machrek* 80: 33–53.

Dwyer, Kevin. 1991. *Arab Voices.* Berkeley: University of California Press.

Entelis, John P. 1986. *Algeria: The Revolution Institutionalized.* Boulder, CO: Westview.

———. 1988. "Algeria under Chadli: Liberalization without Democratization or, Perestroika, Yes; Glasnost, No." *Middle East Insight* (Fall): 47–64.

Entelis, John P., and Lisa Arone. 1992. "Algeria in Turmoil." *Middle East Policy* 1: 23–35.

"Etat, ville et mouvements sociaux au Maghreb et au Moyen Orient." 1987. *Maghreb-Machrek* 115: 53–69.

La Guerre du Golfe et l'avenir des Arabes: débats et réflexions. 1991. Tunis: Cérès.

Hermassi, Elbaki. 1984. "La société tunisienne au miroir islamiste." *Maghreb-Machrek* 103: 39–56.

Huxley, Fred. 1993. "Moroccan Public Backs PLO-Israel Peace Plan, Views U.S. Positively." Washington, D.C.: USIA Opinion Research Memorandum, December 13.

Ibrahim, Youssef. 1990. "Militant Muslims Grow Stronger as Algeria's Economy Grows Weaker." *New York Times,* June 25.

———. 1991. "In Algiers, Curfew and Threats of Worse." *New York Times,* June 7.

———. 1992a. "Jordan Feels Change within as Muslims Pursue Agenda." *New York Times,* December 26.

————. 1992b. "PLO Is Facing Growing Discontent." *New York Times*, April 5.

"L'Islam contestataire en Tunisie." 1979. *Jeune Afrique*, March 14, 21, and 28.

Jansen, Willy. 1987. *Women without Men*. Leiden: Brill.

Karawan, Ibrahim A. 1992. "'ReIslamization Movements' according to Kepel: On Striking Back and Striking Out." *Contention* 2 (Fall): 161–79.

————. 1993. "Arab Dilemmas in the 1990s." Unpublished paper, October.

Khouri, Rami G. 1990. "The Arab Dream Won't Be Denied." *New York Times*, December 15.

————. 1991."A Lesson in Middle East History and Humanity." *Jordan Times*, May 28.

Kokan, Jane. 1994. "Morocco: Riot Deaths as Hassan Faces Challenge." *London Times*, February 20.

Krämer, Gudrun. 1992. "Liberalization and Democracy in the Arab World." *Middle East Report* 174 (January–February): 22–25.

Labib, Taher. 1991. "L'intellectuel des sept mois." In *La Guerre du Golfe et l'avenir des Arabes: débats et réflexions*. Tunis: Cérès.

Layachi, Azzedine. 1992. "Government, Legitimacy and Democracy in Algeria." *Maghreb Report* (January–February).

Layachi, Azzedine, and Abdel-kader Haireche. 1992. "National Development and Political Protest: Islamists in the Maghreb Countries." *Arab Studies Quarterly* 14 (Spring–Summer): 69–92.

Lesbet, Djaafar. 1994. "Effets de la crise du logement en Algérie: Des cités d'urgence à l'état d'exception." *Maghreb-Machrek: Monde Arabe—villes, pouvoirs et sociétés* (numéro spécial) 143 (January–March): 212–24.

Marks, Jon. 1994. "Special Report on Morocco." *Middle East Economic Digest*, April 1.

Moffett, George D. 1989. "North Africa's Disillusioned Youth. *Christian Science Monitor*, May 17.

Munson, Henry. 1992. "Islamist Political Movements in North Africa." Paper presented at a workshop on "Politico-Religious Movements and Development in the Near East," Washington, D.C., June.

Parker, Richard B. 1984. *North Africa: Regional Tensions and Strategic Concerns*. New York: Praeger.

Paul, James. 1984. "States of Emergency: The Riots in Tunisia and Morocco." *MERIP Reports*, no. 127 (October).

Pollock, David. 1992. *The "Arab Street"? Public Opinion in the Arab World*. Washington, D.C.: Washington Institute for Near East Policy, Policy Paper no. 32.

Quarterly Economic Review of Morocco. 1987. No. 1.

Riding, Alan. 1990. "Tunisians, in Search of Roots, Turn toward Iraq." *New York Times*, October 10.

Sabagh, Georges. 1993. "The Challenge of Population Growth in Morocco." *Middle East Report* (March–April): 30–35.

Seddon, David. 1989. "The Politics of 'Adjustment' in Morocco." In Bonnie K. Campbell and John Loxley, eds., *Structural Adjustment in Africa*. New York: St. Martin's.

Soudan, François. 1989. "Tunisie: islamistes contre 'Albanais.'" *Jeune Afrique*, February 12.

Stone, Russell. 1982. "Tunisia: A Single-Party System Holds Change in Abeyance." In I. William Zartman et al., eds., *Political Elites in Arab North Africa*. New York: Longman.

Suleiman, Michael W. 1987. "Attitudes, Values and the Political Process in Morocco." In I. William Zartman, ed., *The Political Economy of Morocco*. New York: Praeger.

Al-Suwaidi, Jamal S. 1995. "Arab and Western Conceptions of Democracy: Evidence from a UAE Opinion Survey." In David Garnham and Mark Tessler, eds., *Democracy, War, and Peace in the Middle East*. Bloomington: Indiana University Press.

Telhami, Shibley. 1992. "Between Theory and Fact: Explaining American Behavior in the Gulf War." *Security Studies* (Fall).

Tessler, Mark. 1980. "Political Change and the Islamic Revival in Tunisia." *Maghreb Review* 5: 8–19.

———. 1981. "Regime Orientation and Participant Citizenship in Developing Countries: Hypotheses and a Test with Longitudinal Data from Tunisia." *Western Political Quarterly* 34 (December): 479–98.

———. 1986. "Explaining the 'Surprises' of King Hassan II: The Linkage between Domestic and Foreign Policy in Morocco; Part I: Tensions in North Africa in the Mid-1980s." *Universities Field Staff International Reports*, no. 38.

———. 1990. "Tunisia's New Beginning." *Current History* (April): 169–84.

———. 1991. "Anger and Governance in the Arab World: Lessons from the Maghreb and Implications for the West." *Jerusalem Journal of International Relations* 13: 7–33.

———. 1993. "The Alienation of Urban Youth." In I. William Zartman and Mark W. Habeeb, eds., *State and Society in Contemporary North Africa*. Boulder, CO: Westview.

Tessler, Mark, and Marilyn Grobschmidt. 1995. "The Relationship between Democracy in the Arab World and the Arab-Israeli Conflict." In David Garnham and Mark Tessler, eds., *Democracy, War, and Peace in the Middle East*. Bloomington: Indiana University Press.

Tessler, Mark, and Jolene Jesse. 1996. "Gender and Support for Islamist Movements: Evidence from Egypt, Kuwait, and Palastine." *Muslim World* 86 (April): 194–222.

Tessler, Mark, and Jamal Sanad. 1994. "Will the Arab Public Accept Peace with Israel: Evidence from Surveys in Three Arab Societies." In Efraim Karsh and Gregory Mahler, eds., *Israel at the Crossroads: The Challenge of Peace*. London: British Academic Press.

Vandewalle, Dirk. 1988a. "Autopsy of a Revolt: The October Riots in Algeria." Hanover, NH: Institute of Current World Affairs.

———. 1988b. "From the New State to the New Era: Toward a Second Republic in Tunisia." *Middle East Journal* 42: 602–20.

———. 1989/90. "Ben Ali's New Tunisia." *Universities Field Staff International Reports*, no. 8.

Waltz, Susan. 1986. "The Islamist Appeal in Tunisia." *Middle East Journal* 40 (Autumn): 651–71.

Witter, Willis. 1993. "Moroccans See Good, Evil in Possible Economic Boom." *Washington Times*, September 22.

Yousif, Sami. 1991. "The Iraqi-U.S. War: A Conspiracy Theory." In Haim Bresheeth and Nira Yuval-Davis, eds., *The Gulf War and the New World Order*. London: Zed.

Zghal, Abdelkader. 1991. "La guerre du Golfe et la recherche de la bonne distance." In *La Guerre du Golfe et l'avenir des Arabes: débats et réflexions*. Tunis: Cérès.

6.

Prospects for Liberalism in North Africa

Identities and Interests in Preindustrial Welfare States

LISA ANDERSON

We are faced now with two alternatives. Either we become a police state and step back from the democratic advances that have been made, or we descend into disorder and perhaps civil war.
—Hala Mostapha, Egyptian writer,
quoted in the *New York Times,* April 1, 1993

This essay is an examination of the impetus to liberal political reform in North Africa and of the impediments to the realization of the fruits of such reform. In the mid-1970s, North Africa well deserved a wide reputation for despotic government. No country enjoyed widespread freedom of speech, opinion, or assembly, not to say contested elections. Only Morocco had more than one political party and Libya permitted none at all. Fifteen years later, multiparty political systems existed in Morocco, Algeria, and Tunisia. None of these were Scandinavian-style democracies, but neither were they the oppressive regimes they had once been. Moreover, economic liberalization in Libya had raised hopes of political reform there as well.

Our first question, then, is, why this change? What prompted the governments of the region to loosen their grip, to accord some political rights, however limited, to their citizens? The second question is a sadder one, at least to those of us attached to liberal institutions. For just as liberalism appeared to triumph in much of the rest of the world, North Africa seemed to opt out. Since the beginning of the 1990s, there has been a subtle but quite palpable reversal in the trend toward liberal politics. The most spectacular setback was the military coup in January 1992 in Algeria that led to cancellation of the results of free and fair elections, suspension of parliament, dismissal of the president, and to what soon looked like a low-grade civil war.

Elsewhere, however, press censorship was tightened—as in Tunisia, elections more carefully manipulated—as in Morocco, and opposition even more ruthlessly repressed—as in Libya.

What happened? The short answer is that the power of Islamist political movements to avail themselves of the newly created political spaces surprised and alarmed the political elites so much that they changed their minds about allowing them (or anyone else) to speak and assemble freely. We still must ask, however, why the regimes created the opportunities in the first place, and why it was Islamists—rather, than, say, secular liberals, or labor unions, or big business—that so quickly took advantage of them.

The following pages provide an explanation for both the initial enthusiasm for and subsequent reluctance to pursue regime change in the Arab world in the 1980s and 1990s. The emphasis is on the international economic factors that have shaped demands for and assessments of political change in the Arab world in general and in North Africa in particular. While this approach is fairly conventional in studies of regime stability and transition elsewhere in the world, it is somewhat unusual in scholarship on the Middle East and North Africa, and some of the alternatives should be addressed briefly.

Perhaps most common is the inclination to attribute primacy to culture and tradition. This perspective almost invariably concludes that the region is irredeemably authoritarian. For a variety of reasons unrelated to scholarly pursuits and very much shaped by current politics—as we shall see—scholars both here and in North Africa often identify Islam as the villain in the piece. The variety of cultural arguments is considerable, however, drawing not only on the presumed dictates of Islamic jurisprudence or Muslim theologians but also, for example, the workings of the tribes of the desert or the legacy of the Ottoman Empire to account for the apparent fact that, as Elie Kedourie put it, "democracy is alien to the mind-set" of the residents of the Arab world (1992: 1).[1] The difficulties with this approach are legion. Some of them have been usefully dissected by Edward Said in *Orientalism* (1978), but perhaps most important for my purposes is the fact that unless novelty is attributed to imports—of ideas, individuals, technologies, and so forth—change itself is inexplicable. Since what I am trying to explain is change, or at least efforts at change, this will not do.

In part, of course, international political factors do serve as a catalyst to change by introducing new ideas and institutions, now as they did in the nineteenth and early twentieth centuries, when the contemporary states of North Africa took shape at the behest and eventually under the tutelage of European powers. While recognizing that international ideological pressures are important, however, we must also acknowledge that they cannot account equally or in the same way for the decisions of, say, Qaddafi in Libya and Ben Ali in Tunisia to open up economically and crack down politically at the beginning of the 1990s.

Finally, changing domestic social structures, particularly the growth of voluntary organizations outside the purview of the state, are also thought to play a significant role in creating eager constituencies and hospitable environments for more democratic politics.[2] Unfortunately, however, where state ownership predominated in the economy, as was the case throughout North Africa, what is sometimes called the resurgence (more appropriately here, the appearance) of civil society may be difficult to discern. Still, liberal democratic discourse grew during the 1980s, and hesitant experiments in more liberal politics were launched virtually across the region. What happened, and why?

The Political Economy of North Africa

Before examining the trajectory of reform in the region, any effort to understand or explain the nature of the regimes in North Africa must take account of the international political economy within which the states of the Arab world were formed. Whether created from pre-existing regencies—Morocco and Tunisia—or invented on terrain once belonging to the Ottoman Empire—Algeria and Libya—they were constituted originally as administrations over, rather than of, the local population. Much of the cost of the administration was borne by the European colonial and protectorate authorities, establishing a political pattern characterized by an exceptionally strong state apparatus, a weak domestic economy, and heavy reliance on external revenues, which would persist well into independence.

Soft Budget Constraints: Income

These very important characteristics distinguish these states from the early developers of Europe and the more recent industrializers of Latin America and East Asia. To put it most succinctly, these are states subject to what have been called soft budget constraints.[3] From the outset, external infusions of funds have been made available to cover budget deficits, and the states derive substantial parts of government revenues from sources outside of domestic production, from what also have been called exogenous rents. The importance of this profile first became apparent in the large oil-producing countries of the Middle East and North Africa. In the early days of oil exploration and production, the governments quite literally drew rents, or royalties, from the concessions they granted to foreign oil companies. In time the governments took increasing control of the oil operations within their borders, but the state remained the recipient of substantial revenues in the absence of virtually any corresponding domestic productive activity.

From the perspective of a country's domestic political economy, other externally generated revenues may also behave like oil income, and from this perspective, substantial rents have accrued directly to the state fairly often in

this part of the world.[4] In the days before independence, metropoles supported colonial state administrations that would later be characterized as
"over developed" by local societal standards. After independence, governments garnered windfalls from foreign exchange reserves that accumulated
during the Second World War; from nationalizations of foreign-owned
property immediately after independence; from the foreign aid they obtained
first as a result of the region's geostrategic location at the height of the Cold
War, and after 1973 within Arab regional politics; and during the 1980s, from
foreign debt incurred, not in the private sector as in much of Latin America,
but by the states themselves.

What difference does such a political economy make for the nature of the
states, of their regimes, and for the prospects of regime change? The
argument can be put in the following way: Historically, states have become
beholden to their citizens through reciprocal obligation. Impersonal, formal,
arbitrary state extraction—taxes and conscription, for example—was the first
sign of government penetration and control in the early modern nation-
states. It was soon followed by demands, particularly among property-
holders, for protection against such arbitrary government exactions and for a
role in decisionmaking about the expenditure of state income. These developments we now think of as the expansion of liberal individual rights and
democratic participation. In extractive states, wealth translates into capacity
to pay taxes to, and extract concessions from, the government—that is,
power.[5]

In states characterized by soft budget constraints, by contrast, the conventional relationship between purse strings and policy in domestic politics is
reversed. The availability of exogenous revenues releases governments from
reliance on domestic taxes for a (substantial though variable) component of
their income. As a result the governments are not subject to ordinary
obligations of domestic accountability. As it is sometimes put, there is "no
representation without taxation." Rather than make themselves beholden to
their people, the regimes use their externally generated income to buy
acquiescence to their rule. Thus have the governments of North Africa
provided generous consumer subsidies, education, health care, and other
services to their people, becoming, in essence, preindustrial welfare states.

Soft Budget Constraints: Expenditures

While elaborate welfare bureaucracies emerged throughout North Africa,
as in all of the Arab world the domestic fiscal systems remained rudimentary
until the mid-1980s. Despite the variety of the regimes, from monarchy to
socialist single-party government, they all proclaimed their solicitude for
ordinary folk while sustaining themselves in power without making significant demands upon or concessions to those very same people.

The generous distributive policies of these governments had several other equally important effects. Not only did they buy for the governments domestic acquiescence, they also retarded or deflected the appearance of demands for participation in government decisionmaking, breeding instead societies dependent upon the state for many of the necessities of modern life. In soft-money states, the relationship between power and wealth characteristic of the typical extractive state is reversed: here wealth derives from power. It is most efficiently generated not in production but through the forging and sustaining of close ties with the regulatory and distributive agencies of the state. Indeed, the "modern" or profitable sectors of the economy are often monopolized by the state itself, in state-owned enterprises. Where they are not, the private entrepreneurs are friends, clients, relatives of the ruler, or even—as in Morocco where the king is by far the largest property-holder— the ruler himself.

Class-based or interest group associations such as business groups or labor unions—organizations based on common positions within a productive process—are less effective in enhancing and protecting wealth than are relations built on personal patronage and bureaucratic clientelism. Thus, from the perspective of appropriation, the utility of the broad-based associations of civil society is markedly diminished, and labor unions and industrialists' syndicates have been notable mostly by their absence or their subservience to the regime.

Equally important is the impact of distribution, or welfare politics, on the development of the social cleavages that do appear in politics.[6] Where taxation is the most important economic relationship between state and society, differential abilities to meet government assessments—that is, different kinds and amounts of property ownership or control—serve as markers of common political interest and identity. By contrast, where distribution is the most significant economic link between government and governed, the criteria by which government goods and services are allocated become critical determinants of common political interest and identity. For a variety of reasons, including the dynamics of both patronage and affirmative action, the criteria of distribution are often noneconomic. This elicits political organization based on common identities—often officially constructed and sanctioned identities—rather than on common interests.

Most advanced industrial societies are now mixed economies and both extraction and distribution (or redistribution) take place. As a result, political groups are reflections of both interest and identity. Where extraction predominates, class politics is prevalent, however, and where distribution predominates, as in the somewhat unusual case of the soft budget state, identity politics eclipses other forms of political organization.

In North Africa, economic distinctions among citizens, particularly differential ownership or control of property, are not significant bases for political identity. Both supporters and foes of the regimes are encouraged, sometimes deliberately, sometimes inadvertently, to organize around noneconomic familial, patronage, or ideological commonalities. Thus have the clients of Morocco's king, the children of the martyrs of Algeria's revolution, the residents of the Tunisian president's natal village, the members of the Qaddafa clan in Libya all enjoyed preferential access to government-controlled benefits. As we shall see, this effect of the structure of the soft budget state has had profound significance for the nature of political opposition. Indeed, it appears to be true in general, and it is certainly true in North Africa, that interest-based movements are weakened by the welfare state, while the importance of identity-based movements is amplified.[7]

Political Reform and Reversal in North Africa

How has the nature of state income and expenditure in North Africa, together with its social structural consequences, influenced the region's patterns of political change? By the late 1980s, many of the sources of externally generated revenues upon which the North African regimes had relied were depleted or exhausted. Oil revenues fell off dramatically; debt service obligations mushroomed; the amount of foreign aid contracted with the end of the Cold War. Governments had to develop alternative sources of revenue. Although at least one regime appears to have attempted to alleviate its difficulties through foreign conquest,[8] for most, extracting resources from previously immune domestic populations was the most plausible untapped source of income. Government coffers that were rapidly emptying were, in other words, the impetus to change.

This policy shift implied the prospect of both a loosening of regime links with foreign patrons and the creation of potential for demands from, and obligations to, various sectors of the domestic society. Political liberalization was therefore intended from the outset to have both international and domestic audiences: It promised to win favor among Western aid donors no longer enthralled by anticommunism and, equally importantly, it constituted an essentially preemptive compensatory political concession to the constituencies likely to be targeted for taxation.[9]

Partly as a result of the nature and interests of these foreign and domestic constituencies, the reforms have been more often liberal than democratic, more concerned with broadening rights than with expanding participation. Thus liberalizing regimes lifted press censorship while postponing genuinely contested elections, or held elections without recognizing significant opposition political parties. In fact, in both intent and content, these reforms were designed *not* to inaugurate a system of uncertain outcomes—democracy— but to solidify and broaden the base of the elites in power, making possible increased domestic extraction. From the perspective of the regime incumbents, the desirability (indeed, the possibility) of retiring from politics to profitable private endeavors is faint at best, since politically generated wealth cannot be transferred reliably into a genuine private sector. In these circumstances, government incumbents have no economic incentives to relinquish power but many reasons to prolong their stay.

That they succeeded in doing so reflected the relatively weak and undifferentiated character of independent associational life in the region.[10] This weakness of civil society is all the more striking since the state itself is sufficiently organized and bureaucraticized to provide elaborate welfare services. Yet the poverty and timidity of class and interest-based organizations, whether professional associations, interest groups, labor unions, or student syndicates, is striking. Very few societal organizations took up the challenge, implied in political liberalization, to actually contest government policy. Those that did, such as the Tunisian Human Rights League, often found that the governments attempted to coopt their members with offers of influential ministerial or ambassadorial appointments. This posed the virtually insoluble dilemma of having to choose between compromising principles or sacrificing access. In part because of these contradictory pressures, from Morocco to Algeria to Tunisia the secular liberal opposition often preferred to boycott elections rather than fully embrace the rough and tumble of campaign politics.

Among those few who have taken up the government challenge to participate in politics are, of course, the Islamist movements. These groups have found support in those social categories that benefited least from government largesse, usually among the poor and the young. Like the new social movements of Europe, however, their claims against the government are cast in terms of personal (religious) identity and moral outrage—in what is fair to characterize as Albert O. Hirschman's (1977) "passions," or perhaps virtues—rather than interpretations of economic interest.

To some extent, the Islamists' reliance on a moral critique of the governments mirrors the rhetoric of those governments themselves. Because only self-defined moral responsibility or ideological commitment, rather than any fiscal incentives or obligations, required the governments to rule responsibly, the idiom of politics was not the prosaic language of budgets but far more often was the righteous rhetoric of war, family honor, ethnic purity, religious virtue—from the nationalist struggle to the myriad regional conflicts. Often, of course, the regimes failed to meet even their own standards, losing at wars and succumbing to the temptations of flesh and spirit that presumably face all absolute rulers. Nonetheless, the divorce between the rulers and the ruled—or, perhaps better, their financial separation—created the conditions for the making of mutual claims on noneconomic grounds. The absence of both taxation and representation enhanced reliance on moral suasion and religious exhortation. Economic corruption became a mere symptom of moral corruption.

The economic class- and interest-based organizations—chambers of commerce, industrial and professional syndicates, labor unions—represented constituencies whose contribution to the government coffers was minimal, and they played relatively little role in the domestic conflicts over government policy. The critical resources were ideological or symbolic, and only secondarily economic. The Islamists thus challenged the regimes where they needed and wanted support—the realm of symbolic production—and the regimes responded in ways that reflected less the economic resources of the religious movements than the role religion had been conceded by the incumbent governments themselves. The role of religion in the Moroccan king's self-portrayal as the "Commander of the Faithful" and in the Libyan regimes' claims to legitimacy as righteous rulers is self-evident. Even the most secular Arab nationalist in Algeria conceded, however, that Islam provided the sole marker that distinguished "Algerians" from their colonial rulers during the war of independence.

Although both the Islamists and their opponents framed the debate in ideological terms, it is important to note that the Islamist movements represented more than simply an ideological challenge to the status quo. Algeria's FIS (Front Islamique du Salut, or Islamic Salvation Front), for example, was often better organized, more efficient, and less corrupt than the government administration. As such, it not only effectively discredited the regime by providing services in its stead but—and this was critical to its capacity to seize the terrain of opposition—it also out-performed the secular political opposition. With the partial exception of ethnically based parties such as the FFS (Front des Forces Socialistes) in Algeria, the secular legal opposition defined its mandate in narrowly political terms such as contesting elections or publishing newspapers—eschewing social and economic activities and thus developing little or no grassroots following. Although through the late 1980s neither the urban sub-proletariat nor the rural peasantry appeared to have been significantly mobilized by Islamist groups anywhere in North Africa, the popularity of the FIS before its prohibition suggested that the support for Islamist movements was increasingly crossing social classes. In 1990, a young Algerian explained his support for the FIS in the following terms:

> [Y]ou have only four choices: you can remain unemployed and celibate because their are no jobs and no apartments to live in; you can work in the black market and risk being arrested; you can try to emigrate to France to sweep the streets of Paris or Marseilles; or you can join the FIS and vote for Islam. (Quoted in Tessler 1991: 17)

As the rulers lined their pockets while continuing to demand sacrifice for the good of the nation, the ruled had begun to reexamine the prerogatives and obligations of righteous rulers in Islam. Although they were quick to take advantage of expanded rights, such as greater press freedoms or opportunities to contest elections to press their cases, the Islamists were not by and large well disposed to liberal democracy, either by ideological inclination or social base. Indeed, many of the Islamic movements look very much like the governments they oppose.[11] A number of them obtain significant resources from patrons abroad, with which they construct and sustain their domestic clienteles.[12] Precisely because they have not worked within the political system of the incumbent government, they are worrisome to that very government. In rejecting the prevailing system outright, they aspire to creating an alternative rather than to participating in a system from which they have been excluded. As such, however, they are no more "liberal" or "democratic" than are the regimes that spawned them.

In very few of the debates about political and moral authority between governments and their opponents has the question of establishing and maintaining institutions by which government might be held accountable for its policies even been raised, much less resolved. In a survey done in Algiers at the end of 1991, for example, only half of those who claimed to support the FIS declared themselves favorable to installation of an Islamic Republic (Burgat with Dowell 1993: 100). The widespread support for Islamist movements among individuals who do not support what would seem to be key elements of their program is a reflection of the ambiguity of the program itself. Like political parties and movements out of power elsewhere, the Islamists attempt to win and keep the widest possible public sympathy through vague and often emotional appeals to popular sentiments rather than through detailed and specific policy proposals that might alienate some of their followers. Moreover, it is a truism of political science that political parties with *no* prospect of gaining power often advocate positions they know to be untenable. For the governments, running on their records is often an awkward proposition and they too prefer to join the contest at the level of emotional appeals rather than concrete policy prescriptions.

The terrain of symbols, of reciprocal moral obligation, may be a passionate, complex, and potentially dangerous one, but it has the singular advantage of being cheap to government and opposition alike. Far more taxing, literally and figuratively, is the construction of the tangible, material means of guaranteeing popular representation and government accountability; this battle has only just been joined (Anderson 1991). Small wonder, then, that the regimes of the region got cold feet about liberalization. What was supposed to be little more than a sop to a timid, largely dependent bourgeoisie, a device to broaden and solidify the regimes' support, soon threatened to seriously challenge those very regimes.

Within the four countries of North Africa, there is considerable variation in levels of reliance upon external revenues, the liveliness of private associational life, the type of regime and prospects for regime change. Of the two monarchies that survived independence, Morocco and Libya, only one remains—Morocco. Indeed, Qaddafi's overthrow of the Libyan king constitutes the only permanent and clear-cut regime change in the region since Algeria's independence in 1962. Single-party socialist regimes were established in the aftermath of independence in Algeria and Tunisia; and although both ruling parties now share the political terrain with other political parties, neither has made any substantive concessions of power to any of those other parties. Nonetheless, it is fair to say that Morocco and Tunisia have been, for some time, the more liberal of the regimes, Algeria and Libya the less so, although Algeria is the only country to have even flirted with genuine democracy.

Though we do not have a large number of cases in North Africa, the correlation between high levels of reliance on external rents and illiberality is perfect. Because of their hydrocarbon exports (gas in the case of Algeria, oil for Libya), the governments of Algeria and Libya have had little need of a domestic productive capacity or of a tax-paying bourgeoisie and working class. Indeed, in both countries, well over half of the active labor force is employed in the public sector, and the regimes have relied on government patronage and bureaucratic clientelism to distribute resources and win acquiescence to their rule. As demonstrated by both Algeria's ill-fated democratic era and the Libyan government's simultaneous promise to distribute half of all oil revenues directly to individuals willing to relieve the pressure on limited water supplies by leaving the country, this pattern of state formation not only narrowly circumscribes the social base of opposition but encourages the resort to symbolic politics on the part of government and opponents alike.

By contrast, the governments of Tunisia and Morocco are more reliant upon domestic economic constituencies; in that sense the Moroccan king, one of the richest individuals in the world, is his own best constituent. The existence of private associations to express and foster common economic interests in both countries has forced those governments to adopt somewhat more of the trappings of liberal politics. Thus did the Moroccan monarch sponsor a referendum to endorse a new constitution delegating somewhat more power to the parliament and prime minister, while the Tunisian government issued a new electoral law designed to permit greater representation of opposition parties in the parliament. Nonetheless, life in the private sector is not sufficiently attractive to constitute a genuine alternative to political power in any of these countries. The Algerian crackdown and the Libyan intimidation campaigns against government opponents reflect the frailty of an alternative organization to that of the state. In Tunisia and

Morocco the apparently more liberal reforms have much the same purpose: The Tunisian electoral reform is expressly designed to retain the majority of Assembly seats for the ruling party and the Moroccan king warned that his delegation of authority should not be understood as its renunciation.

Insofar as this analysis is correct, the prospects for further democratization in North Africa are not bright. Democracy is predicated on public institutions and private associations that permit expression of the common interests of citizens in the disposition of their contribution to their own governance. Structural adjustments of the region's economies, on much the same scale as those now being attempted in Eastern Europe, would appear to be a virtual prerequisite to the appearance of political and societal alternatives to the state as patron. Such adjustments are inevitably painful, and pain, at least of this magnitude, probably precedes rather than accompanies the birth of democracy. Therefore economic liberalization—that is, the decoupling of wealth and power—and greater respect for human rights and the rule of law are probably necessary conditions for the establishment and maintenance of institutions and associations that are themselves prerequisites for democratic politics.

One (perhaps one more) irony needs to be noted. As should be apparent by now, the regimes of North Africa have for decades adroitly played what political scientists call "two-level games" (Putnam 1988) by employing domestic policy for foreign purposes—providing "labor peace" for potential investors and undertaking economic reform to obtain conditional loans—and using foreign policy for domestic purposes—claiming that their hands are tied by the International Monetary Fund or by the demands of national security. Since in these polities as elsewhere, he who pays the piper calls the tune, the governments have danced to rhythms emanating from corporate board rooms and policy situation rooms in Washington, Houston, Paris, and Moscow with far more alacrity than they have responded to the faint and sorrowful tunes wafting from their own hinterlands and bidonvilles. They were therefore all the more profoundly disturbed by the end of the Cold War and the prospect that they would have to look to their own populations for financial support. In addition to the liberalizations described here, therefore, they have continued to carefully monitor the international scene, hoping to replace the international leverage their strategic position had provided during the Cold War with some new claim on Western attention. The idea that the litmus test for American aid would no longer be anticommunism but, say, actual observance of human rights was for obvious reasons genuinely worrisome.

The more Machiavellian or more desperate regimes were able to make a virtue of necessity, however, and use what has become known as "the Islamist threat"—ostensibly revealed in the liberalization—to win international support for a return to the old authoritarianism. Were it not for the shared perception of the dangers of the Islamist movements on the part of policy-makers within the region as well as in the West, Western governments might have held the regimes in North Africa to a higher standard. As it is, thanks to a Western revulsion at the prospect of Islamists in power, assiduously culti-vated by Tunisian President Ben Ali and the Algerian junta among others, the regimes were not only permitted to revert to their authoritarian ways but also were paid for it.

The stance toward liberal and democratic politics, ambivalent at best, on the part of government and opposition alike in North Africa reflects the region's particular political economy. The necessity for domestic political and economic, including fiscal, reform; the marked reluctance of the political elites to concede power; the relative weakness of the interest-based associa-tional life of civil society; and the apparently disproportionate importance of identity-based political movements are all legacies of the particular character of the region's insertion into the international economy and of the influence of the welfare state in structuring political cleavages.

Notes

1. See L. Anderson 1995 and Leca 1988. This quotation is from Kedourie 1992: 1.

2. See the special issue of the *Middle East Journal* 47, no. 2 (Spring 1993), particularly the lead article by the issue's guest editor, Augustus Richard Norton, "The Future of Civil Society in the Middle East."

3. See Kornai 1992: 140–44 and passim, for the argument that the availability of "soft money" has regular and predictable consequences for the organization of the recipient institutions.

4. See, within the now considerable literature on rentier, distributive, and allocative states in the Middle East, Mahdavi 1979, Beblawi and Luciani 1987. On the general questions of reform in such economies, see both Harik and Sullivan 1992 and Barkey 1992.

5. On these relations see the provocative formulations in P. Anderson 1979, Bates and Lien 1985, Hirschman 1978, and Tilly 1975.

6. This point was made (somewhat obliquely) in the remarkably prescient article of Delacroix 1980.

7. This observation is consistent with much of the contemporary literature on new social movements in industrial Europe although, obviously, the preindustrial context of the Middle East and Africa throws the significance of distribution in welfare states into sharper relief. See, for example, Melucci 1985, Offe 1985, and Dalton and Kuechler 1990.

8. Morocco's annexation of the Western Sahara is believed likely to produce substantial revenues in increased phosphate exports; foreign conquest appears to have presented an apparently viable alternative to domestic extraction. Despite the record of very uneven, if not to say dismal, returns-to-conquest in the Arab world as a whole since World War II, the potential financial rewards should not be overlooked as a factor in the willingness of soft budget states to pursue "foreign adventures."

9. For a succinct account of the initial enthusiasm for and ultimate opposition to tax reform on the part of the Tunisian bourgeoisie, for example, see Marks 1993: 170–72.

10. As René Gallissot (1985: 322) has suggested, "Colonial history created a paradox in the Maghreb . . . the workers' movement preceded the class." As a result, the syndicates and unions of the region are peopled with civil servants, government employees—the "administrative intelligentsia"—rather than with classical laborers; and they routinely serve as organs of government communication and control rather than as associations fostering the interests of labor.

11. This observation was brought to my attention by Lahouari Addi. On related subjects, see Addi 1990 and 1991.

12. See, for example, reports of Saudi funding of the FIS in Porteous 1991.

References

Addi, Lahouari. 1990. *L'impasse du populisme –L'Algérie: Collectivité politique et état en construction.* Algiers: ENAL.

——. 1991. "Peut-il exister une sociologie politique en Algérie?" *Peuples meditérraneens* 54–55 (January–June).

Anderson, Lisa. 1991."Obligation and Accountability: Islamic Politics in North Africa."*Daedalus* 120, no. 3 (Summer).

——. 1995. "Democracy in the Arab World: A Critique of the Political Culture Approach." In Rex Brynen, Bahgat Korany, and Paul Noble, eds., *Political Liberalization and Democratization in the Arab World.* Boulder, CO: Lynne Rienner.

Anderson, Perry. 1979. *Lineages of the Absolutist State.* London: Verso.

Barkey, Henri J., ed. 1992. *The Politics of Economic Reform in the Middle East.* New York: St. Martin's.

Bates, Robert H., and Da-Hsiang Donald Lien. 1985. "A Note on Taxation, Development and Representative Government." *Politics and Society* 14, no. 1.

Beblawi, H., and G. Luciani, eds. 1987. *The Rentier State.* London: Croom Helm.

Burgat, François, with William Dowell. 1993. *The Islamist Movement in North Africa.* Center for Middle Eastern Studies at the University of Texas at Austin.

Dalton, Russel, and Manfred Kuechler, eds. 1990. *Challenging the Political Order: New Social and Political Movements in Western Democracies.* New York: Oxford University Press.

Delacriox, Jacques. 1980. "The Distributive State in the World System." *Studies in Comparative International Development* 15, no. 3.

Gallissot, René. 1985. "Interrogation critique sur la centralité du mouvement ouvrier au Maghreb." In Noureddine Sraieb et al., *Le mouvement ouvrier Maghrebin.* Paris: Editions du CNRS.

Harik, Iliya Harik, and Denis Sullivan, eds. 1992. *Privatization and Liberalization in the Middle East.* Bloomington: Indiana University Press.

Hirschman, Albert O. 1977. *The Passions and the Interests: Political Arguments for Capitalism before Its Triumph.* Princeton: Princeton University Press.

——. 1978. "Exit, Voice and the State," *World Politics* 21, no. 1 (October).

Kedourie, Elie. 1992. *Democracy and Arab Political Culture*. Washington Institute for Near East Policy.

Kornai, Janos. 1992. *The Socialist System: The Political Economy of Communism*. Princeton: Princeton University Press.

Leca, Jean. 1988. "L'economie contre la culture dans l'explication des dynamiques politiques." *Bulletin du CEDEJ* (Cairo) 23, no. 1.

Mahdavi, Hossein. 1979. "The Pattern and Problems of Economic Development in Rentier States: The Case of Iran." In Michael Cook, ed., *Studies in the Economic History of the Middle East*. London: Oxford University Press.

Marks, Jon. 1993. "Tunisia." In Tim Niblock and Emma Murphy, eds., *Economic and Political Liberalization in the Middle East*, pp. 170–72. London: British Academic Press.

Melucci, Alberto. 1985. "The Symbolic Challenge of Contemporary Movements." *Social Research* 52, no. 4.

The Middle East Journal. 1993. 47, no. 2 (Spring).

Norton, Augustus Richard. 1993. "The Future of Civil Society in the Middle East." *Middle East Journal* 47, no. 2 (Spring).

Offe, Claus. 1985. "New Social Movements: Challenging the Boundaries of Institutional Politics." *Social Research* 52, no. 4.

Porteous, Tom. 1991. "The Crisis in Algeria: What Chance Democracy?" *Middle East International* 404 (July 12): 17.

Putnam, Robert D. 1988. "Diplomacy and Domestic Politics: The Logic of Two-Level Games." *International Organization* 42, no. 3 (Summer).

Said, Edward. 1978. *Orientalism*. New York: Pantheon.

Tessler, Mark. 1991. "Anger and Governance in the Arab World: Lessons from the Maghrib and Implications for the West." *Jerusalem Journal of International Relations* 13, no. 3.

Tilly, Charles, ed. 1975. *The Formation of National States in Western Europe*. Princeton: Princeton University Press.

7.

From Social Contracts
To Extraction Contracts

The Political Economy of
Authoritarianism and Democracy

JOHN WATERBURY

The subtitle of this chapter bears the promise that political regimes—authoritarian and democratic—generate or are accompanied by predictable political economic arrangements. The promise, I fear, cannot be kept. The most that can be said is that there are elective affinities between regime types and certain patterns of resource utilization, but just about anything can go with anything else.

The main title of this chapter suggests a political economic transition along two major dimensions: a shift from inward-looking, state-dominated to outward-looking, private sector and market-oriented development; and from corporatist, inclusionary to more pluralist, exclusionary political arrangements. What propels the transition is economic crisis of both a structural and conjunctural nature: structural in the sense that state-led, import-substituting industrialization (ISI) is no longer economically viable, and conjunctural in the sense that the collapse of oil rents in the decade since 1982 has laid bare the structural flaws of decades of inward-looking growth strategies.

With the exceptions of "simple" economies in the regions, such as those of Somalia and Mauritania, or of oil-exporters such as Libya, Kuwait, Oman, and the UAE, virtually all countries (including Israel, but not Lebanon) experimented with and relied upon ISI that was built around large public sectors (Richards and Waterbury 1996: chap. 7; Waterbury 1993: chap. 3; World Bank 1995; Amirahmadi 1990: 145). It is an empirical fact with no obvious deductive corollary that these experiments were accompanied by political authoritarianism. That authoritarianism, in turn, was founded on broad-based corporatist coalitions that were party to "social contracts," according to which regimes pledged welfare benefits in exchange for political discipline and quiescence. Conventional forms of direct political accountability were eschewed with the result that dissatisfaction could be expressed and accountability exerted only by indirect means. Those means included (and still include) shirking and moonlighting in the public sector workforce, government crop sabotage by smallholders, and capital flight by both entrepreneurs and migrant workers.[1]

Political legitimacy, therefore, was rooted not in approbation through the ballot box but in the ability of the regime to meet its welfare commitments. Success was measured by the absence of contestation; and if one looks at Algeria (1967–88), Tunisia (1970–90), Morocco (1972–90), the Sudan (1970–83), Egypt (1952–91), Syria (1970–), and Iraq (1975–91), the record of stability and noncontestation is depressingly consistent. I do not mean to belittle cost-of-living riots or bloody events such as the Hama massacre, but these merely showed that, although coerced as much as bought by state largesse, quiescence it was.

For the most part, then, authoritarianism and broad-based coalitions went hand in hand. But there are important exceptions which suggest that there is no necessary connection between the two, nor between political repression and inward-looking growth. For example, between 1965 and 1980, Turkey sustained a formal multiparty democracy with alternation of power (there was a blip in 1970) *and* inward-looking, state-led industrialization. In this case, political accountability was exacted through conventional means, and elected coalition governments serviced broad-based constituencies through state largesse. Since 1947, and until 1990, India has exhibited the same ability to combine an inward-oriented growth strategy and electoral democracy. The converse is also true: Outward-oriented growth strategies, relying on private sector initiative, can be combined with authoritarianism, as both Taiwan and South Korea demonstrated for nearly three decades. It is safe to say that the incumbent political elites of the Mid-dle East and North Africa, having variously recognized that their economies need far-reaching restructuring, would like to emulate the authoritarian controls that the East Asian newly industrializing countries (NICs) have successfully maintained.

It has become commonplace to argue that existing social contracts can no longer be maintained due to the overall economic crisis. Subsidies to urban consumers, protection and soft-budget constraints for public enterprise, bloated civil service ranks, university-biased educational systems, and military establishments routinely claiming a tenth or more of the national product constituted demands on public expenditures that could no longer be met short of fueling triple-digit inflation.

Indeed, this fiscal crisis had existed for years but had been masked by flows of petroleum rents, worker remittances, and foreign borrowing from governments.[2] All these sources began to dry up nearly simultaneously. The collapse of international oil prices had its corollary in contracting labor markets in the oil-exporting states and diminishing worker remittances to the labor-rich, oil-poor. The end of the Cold War reduced the incentives for the two superpowers to pay strategic rents to their regional clients, and in the case of Russia, continued payments were no longer economically possible.

In schematic form, the transition we have been witnessing in the Middle East and elsewhere consists in the following failed expectations: For decades most countries of the region tried to avoid foreign direct investment, while relying on foreign borrowing and external assistance; many eschewed domestic private investment, replacing it with nationalization and the expectation that state-owned enterprises (SOEs) would generate a constant surplus for the state treasury; most saw only risk in exports and instead expected domestic and regional markets to expand exponentially.

When SOEs generated consistent losses instead of surpluses; when Cold War lending dried up (although Saudi Arabia and Kuwait continued to lend to Iraq during its hot war with Iran); when domestic demand grew and domestic production failed to keep pace; when imports swamped exports, then crisis drove economic reform which in turn drove political experimentation.

By and large, then, most countries in the Middle East entered into the era of structural adjustment by the mid-1980s. The experience was more or less brutal according to the case. There may be a political economy of adjustment, but as was the case with ISI, there is no obvious politics of adjustment. The general pattern consists of the following elements: Government expenditures are more or less sharply curtailed, the tax burden—direct or indirect—is increased, the coalitional base of the regime is narrowed, and compensatory payments are allocated to (a) crucial strategic allies and (b) those most severely affected by the adjustment process. There may not be much overlap between the two. Compensation functions like a lottery: Everyone has a theoretical possibility of benefiting, but only a few will actually be compensated.

Even more than was the case with ISI, we do not know if adjustment requires, or is enhanced by, authoritarian controls or by greater political liberalization. There are plausible arguments on both sides of this issue. Because public resources are so curtailed and the victims of adjustment so numerous, only authoritarian regimes, it is argued, can contain the demands of society and impose the discipline necessary to weather the crisis. Chile under Pinochet would be the model for this kind of adjustment. By contrast there are those who argue (myself included, but see Przeworski 1991 or Richards 1992) that political liberalization can help sustain the reform process in essentially two ways. First, by breaking down the state's monopoly on the allocation of resources, liberalization obliges all or most elements of civil society to share in the apportionment of the pain of adjustment. Second, economic adjustment is often popular, *if the antecedent crisis has been deep enough,* and the architects of adjustment do not always do poorly at the polls. In short, by allowing zones of autonomous political and financial power to develop (what are commonly referred to as the components of civil society), states can displace some portion of the welfare burden and the setting of the social agenda onto the shoulders of private or quasi-private actors.

There is, of course, a price to be paid, and it is not merely the relative loss of political control that the state must absorb. Rather, it may include steps toward a new kind of contract, one that I see as approximating contracts of extraction. Part of what is at stake is the old injunction: no taxation without representation. But as I shall argue below there is far more to extraction than taxation.

Throughout the 1970s, inclusionary social contracts could be maintained through high levels of public spending and subsidy outlays. It did not much matter if one exported oil or exported labor (or, as in Algeria, both). Petroleum rents rolled in to the exporters while the oil-poor found they could borrow at negative real rates of interest. In addition, they exported their labor to the oil-rich and received substantial financial assistance from them as well.

Between 1982 and 1986 the bottom dropped out of international petroleum markets, rents shrunk, labor markets contracted, and most of the financial assistance of the regional oil-rich was redirected to Iraq—a fact that allowed a few other regional actors, principally Jordan and Turkey, to benefit by supplying the burgeoning demands of Iraq's war economy. The collapsing regional oil economy had the added effect of scaring off nonregional foreign investment that had begun to enter in the 1970s. In 1980, Arab oil exporters alone had earned $178 billion from petroleum sales, while by 1986 that figure had plummeted to $41 billion (Sadowski 1993: 6). The trends in major economic indicators are represented in figure 7.1. The only indicator that is up over the period is debt service, while arms imports on average hold their own.

Whether one tries to account for the inception of ISI and its accompanying broad-based coalition, or for its collapse, the external environment is crucial. I do not go as far as Barbara Stallings (1992) or Stephan Haggard (1990) to argue that it is, or can be, determinant, but it must be taken into account in explaining far-reaching change in economic strategies and perhaps in political arrangements as well.

The regional shifts we see today could not be explained without reference to the collapse of socialist economies and of the former USSR, which could no longer project its military power or extend economic support to its erstwhile clients in the Middle East. The statist, populist, "secularizing" regimes of the

Figure 7.1. Trends in Hard Currency Revenues and Expenditures of Arab States, 1980–88 (1980 value = 1)

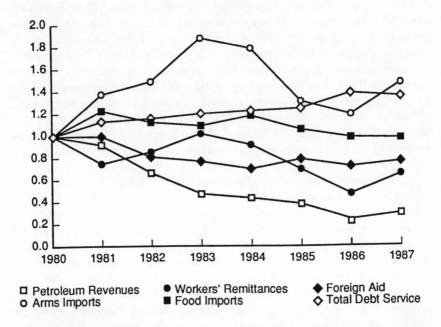

Source: Sadowski 1993: 7.

Middle East fell simultaneously into economic crises that resulted from inherent flaws in the growth strategies they themselves had pursued, and into crises of legitimacy resulting from years of military humiliation coupled with the loss of successful external referents and models for their statist experiments.

There are, as well, substories that can be told only in an international context. Turkey's quest since the 1960s to join the Common Market, or now the European Union, necessitated both political and economic changes in order to bring Turkey into greater conformity with European standards and practices.

In brief, the political economy of authoritarianism and democracy does not stop at a given country's border but is in fact closely connected to international markets, sources of credit and arms, investment flows, strategic rents, and the instruments of international clientage and dependency.

Praetorianism

I have written elsewhere (Waterbury 1994) that if there is one factor that sets the Middle East apart from most of the rest of the developing world, it is the level of armed conflict that has prevailed in the region since 1947/48. It may be futile to debate whether or not praetorian regimes[3] have been the principal cause of military conflict or the result of it, but the fact remains that the Middle East has suffered six large-scale conventional wars and five major and prolonged civil wars. No other region of the world has devoted so large a share of its gross product to the military as the Middle East. Because in several states the military has monopolized political and coercive power, its invasion of the civilian economy has been inevitable and extensive (see Stork 1987; Richards and Waterbury 1996: chap. 13; Sayigh 1993).

It is for these reasons that the nature of the military's economic and political entitlements is the single most important variable in determining the political economy of authoritarianism and democracy. Only in Israel and Turkey do we have evidence of the possible accommodations that powerful military establishments may make with civilian, democratic regimes—and even in these two instances the evidence is not always reassuring. Turkey's military has seized power three times, in 1960, 1970, and 1980. While the country has been under civilian control since 1983, the military has received a virtual blank check to crush the Kurdish Workers Party (PKK) in the southeast of the country. One can only suppose that Turkey's civilian leaders believe that if they were to restrain the military, a coup might well follow. In Israel, the possibility of a coup appears remote, but the fact is that military leaders play a direct role in civilian politics (Rabin, Dayan, Eytan, Sharon, Allon, Weizman, etc.) and the military's claims to resources have seldom been seriously challenged.

Most other Middle Eastern countries are under the direct or indirect control of their military establishments. Those under direct control are Syria, Iraq, Libya, the Sudan, and Algeria. These are the true praetorians of the region.[4] Those under indirect control include Egypt, Tunisia, and Yemen. The military in those three countries can exercise veto power over virtually any aspect of national policy, and they maintain unchallenged claims to national resources. The Tunisian case is of particular interest. It was a commonplace that the civilian head of state, Habib Bourguiba, maintained a small military establishment in order to avoid the plague of coups that had swept the Middle East in the 1950s, as well as Algeria in 1965 and Libya in 1969. Although the evidence is inconsistent, sometime in the mid-1980s, Tunisia's defense outlays began to rise sharply. Leveau (1993: 105 and 226–27; see also Zartman 1993 and appendix, p. 306) claims that they reached over 5 percent of GDP by 1990. Standard military expenditure yearbooks show a somewhat lower rate of expenditure (see fig. 7.2). It is unwarranted to claim that the deposition of Bourguiba in November 1987, and the assumption of the presidency by General Ben Ali, was the result of this growing assertion of military claims; but the startling fact is that by 1992, while "praetorian" Algeria's military expenditures had fallen to 2.7 percent of GDP, Tunisia's were (at least) 3.3 percent of GDP.

Lebanon offers a unique case of indirect control by the military of other countries, primarily that of Syria but also that of Israel. There are three cases of ruling monarchs—Saudi Arabia, Morocco, and Jordan—who ultimately rely on the loyalty of their military establishments to remain in power. We come finally to Iran which, perhaps surprisingly, exhibits well-entrenched civilian rule, a highly circumscribed democracy, and a relatively well-contained military establishment. Huntington gave us no category to encompass rule by fractious mullahs and militias, but that is what Iran displays.

I have gone through this exercise to make the point that the most important vested interests in the Middle East are the region's military establishments. They were the linchpin of the dominant coalitions that held

Figure 7.2. Military Expenditures as a Percentage of GNP: Select Middle East Countries

	1960	1978	1983	1990	1992
Algeria	2.0	5.5	3.4	1.8	2.7
Egypt	5.5	16.0	13.4	5.1	6.0
Iran	4.5	15.3	5.2	2.1	7.1
Iraq	7.3	19.2	45.3	27.4	21.0
Israel	6.5	23.0	23.1	13.0	11.1
Jordan	16.7	27.9	19.8	12.2	11.2
Kuwait	–	3.6	5.3	5.0	62.4
Lebanon	1.7	4.8	8.2	–	5.0
Libya	1.2	16.7	15.3	7.2	5.0
Morocco	2.0	6.0	8.4	4.5	4.0
Saudi Arabia	5.7	–	–	14.0	11.8
Sudan	1.5	3.0	2.0	4.0	15.8
Syria	7.9	14.6	21.8	13.5	16.1
Tunisia	2.2	1.5	4.9	2.1	3.3
Turkey	–	5.2	5.0	–	4.7
Yemen (Aden)	–	26.2	21.0	–	–
Yemen (Sanaa)	–	26.6	33.9	14.9	93.0

Source: Columns 1 and 4, Sivard, ed. 1993: 44–45; columns 2 and 3, United States Arms Control and Disarmament Agency 1989: 36–70; column 5, IISS 1993: 224–26. Inconsistencies among those sources are glaring and not easily reconciled. One can only hope that trends and relative orders of magnitude are not grossly distorted.

sway during the decades of import-substituting industrialization and inward-looking growth. They will determine the nature, speed, and ultimate success of any transitions toward democracy. We know from the voluminous transitions literature on southern Europe and Latin America how crucial it is for civilian challengers to reach accommodations with military incumbents, whose hands are inevitably bloody and dirty. Eastern Europe's experience is too recent and too much in flux to have provided a similar literature (although see Przeworski 1991).[5]

Some analysts have discerned in the economic crisis prevailing in the region the signs of a necessary and perhaps bristling reengagement of governments with their citizens. The reengagement comes about through the needs of regimes to deal with their fiscal crises through higher direct and indirect taxation. Equally, if not more, important are signs that the resource entitlements of the military establishments of the Middle East are diminishing as a result of the economic crisis. Nonetheless, as figure 7.2 shows, the pattern is very uneven, and even in those cases where a substantial decline has occurred, it has been from a very high base. The total of the resources devoted to the military in the Middle East is quite simply appalling.

A second development, the uncertain steps taken toward a settlement of the Israeli–Palestinian conflict, may also contribute to the erosion of military entitlements. Thus economic crisis and conflict containment, if not resolution in one critical theater, are weakening the war economy (Sadowski 1993: 25–32). Regular military personnel per 1,000 inhabitants may be declining as well. Diminished resources for the military do not, however, have clear implications for the loosening of authoritarian controls. Praetorianism is not solely a function of the size of the military establishment nor of its control over resources, but of its ability to preempt the political arena through repression and delegitimization of all rivals. For instance, in Algeria the level of resources devoted to the military has steadily declined in the last decade, but since the aborted elections of 1991 the level of praetorianism has steadily risen.

It is also important to keep in mind that democracies do not always devote fewer resources to the military than authoritiarian regimes. Israel's electorate, for example, has consistently tolerated high outlays of national wealth on the Israeli Defense Force, and the same can be said for Turkey's electorate.

A further cautionary note is in order. The huge outlays for imported arms and for the maintenance of armed forces out of all proportion to their population bases have not been driven by the Arab–Israeli conflict. If that conflict is somehow ended we can expect the following conflicts to endure:

Turkey–Greece	Yemen–Saudi Arabia
Iran–Iraq	Saudi Arabia–Iraq
Iraq–Syria	Saudi Arabia–Iran
Turkey–Syria/Iraq	Egypt–Upper Nile states
Libya–Chad	Morocco–Algeria

I have broken these conflicts down into oversimplified dyads; reality is far more complex. I have also left out civil wars such as those raging in the southern Sudan, on hold in Lebanon, and perhaps on the horizon in Iraq. Turkey's Deputy Prime Minister, Murat Karayalçin, stated in 1994 that 5 percent of Turkey's GDP was then being devoted to the "suppression of terrorism" in the southeast of the country and that 160,000 troops were taking part in the operations there (*Turkish Times,* January, 15, 1994).[6] The military in Turkey and elsewhere will continue to invoke internal and external threats to national security in order to protect its entitlements. The best that can be hoped is that the military will do no more than hold its own.

Extraction and Accountability

Political theory, and sometimes practice, has posited that taxes constitute the implementation of a contract between citizens and their government. Taxes go to pay for public goods that private agents would not provide. Taxpayers are the consumers of those public goods, and public officials are subject to the contractual obligation to provide them honestly and impartially. Citizens have the right to hold public officials accountable for the kind, quality, and cost of public goods. Democratic theory suggests that the most efficient way to monitor implementation of the contract is through elected representatives of the taxpayers. Hence "no taxation without representation."

It flows logically from the above that the process of democratization or its absence may have a great deal to do with the incidence, nature, and variability of taxes. Lisa Anderson (1992) takes this logic a step further and argues that "the taxed devise ways to be represented." Something causal is being suggested here, but just what it is, is very hard to pin down. I want to broaden both sides of the equation, expanding taxation to include all forms of extraction, and representation to include all forms of accountability. The question then becomes, how do we measure extraction, and having measured it, what do we expect in terms of the effective holding of public officials to account? I begin the analysis by considering conventional tax regimes.

On the issue of "optimal" taxation, political scientists and economists have sailed past each other in the night. When (some) economists talk about optimal taxation, they have in mind levies that minimize distortions in markets, correct for market failures, maximize welfare, and maximize government revenues (see Newberry 1987 and Stern 1987). There is an implicit assumption of a benevolent leviathan with legitimate claims to revenue to cover expenditures for the public good.[7] The question then becomes finding the most efficient way to raise those revenues.

Some political scientists, perhaps especially those who have studied the rentier state phenomenon in the Middle East, have come to the conclusion that external rents impede accountability, and that only when states have to extract their revenues from their own citizens will the demand for accountability rise (inter alia see Anderson 1992; Von Sivers 1992; Brand 1992; Beblawi and Luciani 1987; Shambayati 1994). Fiscal engagement between citizens and governments is thus to be welcomed, and the more that engagement is mediated by *direct* taxation the better.

With respect to the issue of direct taxation, the conventional economic wisdom appears to be on a different wave length. A few decades ago, those who advised developing countries on tax regimes, such as Nicholas Kaldor or Richard Musgrave, advocated reliance on direct taxes accompanied by some redistribution. But the tide has changed dramatically since then. The conventional wisdom now stresses indirect taxes, especially value-added taxes (VATs), despite their regressivity (Burgess and Stern 1993: 778). Redistribution through taxation is no longer on (Goode 1993; Due 1988). Poor administration and powerful upper income groups will probably defeat any attempts at redistributive taxation, and the costs of collection will probably outweigh the yield (Bahl 1989). Indeed, as Stern argues (1987: 51), it is through subsidies, infrastructure, and other public goods that redistribution may be effected, and the challenge then becomes to link *indirect* taxes to the financing of subsidies and infrastructure.

As economists dealt with the crises that emerged in the late 1970s and 1980s in both developing and developed countries, what passed for optimal conditions changed in subtle and not so subtle ways. Gross imbalances in macroeconomic equilibria had obvious short- and long-term negative consequences for welfare. Most of the imbalances stemmed from the governments' expenditure patterns themselves so that markets could not be expected to correct them. Large budget deficits, monetized debt, inflation, overvalued exchange rates, trade imbalances, and escalating foreign borrowing were all standard features. To begin to deal with the crises, governments had to lower expenditures and increase revenues. Tax advice focused on the latter challenge, and the standard advice became to simplify and reduce direct taxation and to increase revenues through various forms of VAT.

The equity implications of this advice escaped no one. Consumers would bear the brunt of most indirect taxation, and inasmuch as the poor devote more of their income to consumption than the rich, the poor would be disproportionately, *but indirectly,* taxed. Targeted consumer and, in the agricultural sector, producer subsidies could cushion some of the impact but obviously not all of it.[8]

Thus trends in economic advice and actual tax regimes moved in the opposite direction from that espoused by the critics of the rentier state, i.e., greater reliance on direct taxation with high progressivity (after all, it is likely to be the wealthy that first demand greater accountability). Developed countries moved in this direction even as swiftly as the developing. The explosion in state-managed or taxed gambling casinos and lotteries in the United States is a case in point.

In the 1970s, specialists in European politics began to discern both a fiscal crisis in the welfare state and a tax "backlash."[9] Backlash, in the eyes of these observers, was bad in that, if successful, it might lead to diminished state revenues. Harold Wilensky analyzed a genus of "success" stories that combined corporatist peak bargaining associations with a reliance on indirect taxes (Wilensky 1976; Hibbs and Madsen 1981). The message in this kind of analysis is clear but not always stated: Governments should have some minimal level of revenues, say 25 to 30 percent of GDP, in order to provide necessary public goods. Citizens, following narrow individual interests, try to and often succeed in evading direct taxes. Therefore, taxes must be taken by stealth, indirectly. A recent International Monetary Fund study on the United States recommends that the IRS rely less on direct taxes and more on VAT so as to "alleviate problems of tax enforcement" (*IMF* 1993: 56). The *Economist* argued for "more VAT" with the following justification: "Deluded taxpayers" accept taxes more readily on goods than on incomes, although a tax is a tax. Their conclusion was: "If people do not feel heavily taxed (although they are), they will behave accordingly" (*Economist,* December 4, 1993, p. 65), that is, they will not resort to a politically destabilizing "backlash." Backlash is a term of disapproving evaluation of citizen behavior, but should it not be seen as a demand for accountability?[10]

What seems to be missing in the economists' and some social scientists' calculus is the nature and quality of public goods. My own feeling is that backlash comes not only because of the level of (and, as in Denmark, sudden increase in) taxes, but also because the public goods provided to citizens— education, health, transportation, policing, communications—decline in quality or are simply denied to significant numbers of taxpayers. It may be only through continued reliance on direct taxation that the kind of accountability necessary to maintain or improve the quality of public goods can be established. Who wants "deluded taxpayers"? They must surely be a frail base on which to sustain democratic government and an impossible starting point for those countries that have not even begun a democratic transition.

Taxes and Extraction in the Middle East

Noneconomists who study the Middle East have frequently come to roughly similar conclusions concerning structural flaws in the region's political economies that allegedly account for the persistent authoritarianism, clientelism, weak civil society, and lack of accountability of political leaders. The major flaw is that Middle Eastern populations are undertaxed and that those taxes which most people bear are indirect rather than direct. Governments have been able to avoid directly taxing their populations because, in the last twenty years or more, they have had access to external rents of various kinds: rents from sales of petroleum, strategic rents paid to clients by the superpowers, strategic rents paid by the oil-rich to the people-rich in the region itself, and worker remittances. Only when these rent streams begin to dry up, it is argued, will governments be obliged to turn to their own citizens for revenues, and only then will the chemistry of accountability be activated (see Beblawi and Luciani 1987, Anderson 1991, Chatelus 1993, Von Sivers 1992, Brand 1992).

Anderson breaks down the issue in the following manner. The colonial era in the Middle East tended to build powerful state structures while stifling the development of indigenous bourgeoisies (1992). Moreover, it was during the colonial era that the states of the region became habituated to a flow of external resources and to weak local tax bases (remarks, Princeton, Near East Studies brown bag meeting, February 2, 1994). This triad of factors has then been accentuated in the post–colonial period: States have become stronger, indigenous bourgeoisies have remained weak, and rents have figured more prominently in government finance. The lack of articulation between the state and civil society has provided an opening for Islamic movements to attack governments, not on issues of the use of tax revenues, but on issues of corruption and moral turpitude in the governments' disposal of rents (Anderson 1991: 95; Von Sivers 1992: 24; Addi 1995).

At the risk of crude reductionism, I will summarize the consensus as follows: Governments that rely on rents for a substantial portion of their revenues will stifle democracy; governments that tax their citizenries will foster democracy. Let us look at the facts of taxation and extraction in the Middle East to test the hypothesis.

Are Middle Easterners undertaxed? At an aggregate level, and in comparison to other developing areas, the answer is no. In 1985, for example, both total taxes as a percentage of GDP (23 percent) and the ratio of direct to indirect taxes (56 : 46) in the Middle East averaged higher than in all other regions of the developing world (see fig. 7.3). When we look at specific countries in the early 1980s (fig. 7.4) we see great variation, with Iran, Kuwait, and Syria perhaps being "undertaxed" while Israel and Egypt exceed or approximate taxation levels of advanced industrial nations. There is no observable correlation between level of taxation and degree of authoritarianism or democracy, although Israel would come closest to conforming to the expectation that high and *direct* taxation may foster democracy.[11]

If level of taxation is an inconclusive indicator of accountability, then we should perhaps turn to trends. Over time most Middle Eastern societies have become more heavily taxed. Askari, Cummings, and Glover assert (1982: 202): "[I]t is clear that over three decades [1950–80] the ratio of taxes to

GNP has risen in every country, and in some cases dramatically. In fact, the weighted average tax ratio nearly tripled to more than 35% of aggregate gross product." The increase was most dramatic among oil-exporting states (9.3 percent in 1950 to 49.3 percent in 1978) while for non oil-exporters the increase was from 16 percent in 1950 to 23 percent in 1978. Thus, part of the surge in the aggregate level of taxation has come about through the taxation of an economic enclave (state-owned petroleum companies or foreign companies) rather than through fiscal engagement with the citizenry at large. Figure 7.5 shows the growing reliance on petroleum rents of nine Middle Eastern oil-exporting countries over the period 1950–77. For these countries, at least, the proposition that rent dependency and authoritarianism are likely companions appears to hold.[12]

So far we can conclude that average tax burdens in the Middle East are not noticeably low, and they have been steadily increasing. Yet, it would be hard to argue that the tax burden has stimulated much government accountability or that the few democratic experiments in the region have anything obvious to do with levels or trends in taxation.[13] How might we account for this? One factor is that all of the states in the region have relied on state enterprises to lead their development efforts. While these are often chronic after-tax loss-makers, they are nonetheless captive sources of tax revenues (see Ahmed 1984; World Bank 1990a: 88). One would hardly expect state-owned enterprises to be at the forefront of demands for accountability. Similarly, the bulk of direct income taxes falls on captive wage and salary earners in the public sector, while those in the professions and private service sector are routinely delinquent. We would not expect to see civil servants and public sector labor lead the charge for greater governmental accountability.

A second factor may be the incidence of indirect as opposed to direct taxation. Most states in the region reveal a ratio of indirect to direct taxes of about 2 : 1 (see, e.g., fig. 7.6). If we assume that taxpayers are more conscious of direct than of indirect tax bites, then we may have a partial explanation of the lack of linkage between tax level and accountability. It appears to be the case, however, that in many Middle Eastern countries the share of direct taxes in total tax revenues has been rising during the last five years or so.

We cannot reject the hypothesis that there is no relation at all between the levels and kinds of taxation and accountability, although intuitively that does not sound plausible. It may also be that it is "only" a matter of time before accountability catches up with the tax burden which, as noted, has been growing over recent decades. The troubling problem here is that democratic systems of accountability have emerged in countries with similar or lower tax burdens, for example, in Latin America, sub-Saharan Africa, and South Asia (above all India). If it takes longer in the Middle East for taxes to do their magic, perhaps we have to turn to other factors to explain the lag (see Waterbury 1994).

Figure 7.3. Variation in Level and Composition of Tax Revenue by Region, 1985 (as Percent)

	Developing Countries				
Item	Sub-Saharan Africa	Middle East and North Africa	Asia	Latin America	Industrial Countries
Revenue level					
Tax revenue–GDP ratio	17	23	15	18	32
Revenue composition					
Income and wealth					
(direct)	39	56*	37	46	69
Company	(20)	(19)	(19)	(10)	(7)
Personal	(12)	(13)	(8)	(5)	(27)
Property	(1)	(3)	(3)	(2)	(2)
Other[a]	(4)	(13)	(7)	(9)	(2)
Goods and Services					
(indirect)	61	46*	63	54	31
Domestic					
Sales, VAT, turnover	(15)	(10)	(14)	(13)	(17)
Excises	(9)	(7)	(19)	(17)	(10)
International trade					
Import	(26)	(22)	(21)	(14)	(2)
Export	(8)	(0)	(2)	(2)	(0)
Other[b]	(3)	(7)	(7)	(8)	(2)

Source: World Bank 1991.

[a]The most significant taxes in this category are manpower and payroll taxes. It also includes some schedular nonrecurrent taxes.
[b]This residual category includes a series of miscellaneous taxes such as stamp duties, airport taxes, and vehicle taxes.

*I cannot account for the fact that indirect and direct taxes total 102 percent of government revenues.

Figure 7.4. Selected Industrial and Developing Countries: Direct and Total Tax Revenue as Percentage of GDP

	Direct Tax		Total Tax
			1980–82 Average
United States			28.9
Austria			41.0
Japan			27.0
United Kingdom			36.0
Iran	(1981–83)	2.2	8.1
Kuwait			3.3
Morocco	(1981–83)	4.5	21.6
Tunisia	(1980–82)	4.9	25.1
India	(1981–83)	2.4	16.0
Korea	(1982–84)	4.3	16.0
Egypt	(1982–84)	7.0	30.0
Israel	(1981–83)	16.1	49.0
Jordan	(1981–83)	3.3	18.0
Syria	(1978–81)	2.5	9.5
Yemen Arab Rep.	(1982–84)	2.9	19.1
Turkey	(1983–84)	9.1	16.0

Source: Gandhi et al. 1987: Tables A1, A2.

Figure 7.5. Oil Revenues Relative to Total Revenues: Major Oil Producers (as Percent)

Country	1950	1962	1970	1973	1977
Bahrain	55.2	72.0	66.2	65.2	78.1
Iran	11.6	40.1	49.7	67.0	73.6
Iraq	17.3	64.1	53.7	80.9	85.5
Kuwait	81.7	94.6	91.2	92.7	96.6
Libya	0.0	7.6	83.1	75.1	83.2
Oman	0.0	0.0	98.0	94.3	92.6
Qatar	84.1	94.0[a]	88.9	92.5	97.0
Saudi Arabia	68.0[a]	86.4	86.9	93.3	88.3
United Arab Emirates	0.0	25.0	96.6	89.3[a]	94.5[a]

Source: Askari, Cummings, and Glover 1982.

Note: Total revenues excludes borrowing.

[a]Estimated.

Figure 7.6.

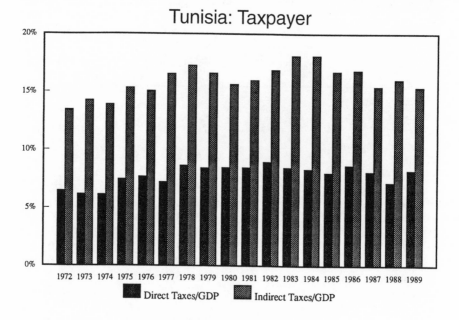

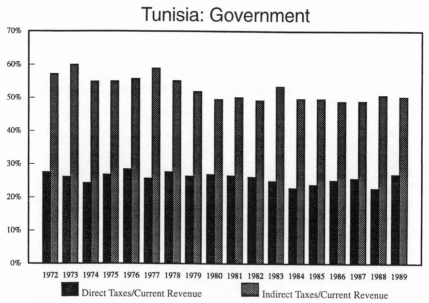

Source: Government Financial Statistics Yearbook 1991.

We need to say something about the actual dynamics of accountability. A first cut would be to imagine two interactive variables. The first is the size of the tax burden to GDP. This would tell us what proportion of national wealth is captured by the government. Hibbs and Madsen (1981) have suggested that anything above 50 percent is politically unsustainable, and as we have shown, Middle Eastern burdens are in the range of 20 to 30 percent of GDP. This variable is a proxy for citizen awareness of government impositions. Yet it says nothing about the quality of the public goods the government delivers back to the taxpayers. It is conceivable that a low tax burden could be associated with such poor quality, or with such a discriminatory delivery of public goods that evasion or a political backlash are provoked. It also says nothing about the perceptual blind spots that may prevail among citizens who are taxed by and large indirectly (through customs, excise, sales, and stamp duties).

The second variable is that of direct and indirect tax revenues to total government revenues. This variable indicates the degree to which governments are dependent upon taxpayers for their revenues. The higher that dependency, the more likely it is that governments will have to listen to their citizens. A combination of high government tax dependency and a high direct tax burden will presumably provide the best enabling environment for accountability. As shown in figure 7.7, Israel comes the closest to satisfying that condition among the countries of the Middle East.

These two variables, though they explain a lot, miss other crucial elements that are not susceptible to ex ante analysis. The rate at which taxes increase (an issue which triggered a backlash in Denmark), the introduction of new taxes (such as that proposed on social security payments in the United States, or the 1991 consumption tax in Jordan), and the horizontal and vertical equity of taxes may all have major implications for the taxpayers' reaction to government impositions.

The preceding discussion presupposes that accountability is driven by conventional fiscal measures. But if the crux of the dynamic is the extraction of private surplus in exchange for public goods, then we must move beyond conventional fiscal measures. Subsidies and their removal must enter into the equation. A subsidy can be conceived of as a negative tax or a positive income transfer. The removal of a subsidy is equivalent to a tax increase. The January 1977 riots in Egypt in that sense can be seen as a taxpayers revolt, and a successful one in that the government rolled back the price increases.

There are many other ways in which governments extract and transfer wealth. Administered prices are common in the Middle East. In Syria, support prices for wheat are well above world market prices and thus constitute an implicit transfer of wealth to wheat farmers. In Egypt, by contrast, administered agricultural prices have generally worked to lower rural incomes by

Figure 7.7.

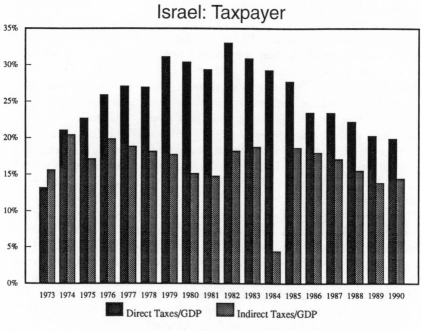

Israel: Taxpayer

■ Direct Taxes/GDP   ▨ Indirect Taxes/GDP

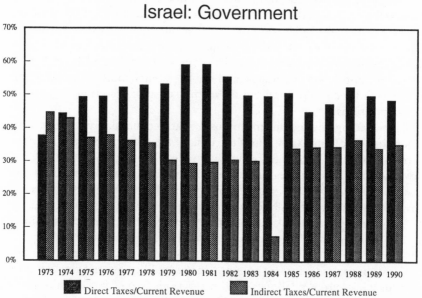

Israel: Government

▨ Direct Taxes/Current Revenue   ■ Indirect Taxes/Current Revenue

Source: Government Financial Statistics Yearbook 1991.

turning the intersectoral terms of trade against agriculture. In addition, overvalued exchange rates have worked against the incomes of exporters of agricultural products (Dethier 1989: 138–45). The counterpart to administered prices in rural areas is consumer subsidies (on food, fuel, and transport) that generally favor urban populations.

Governments often set wage levels for specific sectors of the workforce, such as civil servants, teachers, and public sector workers. If they allow real wages to lag behind the rate of inflation, an implicit tax is being levied. On the other hand, the government may routinely supply a considerable portion of income to its employees in the form of allowances, bonuses, and free services that are untaxed.

Finally (though this list is not exhaustive), there is the inflation tax. The economic boom years of the 1970s triggered inflationary episodes in several Middle Eastern countries. As the crisis of the 1980s evolved, inflation continued at the same rate or worsened as governments failed to curtail expenditures while their revenues declined. Through deficit financing, governments fueled inflation but enjoyed first advantage in using the money they printed while all subsequent users received diminishing real value for each unit of currency.[14] Turkey, Egypt, the Sudan, Iran, and Algeria have all levied high inflation taxes at different times.

The point I wish to make is that any citizen may act according to a complex calculus of state extraction that combines levels and kinds of conventional taxes, reactions to sudden price shifts, diminution of entitlements, perceptions of the inflation tax, and attention to the quality of public goods. Because the calculus is not likely to be uniform across entire sectors of the citizenry, it is hard, if not impossible, to predict the conditions under which citizens will take action, let alone what the dominant form of action will be (cf. Hettich and Winer 1993: 8).

Having said that, I will nonetheless consider some likely possibilities. The inflation tax is seldom perceived as such. Few people see the direct connection between government expenditures, monetized public debt, and inflation. They may cope with inflation by increasing their labor in both the formal and informal sectors, or by migration. The inflation tax cannot be gathered indefinitely, however. The Shah of Iran may have paid a high political price for the inflation of the late 1970s, while the Motherland Party in Turkey experienced electoral setbacks in the late 1980s that can be attributed in substantial measure to unhappiness with continued inflation. In the first instance, protest was violent and formally illegal while in the second it was expressed legally through the ballot box.

Similarly, administered pricing systems that turn the terms of trade against specific sectors can generate public revenues without any immediate reaction from the taxed. We may posit, however, that sooner or later persistently negative price signals will lead to altered economic activity. Egyptian farmers have been evading cotton cultivation for a couple of decades, and to some extent the government, in the face of this behavior, has had to concede substantial procurement price increases in recent years.[15] As Goren Hyden demonstrated years ago in Tanzania (1980), the cumulative impact of thousands of individual cultivator decisions can force governments to change policies. In this same vein, we may consider migrant workers faced with an overvalued exchange rate (again, the overvaluation leads to an implicit tax on their foreign earnings). Their likely response is to hold their earnings offshore or to repatriate them through "black market" channels. Governments in the Middle East have devalued in recent years, partially in response to the loss of remitted earnings through official intermediaries. In both instances, we have accountability of a sort, but certainly not of the democratic variety.

Erosion of real wages and of consumer subsidies may provoke strikes and riots; but it is just as likely they will provoke continued migration from the formal into the informal sector, where second jobs can raise incomes and where goods, albeit expensive, can be found without queuing. If a large part of economic activity is informal, and hence beyond the fiscal reach of the state, then governments may extend legal recognition to a range of activities, such as money changing or unlicensed manufacturing, vending, and transportation, so that they can be registered and taxed. Deregulation of private activity may be the government's response to a growing exodus from the formal economy. Here, too, we are not dealing with formal mechanisms of accountability.

Private Interests, Mobile Capital, and Extractive Contracts

The most crucial economic agents in the extractive equation are the providers of private capital and investment. The structural strength of capitalist interests can counter the numerical weight of, and force concessions from, those who own physical or intellectual capital, even in democratic systems (see Przeworski and Wallerstein 1988). In the setting of systemic crisis described in the first section of this chapter, capitalist interests may wield unusual leverage in bringing about governmental accountability. The governments of the region can no longer mobilize or borrow the investment resources needed to stimulate real growth in the economy. They must attract indigenous, regional, or foreign capital to undertake that task. They must trade policy concessions for investment. Those concessions will take the form of liberalized banking procedures, deregulation of markets, privatization, expansion of capital markets, and elimination of discriminatory taxes and reduction of corporate tax rates.

Initially, this process may not involve any direct bargaining between capitalist interests and the state. The government may try to anticipate the policy measures required to attract capital investment and financial flows to the country. What the government most wants to avoid is the resort on the part of private interests to the twin weapons of investment strikes and capital flight. On a trial and error basis, the government will gauge the success of policy concessions and make more if necessary.[16] Policy changes may come about initially through the pressures of the international financial institutions rather than through the efforts of investors themselves.

The crucial turning point comes when indigenous private capital organizes and lobbies for policy changes. That moment came in 1979 in Turkey when, in the midst of Turkey's economic crisis, the Turkish Industrialists and Businessmen's Association (TÜSIAD), went public with a stinging critique of the government's economic policies. Since then, TÜSIAD has been a proactive force for large-scale capital interests in Turkey.[17] A similar turning point may be taking shape in Egypt today, where government ministers regularly appear before the Egyptian Businessmen's Association to explain government policy and to enter into dialogue over policy reform.

While business interests bargain on their own behalf, they may still provide public goods, in the form of policy changes, that benefit much broader strata of society. More important, when state officials recognize such bargaining as legitimate, it is harder for those officials to deny the same legitimization to bargaining with other interests in civil society—from labor and commercial farmers to feminists, Islamists, and human rights advocates. The more such bargaining goes on, the greater the likelihood that accountability will grow. Economic crises are good enabling environments for policy bargaining.

The interaction one would want to see goes like this: Private investment and entrepreneurship are seen as necessary to stimulate real growth in the economy; real growth will yield higher tax revenues to the government; the government accepts being held to account by private interests. Eventually, formal institutions of representation, perhaps dominated by private economic interests, will be allowed to develop.[18] Crystal provides a vivid example of this dynamic. In 1909 the Shaykh of Kuwait attempted to impose new levies on merchant wealth. The merchants in turn "exited" to Bahrain. The Shaykh backed away from his exactions, and the merchants returned. During the 1920s there was a gradual enfranchisement of the merchant class, culminating in the legislative assembly of 1938. However, as the argument of Beblawi and Luciani (1987) would suggest, once the Shaykh got access to petroleum rents in the 1950s, the merchant class was politically marginalized and the assembly atrophied (Crystal 1990: 24–25 and 47–48).

The Kuwaiti merchants who fled to Bahrain had moveable assets and capital. The degree of capital mobility raises an important consideration. It has been argued by Albert Hirschman and others that historically it has been the owners of immovable assets (above all, land) who are most likely to contest tax-gathering states and to hold public authorities accountable. A counterargument has been advanced by Bates and Lien (1985) and Bates (1989) that it is in fact the owners of moveable assets who enjoy the best bargaining position vis-à-vis the state because they are able to hide or transfer their wealth with relative ease.[19]

Bates and Lien do not adequately explain what the owners of moveable assets would bargain for, short of an exemption from any form of taxation. If it is costless for those owners to move their assets, then there is no reason why they would accept any form of imposition. If the dynamic suggested by Bates and Lien is to work, there must be transaction costs involved in the movement of capital and assets. That is obvious in closing down a factory and moving it elsewhere but not as clear in the case of capital movements. The incentive to bargain must lie in a combination of three factors: a preference to stay put, real costs incurred in moving, and alternative environments that may or may not be more accommodating.

Certainly in this day and age of computerized portfolio movements and currency transfers, the investment resources Middle Eastern states seek are extremely difficult to capture. How important are they? Diwan and Squire estimate the stock of savings abroad for nine Middle Eastern countries at $179 billion (1993: 23). In figure 7.8 they show capital flight for these same countries over the period 1970–90 as a proportion of GNP. "Native" capital in very large amounts is either held or is fleeing abroad. It is at least hypothetically possible that it could be lured back through the proper policy environment (and fig. 7.8 in fact shows a net inflow in recent years in some countries). In turn, that environment could be nurtured through direct, formal consultation between the governments of the region and the owners of capital.

A reverse image of this is the continued weakness of Middle Eastern capital markets. Compared to other emerging markets among the less developed countries (LDCs), such as Mexico, Malaysia, or India, Middle Eastern capital markets—with the exception of Israel's, and to a lesser extent, Turkey's (see fig. 7.9)—are distinctly undercapitalized. Only in those two countries is the policy environment sufficiently attractive to bring in substantial portfolio investment.

The changing balance between public and private investment in the countries of the Middle East is an important part of the accountability matrix. In nearly all countries, the private share has been growing relative to the public. This is, once again, a reflection of the economic crisis and of the general cutback in public outlays. In Iran, for example, where recession began in 1976 and has been sustained ever since because of the war economy, the share of the private sector in gross fixed capital formation rose from 44 to 50 percent in less than a decade. In the same period of time, the share of the Egyptian private sector rose from about 10 to 25 percent and by 1990 may have been close to 40 percent. The data in figure 7.10 show the level of private investment in select countries as a proportion of GDP.

Figure 7.8. Estimates of Capital Flight* as a Share of GNP (as Percent)

Country	1970–74	1975–79	1980–84	1985–89	1990
Algeria	3.1	4.5	-0.4	3.4	1.4
Morocco	2.1	1.1	1.1	5.6	-3.2
Tunisia	1.4	2.2	-1.7	3.5	0.3
Maghreb	2.4	3.1	-0.3	3.2	-0.6
Egypt	-0.1	14.5	12.5	9.2	-6.4
Jordan	1.8	1.7	6.2	9.7	5.4
Syria	2.5	7.4	5.5	9.6	–
Yemen[a]	–	–	–	1.6	–
Mashreq[b]	0.5	10.0	9.8	9.8	-4.0
Israel	5.1	6.6	3.6	1.9	3.1
Region[b]	1.8	5.9	3.6	5.1	0.2

Source: Diwan and Squire 1993: 9.

*Capital Flight = (External Borrowing + Foreign Direct Investment) - (Current Account Deficit + Increase in Reserves)

[a]1985–89 average refers to 1989 only.

It is important to recognize that the structural adjustment process (i.e., dealing with the economic crisis) has fostered a peculiar kind of owner of moveable assets. First, as interest rates are adjusted to positive levels, the domestic holders of debt begin to earn large returns. For example, Turkish government interest payments on domestic debt rose from 4.4 percent of total expenditures in 1981 to 20 percent in 1990 (Karatas 1992: 70). Turkey, and now Egypt, have resorted to the sale of treasury bills to finance their domestic debt. The interest paid on T-bills is tax free. Most of the Turkish public domestic debt is financed in this manner. Korkut Boratav (1990: 4; and see Handoussa 1993) has estimated "rentier" incomes in Turkey in 1988 at 14 percent of GDP.[20] While these domestic "rentiers" claim a very large portion of GDP, they are presumably atomized and do not act as an organized interest that might be moved to exact accounts from their government. If interest rates on T-bills are lowered, the holders of the bills will typically exit into the capital market or into gold. They will not take to the streets or the corridors of parliament.

In summary, economic crisis has forced states not only to cede pride of place to private capitalists but in many instances to woo and legitimize them. This is as true for Iran as it is for Egypt and Algeria, while Turkey and Morocco

Figure 7.9. Market Capitalization* in Select Developing Countries, 1992

Country	Market Capitalization in Billions of U.S. $
India	108.0[a]
Malaysia	94.0
Mexico	139.0
Egypt	2.6
Iran	1.2
Israel	50.0
Jordan	3.3
Morocco	1.8
Tunisia	0.046
Turkey	10.0

Source: Stock Markets Fact Book 1993.

*Market Capitalization = share price x number of shares outstanding.

[a]For 1994.

have for decades granted local capital a fully legitimate *economic* role. With tens of billions of dollars seeking higher returns outside the region, the era in which public officials called upon indigenous capital to do its patriotic duty has come to an end. Most policymakers now recognize that patriotic duty is a function of competitive returns to investment.

To reiterate an earlier point, owners of capital do not necessarily promote democratic accountability, but as a kind of by-product of their bargaining for favorable policy responses from the state, they may foster habits of interaction between the governments and citizens that can lead to a transition. There is nothing inevitable about this, as the happy cohabitation of Sunni capitalists

Figure 7.10. Private Sector Investment as a Proportion of GDP: Select Countries 1982–92

Country	1982	1983	1984	1985	1986	1987	1988	1989	1990	1991	1992
Egypt	9.1	6.5	5.8	6.1	6.4	6.0	8.7	10.5	9.1	8.7	7.8
Morocco	13.4	11.8	11.2	12.1	12.2	11.6	11.8	13.2	15.4	12.2	13.4
Tunisia	15.4	14.2	13.6	12.3	10.5	9.3	9.7	10.7	11.3	9.8	10.7
Turkey	8.1	8.3	8.3	8.4	9.8	11.2	12.6	12.4	12.8	12.3	11.7

Source: International Finance Corporation data, unpublished.

with Alawite praetorians in Syria has demonstrated for some twenty years. Put another way, democracies need strong bourgeoisies more than bourgeoisies need strong democracies.

Nonetheless, there are many signs of growing accountability. In Jordan, a combination of the Jordanian Businessmen's Association and the Chambers of Commerce successfully lobbied to block a proposed sales/consumption tax that was billed as a precursor of a VAT. Moreover, one analyst has argued that the Jordanian government's effort to capture private surplus through reserve requirements in licensed banks was read by private interests as a signal of the government's dependence upon private wealth. This realization, in turn, has contributed to ongoing political liberalization (Roberts 1993: 10, 28; also Chemonics International 1993). In fact, Jordan has manifested a sequence that may be replicated elsewhere: macroeconomic crisis in late 1988 and early 1989; followed in 1989 by structural adjustment, increased taxes, and riots; followed by legislative elections in the same year; followed by increased business involvement in newly founded parties.

A sales tax was successfully introduced in Egypt in 1990, and by 1993 it accounted for over 23 percent of total tax revenues (*al-Ahram al-Iqtisadi,* November 22, 1993, p. 76). While a success from the point of view of enhanced government revenues and deficit reduction, this indirect tax has provoked a reaction from the normally docile Federation of Chambers of Commerce and its president, Mahmud al-Arabi. Noting that the business community had not been consulted before the introduction of the tax, he complained that it falls most heavily on middle- and lower-income consumers, reducing their buying power significantly. He went on to protest the confiscatory nature of stamp duties on businesses and to recommend that direct taxes at the source, but at lowered marginal rates, replace many of Egypt's indirect taxes. Finally, he called for the abolition of all laws of exception, including Egypt's emergency law, which has been the bane of human rights advocates for decades (al-Zayati 1993: 28–30).

A final sign worth noting is the storm provoked in Kuwait over the misappropriation or outright theft of $4 billion of the country's $100 billion Fund for Future Generations. This Fund had been fed by Kuwait's petroleum rents over several years. The newly elected Kuwaiti parliament debated setting up a watchdog system over management of public funds, which had been under the control of the ruling Sabah family and business interests allied to the family (Ibrahim 1993). In short, even the rentier state may be held to account.

Structural Adjustment and the Extraction Contract

Democracies are supposed to reflect the preferences of the numerical majority of voters. These, in turn, are most often influenced in their voting by the economic situation they currently face. They are particularly sensitive to unemployment and the cost of living. The paradox is that the owners of capital, very much a minority among voters, are crucial to the economic growth that can generate employment and reduce inflation by putting more goods and services on the market. The paradox is that minority interests must often be served to the short-term detriment of the majority. For decades, Middle Eastern governments sought to undo this paradox by substituting state agencies for entrepreneurs and planned allocation of goods and services for markets. The process of substitution, with its emphasis on the state-determined allocation of consumption entitlements, obviated democratic accountability.

The economic crises of the 1980s and early 1990s have thoroughly handicapped, if not brought to an end, the Middle Eastern state's capacity to carry on as usual. Thus, at the same time that the state must turn to private capital to spur growth, it must sharply curtail a broad range of entitlements that it had fostered in previous decades. The major political challenge facing the regimes of the Middle East is thus the transition from social contracts to extractive contracts, under which states must concede greater accountability in exchange for shifting the burden of social costs directly to their citizens.

Middle Eastern states are by no means alone in confronting this challenge. There, as elsewhere, the result has been three-fold: a narrowing of the coalition that sustains regimes, rising unemployment, and stagnant or declining per capita income (see fig. 7.11; see also Waterbury 1989 and 1993). The evidence on worsening income distribution is not clear-cut.[21] Inflation may or may not be brought under control. If and when it is, it is usually because the crisis has placed limits on demand, not that there are more goods and services available. Two caveats are in order: First, these adjustments most often do not *cause* unemployment and inflation so much as reveal them. Second, the inflation and employment figures often reflect only the *formal* economy, thereby omitting the value of labor and production in the informal sector that may account for a third of GDP.

Summary and Conclusion

The constraints faced by Middle Eastern states are similar and are tending in the same direction. They are as follows:

1. The military establishment is witnessing the weakening of its grip on national wealth. Economic constraints will continue that trend.

2. Rents of all kinds have diminished. While international petroleum markets may tighten marginally in the next five years, the new producers of Central Asia and the return of Iraq to production will ensure that these markets remain soft. Thus, the Cold War–driven strategic rents, and the

Figure 7.11. Per Capita Real GNP Growth (as Percent)

Country	1970–75	1975–80	1980–85	1985–90	1990	1991	1992
Algeria	2.3	2.6	2.1	-3.0	-4.0	-3.2	-1.7
Morocco	2.2	3.6	0.4	2.0	2.9	2.2	-4.6
Tunisia	6.6	3.6	1.3	1.3	6.6	0.7	7.6
Maghreb (average)	2.9	3.1	1.9	-1.5	-1.4	-1.5	-1.2
Egypt	3.2	7.4	3.6	0.6	-2.4	0.0	0.3
Jordan	2.5	13.2	0.2	-15.8	-19.2	-9.9	8.8
Occupied Territories	11.2	5.5	-1.0	3.8	12.4	-9.1	–
Syria	9.5	3.2	-0.7	-0.9	11.9	4.1	3.0
Mashreq[a] (average)	5.3	6.9	1.7	-0.8	0.5	0.2	-0.6
Israel	4.1	1.5	1.1	2.5	3.1	1.6	2.8
Region	3.9	3.7	1.5	-0.6	0.1	0.2	0.6

Source: Diwan and Squire 1993: Annex 2, table 3.

[a]Does not include Lebanon and Yemen.

strategic rents paid by regional oil-exporting countries in the past fifteen years, will not resume.

3. Middle Eastern governments have nowhere to turn but to their citizens in order to finance the programs they regard as essential. Once-and-for-all nationalizations and land reforms, such as those witnessed throughout the region in the 1950s and 1960s, cannot be repeated and therefore do not offer a way out of the resource crisis.

The citizens of the Middle East, as we have seen, are not now, and historically have not been, undertaxed. The burden they bear through direct and indirect taxes will not go down, and the indirect tax burden is likely to go up. More important is that negative taxes provided through various kinds of direct and indirect subsidies will be, to varying degrees, eliminated, representing real income loss for many citizens.

Governments must try to arrive at contractual understandings with two constituencies whose short-term interests diverge. On the one hand, private capital, both domestic and foreign, must be granted a set of incentives—including well-established property rights, simplified regulatory regimes, and the right to influence the hiring and firing of employees—in order to invest in the economy. Rates of profit, net of the transaction costs of moving capital elsewhere, must equal or exceed rates that can be earned outside the region.

The social costs of adjustment, that is, the scrapping of social contracts, will be borne by the bulk of the citizenry, and it is with its members that the second understanding will be struck. It is moot whether or not the partial casting loose of entire segments of the active population will necessarily yield greater accountability. Many people will continue to resort to self-exploitation or to exit from the country or the formal economy in order to survive. Such reactions pose no direct political threat to incumbent rulers. Inevitably some of those most affected by the adjustment process will give voice to their grievances as they have done in the past, particularly through Islamic movements.

Turkey, for a time, found a way to meet the needs of private capital and of some of the aggrieved portions of the population. The strategy contains two crucial elements: First, there has to be growth in the economy so that there is some taxable surplus; and second, a portion (but not all) of that taxable surplus must be distributed in compensatory payments to carefully targeted groups such as organized labor, farmers, schoolteachers, shanty-town dwellers, or the Kurds of southeast Anatolia (Waterbury 1992).

Since 1987, however, the pressures of the electoral cycle have restimulated deficit spending through "populist" settlements of one kind or another in a manner that cannot be sustained (Öniş 1993; Karataş 1992). A direct effect of the reaffirmation of old populist entitlements was increased inflation and rising interest rates, which in turn dampened investment and curtailed growth. Sunar and Öniş (1992) have proposed that the only way out is through tripartite pacts on wages and prices, negotiated in a Social and Economic Council in which the government and peak organizations of business and labor would meet.

The constraints I have outlined can be defied for a time, but not indefinitely. The military may claim, by force so to speak, an economically unsustainable share of national resources; Saddam Hussein showed how it is done, and General Bashir in the Sudan is following in his footsteps. Algeria today resembles nothing so much as General Jaruzelski's Poland with the Islamic Salvation Front (FIS) playing the functional but unfortunately not the ideological role of Solidarity.

Praetorians, or even civilian authoritarians, can attempt to rule on the strength of an alliance with capital at the expense of the citizenry at large. No regime in the Middle East approximates this "Chilean" model, but there are hints of it in Syria, Morocco, and Tunisia. In these cases, and in contrast to that of Turkey, the dual contracting process evoked above is tilted in favor of capital at the expense of compensatory payments and enhanced accountability. Given the strong growth records in Tunisia and Morocco in recent years, this may be sustainable.

Egypt has come to the same kind of equilibrium as Turkey with two key ingredients missing. Egypt does not have an indigenous bourgeoisie of the size, strength, and organizational capacity of that in Turkey. Its adherence to democratic forms is shallow and unconvincing. Populist settlements in Egypt are prompted not by the electoral cycle but by fear of political Islam. Further political liberalization, through which responsibility for the economic reform process would be shared with elements of civil society, may be the only way to avoid a slide toward a politically untenable situation on the Algerian model.

Iran provides a model that is not easily described, much less analyzed. Its military is under "civilian" control, but the long conflict with Iraq has left the economy on a war footing. It has maintained a big state sector and has made a range of populist settlements through special funds, foundations, and revenues from confiscated properties. At the same time the Islamic regime has had allies in the merchant "bazaar" class, and under Rafsanjani there has been an active attempt to lure back Iranian entrepreneurs and Iranian flight capital. Inflation and joblessness are both high, but the country boasts a peculiar kind of democracy for club members only. If one is male and certifiably Muslim, one may participate fully in a system that tolerates wide-ranging debate over social, economic, and some religious issues. Elections for club members are not meaningless. One could easily imagine this system gradually tilting away from its populist base and toward the interests of private capital without the rules of membership in the club being changed.

Throughout the region, the major sources of demand for accountability today are the various embodiments of the Islamic movement. It is unlikely that these movements seek democratic forms of government per se. Rather, as Lahouari Addi has argued, Islamic groups denounce the failure of secular populist experiments and claim that once such experiments are properly Islamic they will succeed. Not only will they succeed socially and economically, but they will succeed militarily, against the Zionist enemy, as well.

As the Iranian example shows, there is no way that Islamic populism can change the fundamental economic reality of the region or of any particular country. If Islamic regimes are truly populist, they will suffer crippling fiscal crises. If they ally with Islamic capital, it will have to be in an institutional setting that honors private property, the sanctity of commercial contracts, and the mobility of capital. The only thing Islamic regimes can do that more secular counterparts cannot do is survive for a time on the religious fervor that would predictably accompany their coming to power. But even in Ayatollah Khomeini's lifetime, the fervor was evaporating.

In sum, citizens' demands for accountability from their government are likely to grow in the near and intermediate future, but the question is, what groups will do the demanding and what forms will accountability take. We have seen that private interests may lead the way in trying to institutionalize channels of consultation, if not of formal representation. It is, indeed, private sector interests that may be most sensitive to indirect tax burdens. Old corporatist interests, cut loose from their entitlements, may also demand an accounting. The Egyptian Federation of Chambers of Commerce offers an example, but we should also expect to see this phenomenon among trade unions and professional associations. They have constituencies and interests that their governments can no longer help. They are not likely to disappear, and they have financial resources, mainly in their pension funds, and experienced leadership that may enable them to bargain with state agencies to which they were formerly corporatist appendages.

Anderson is probably right that the taxed will find ways to be represented; but it is likely that those ways will include exit from the system, sabotage, and violence as frequently as the search for conventional political representation. People will exact accounts in these various ways not merely because they are taxed at higher rates or more directly, but also because the public goods the state provides are no longer of acceptable quality. Does all of this add up to unavoidable transitions to democracy? The answer is clearly no. But what does appear unavoidable is a situation in which governments and regimes can no longer legislate by decree and in which they must bargain with the constituted interests—economic, religious, and ethnic—of their societies. That is enough of a break with the political status quo of past decades to stir cautious optimism.

Notes

1. Direct but unconventional movements for accountability have taken the forms of street demonstrations; cost-of-living riots; and, as in the Sudan, Turkey, Iraq, and perhaps today in Algeria, civil war.

2. Diwan and Squire (1993: 7) report that in the period 1970–89, the loans and grants, net of repayment, that accrued to the public sectors of Algeria, Morocco, Tunisia, Egypt, Jordan, Syria, North Yemen, and Israel amounted to an astounding $180 billion. On remittances, see Diwan and Squire (1993: 14) and Chatelus (1993: 151).

3. The term is borrowed from Samuel Huntington (1968: chap. 4), and means rule by the military in both the political and economic spheres. Huntington notes: "The stability of a civic polity thus varies directly with the scope of political participation; the stability of praetorian society varies inversely with the scope of political participation" (1968: 198).

4. Elizabeth Picard (1993: 263) has argued that by and large what we have witnessed in the last decade or more is the gradual evolution of military establishments toward less encompassing intervention in the political realm except insofar as "security" matters are concerned. In Syria, Egypt, and Algeria, she contends, "The army has lost its leading role within the polity." That judgment is certainly premature with regard to Algeria, and the distinction between internal security threats and external challenges may have little relevance for the constraints the military place on any forms of political liberalization.

5. The Islamic revolution of Iran reached no accommodation with the Shah's military. The collapse of the Shah's regime was accompanied by the total discrediting of the senior officers corps. In Eastern Europe, the collapse of regimes has been

accompanied by a total discrediting of the police apparatus, but according to Przeworski (1991), the military was largely supportive of change.

6. It is possible that the Turkish government of Tansu Çiller has purposely exaggerated these outlays in order to attribute the sharp rise in inflation to the internal security effort.

7. For critiques of this assumption, see Gwartney and Wagner (1988), Buchanan (1988), and Knut Wicksell (1988). Hettich and Winer (1993) present more formal critiques. I am grateful to Tim Besley for calling these sources to my attention.

8. In the 1980s, Turkey devised an ingenious rebate system on its VAT that at once gave incentives to consumers to make sure the tax was calculated and provided them cash rebates that varied with income level. See Waterbury (1992).

9. Joseph Schumpeter had anticipated this backlash half a century earlier. See his "Crisis of the Tax State," which was first published in 1918, reprinted in 1991.

10. The *Economist* forgot the turn-of-the-century wisdom of Knut Wicksell, who wrote (1988: 128): "The true magnitude and significance of the tax load have in the past been concealed from the people. The fiscal principle would have to yield to the economic principle; the *direct method* [emphasis added] of raising state revenues should become the rule and the indirect method the exception."

11. To show how complicated the issue of causality is, let us note that with the exception of three years, during the period from 1976 to 1987, direct taxes significantly exceeded indirect taxes in Iran. One might be tempted to attribute Iran's peculiar Islamic democracy to that fact until we see that the total tax burden to GDP in those years ranged only between 5 and 8 percent (Amirahmadi 1990: 167). Petroleum rents and income from public property were far more significant sources of revenue.

12. Kuwait has sporadically held parliamentary elections confined to males of proven Kuwaiti ancestry.

13. Israel may be the exception. Other experiments include Turkey (1950–60, 1965–70, 1971–80, 1983–), the Sudan (1956–59, 1965–69, 1986–89), Jordan (1989–), Morocco (1956–65), Egypt (1976–), Yemen (1993–94). Needless to say, the quality of democratic practice varies enormously among these countries. Only Israel and Turkey have come close to adhering to western European standards, but even in these two instances there have been egregious lapses.

14. The right to issue currency is referred to as seignorage. As growth is likely to stimulate demand for monetary instruments, seignorage need not be inflationary. However when governments monetize debts, inflation results. Burgess and Stern (1993: 769) usefully warn that the resulting "tax" does not represent real revenue to the government but rather capital losses to the holders of monetary instruments.

15. These concessions have come in at least equal measure as a result of pressure from the World Bank, the IMF, and USAID.

16. In 1974, Egypt passed Law 43 to attract Arab and foreign investment to the country. In 1977, it rewrote that law as Law 32, making several new concessions in light of the weak response of investors to Law 43. Then in 1981, it extended many of the concessions in both laws to private domestic capital. In no instance did it enter into dialogue with the interests it sought to attract.

17. Its power and cohesion have been questioned by several Turkish experts who emphasize continued Turkish corporatism, weak civil institutions, and governmental contempt for private interests. See Arat, Bura, Kalayçiolu, and Heper, in Heper, ed. (1991).

18. It was the debt crises of the late nineteenth century, and the search for tax revenues, that obliged the Ottoman sultan and the Egyptian khedive to dabble with

the first parliamentary institutions in the region's history. Iran was not far behind with the election of the *majlis* and the drafting of a constitution in 1906.

19. As suggested above, no bargaining between owners of moveable assets and governments need take place, because it is inherent in this situation that moveable factors are taxed at lower rates than tax-inelastically supplied factors.

20. Rentier is used here to refer to the domestic earners of rents, in this instance holders of deposits in financial institutions or of other debt instruments. Heretofore the term rent has been used to refer to external flows of rents accruing to countries.

21. We have few good studies of income distribution in the Middle East. It is probably the case that distribution in Egypt has become more skewed in the last decade (see Handoussa and Potter 1991, and World Bank 1990a). There has been very little change in Turkey over the entire period from 1963 to 1987 (see Sunar and Öniş 1993: 72). An unreleased study in Iran shows worsening distribution since the revolution in 1979. There is a prima facie case for worsening distribution when there are substantial shifts in national income from wage and salary to interest payments.

References

Addi, Lahouari. 1995. *L'Algérie et la démocratie*. Paris: Editions de la Découverte.

Ahmed, Sadiq. 1984. *Public Finance in Egypt: Its Structure and Trends.* World Bank Staff Working Papers, no. 639.

Amirahmadi, Hooshang. 1990. *Revolution and Economic Transition: The Iranian Experience*. Albany: State University of New York Press.

Anderson, Lisa. 1991. "Obligation and Accountability: Islamic Politics in North Africa." *Daedalus* 120, no. 3: 93–112.

———. 1992. "Liberalization in the Arab World." Discussion paper for the Mellon Seminar, Near East Studies Department, Princeton University, February 14.

Askari, Hossein, John Cummings, and Michael Glover. 1982. *Taxation and Tax Policies in the Middle East*. London: Butterworth Scientific.

Assaad, Ragui. 1989. *The Employment Crisis in Egypt: Trends and Issues*. American University in Cairo, unpublished discussion paper.

Bahl, Roy. 1989. "The Political Economy of Jamaican Tax Reform." In Malcolm Gillis, ed., *Tax Reform in Developing Countries*, pp. 115–76. Durham: Duke University Press.

Bates, Robert. 1989. "A Political Scientist Looks at Tax Reform." In Malcolm Gillis ed., *Tax Reform in Developing Countries*, pp. 473–91. Durham: Duke University Press.

Bates, Robert, and Da-Hsiang Lien. 1985. "A Note on Taxation, Development, and Representative Government." *Politics and Society* 1: 53–70.

Beblawi, Hazem, and Giacomo Luciani, eds. 1987. *The Rentier State*. London: Croom Helm.

Boratav, Korkut. 1990. "Contradictions of Structural Adjustment: Capital and the State in Post-1980 Turkey." Conference on Socioeconomic Transformation, State and Political Regimes: Egypt and Turkey. Istanbul, July 26–28.

Brand, Laurie. 1992. "Economic and Political Liberalization in a Rentier Economy: The Case of the Hashemite Kingdom of Jordan." In Iliya Harik and Denis

Sullivan, eds., *Privatization and Liberalization in the Middle East,* pp. 167–88. Bloomington: Indiana University Press.

Buchanan, James. 1988. "The Constitution of Economic Policy." In James Gwartney and Richard Wagner, eds., *Public Choice and Constitutional Economics,* pp. 103–14. London: Jai Press.

Burgess, Robin, and Nicholas Stern. 1993. "Taxation and Development." *Journal of Economic Literature* 31: 762–830.

Chatelus, Michel. 1993. "From the Mirage of Rent to the Burden of Debt: Adjustment and Insecurity in Arab Economies." In Bahgat Korany, Paul Noble, and Rex Brynen, eds., *The Many Faces of National Security in the Arab World,* pp. 145–68. Houndmills: Macmillan.

Chemonics International. 1993. *Political Economy Review of Jordan.* A report submitted to the Near East Bureau, USAID, May 28.

Crystal, Jill. 1990. *Oil and Politics in the Gulf: Rulers and Merchants in Kuwait and Qatar.* New York: Cambridge University Press.

Dethier, Jean-Jacques. 1989. *Trade, Exchange Rate, and Agricultural Pricing Policies in Egypt.* Vol. 1. Washington, D.C.: World Bank.

Diwan, Ishac, and Lyn Squire. 1993. *Economic Development and Cooperation in the Middle East and North Africa.* Discussion Paper Series, no. 9 (November). Washington, D.C.: World Bank.

Due, John F. 1988. *Indirect Taxation in Developing Economies.* Baltimore: Johns Hopkins University Press.

Gandhi, Ved P., et al. 1987. *Supply-Side Tax Policy: Its Relevance to Developing Countries.* Washington, D.C.: International Monetary Fund.

Gersovitz, Mark, Roger Gordon, and Joel Slemrod. 1993. *A Report on the Egyptian Tax System.* Discussion Paper Series, no.8, Middle East and North Africa. Washington, D.C.: World Bank.

Gillis, Malcolm, ed. 1989a. *Tax Reform in Developing Countries.* Durham: Duke University Press.

———. 1989b. "Tax Reform: Lessons from Postwar Experience in Developing Countries." In Malcolm Gillis, ed., *Tax Reform in Developing Countries,* pp. 492–520. Durham: Duke University Press.

Goode, Richard. 1993. "Tax Advice to Developing Countries: An Historical Survey." *World Development* 21, no. 1: 37–53.

Government Finance Statistics Yearbook. 1991. Washington, D.C.: International Monetary Fund.

Gwartney, James, and Richard Wagner, eds. 1988. *Public Choice and Constitutional Economics.* London: Jai Press.

Haggard, Stephan. 1990. *Pathways from the Periphery.* Ithaca: Cornell University Press.

Handoussa, Heba. 1993. "The Role of the State: The Case of Egypt." First Annual Conference on Development Economics, Cairo, June 4–6.

Handoussa, Heba, and Gillian Potter, eds. 1991. *Employment and Structural Adjustment: Egypt in the 1990s.* Cairo: American University Press.

Heper, Metin, ed. 1991. *Strong State and Economic Interest Groups: The Post-1980 Turkish Experience.* Berlin: Walter de Gruyter.

Hettich, Walter, and Stanley Winer. 1993. "The Political Economy of Taxation," prepared for Dennis Mueller, ed., *The Handbook of Public Choice,* December (unpublished paper).

Hibbs, Douglas, and Henrik Madsen. 1981. "Public Reactions to the Growth of Taxation and Government Expenditure." *World Politics* 33, no. 3: 413–35.

Horton, Brendan. 1990. *Morocco: Analysis and Reform of Economic Policy.* Washington, D.C.: Economic Development Institute, World Bank.

Huntington, Samuel P. 1968. *Political Order in Changing Societies.* New Haven: Yale University Press.

Hyden, Goran. 1980. *Beyond Ujamaa in Tanzania.* Berkeley: University of California Press.

Ibrahim, Youssef. 1993. "Financial Scandal Is Shaking Kuwait." *New York Times,* January 10.

IISS (International Institute of Security Studies). 1991. *The Military Balance, 1993–94.* London: Brasseys.

IMF (International Monetary Fund Survey, February 22). 1993.

Karataş, Cevat. 1992. "Public Debt, Taxation System and Government Spending Changes in Turkey: 1980–1992." *Journal of Economics and Administrative Studies* 6, no. 1–2 (Boğaziçi University): 41–82.

Leveau, Remy. 1993. *Le sabre et le turban: l'avenir du Maghreb.* Paris: Editions François Bourin.

Newberry, David. 1987. "Taxation and Development." In David Newberry and Nicholas Stern, eds., *The Theory of Taxation for Developing Countries.* pp. 165–204. New York: Oxford University Press.

Öniş, Ziya. 1993. "The Dynamics of Export-Oriented Growth in a Second Generation NIC: Perspectives on the Turkish Case, 1980–1990." *New Perspectives on Turkey* (Boğaziçi University), no. 9 (Fall): 75–100.

Oualalou, Fathallah, and Larbi Jaidi. 1987. "Fiscal Resources and Budget Financing in the Countries of the Maghreb (Algeria, Morocco, Tunisia, Libya, Mauritania)." In Hazem Beblawi and Giacomo Luciani, eds., *The Rentier State,* pp. 172–93. London: Croom Helm.

Picard, Elizabeth. 1993. "State and Society in the Arab World: Towards a New Role for the Security Services?" In Bahgat Korany, Paul Noble, and Rex Brynen, eds., *The Many Faces of National Security in the Arab World,* pp. 258–74. Houndmills: Macmillan.

Przeworski, Adam. 1991. *Democracy and the Market.* New York: Cambridge University Press.

Przeworski, Adam, and Michael Wallerstein. 1988. "Structural Dependence of the State on Capital." *American Political Science Review* 82: 11–31.

Richards, Alan. 1992. "The Influence of Economic Imperatives of State Systems in the Middle East and North Africa." Santa Monica: Rand Corporation Conference paper, September 2–3.

Richards, Alan, and John Waterbury. 1996. *A Political Economy of the Middle East: State, Class, and Economic Development.* 2nd ed. Boulder, CO: Westview.

Roberts, John M. 1991. "Prospects for Democracy in Jordan." *Arab Studies Quarterly* 13, no. 3–4: 119–38.

————. 1993. "The Political Economy of Identity: State and Civil Society in Jordan." Ph.D. diss., University of Chicago.

Sadowski, Yahya. 1993. *Scuds or Butter?: The Political Economy of Arms Control in the Middle East.* Washington, D.C.: Brookings Institution.

Sayigh, Yezid. 1993. "Arab Military Industrialization: Security Incentives and Economic Impact." In Bahgat Korany, Paul Noble, and Rex Brynen, eds., *The Many Faces of National Security in the Arab World*, pp. 214–39. Houndmills: Macmillan.

Schumpeter, Joseph. 1991. "The Crisis of the Tax State." In Richard Swedberg, ed., *Joseph Schumpeter: The Economics and Sociology of Capitalism*, pp. 99–140. Princeton: Princeton University Press. (Originally published in 1918.)

Shambayati, Hootan. 1994. "The Rentier State, Interest Groups, and the Paradox of Autonomy." *Comparative Politics* 26: 307–31.

Sivard, Ruth Leger, ed. 1993. *World Military and Social Expenditures.* Washington, D.C.: World Priorities.

Stallings, Barbara. 1992. "International Influence on Economic Policy: Debt, Stabilization and Structural Reform." In Stephan Haggard and Robert R. Kaufman eds., *The Politics of Economic Adjustment: International Constraints, Distributive Conflicts, and the State*, pp. 41–88. Princeton: Princeton University Press.

Stern, Nicholas. 1987. "Aspects of the General Theory of Tax Reform." In David Newbury and Nicholas Stern, eds. *The Theory of Taxation for Developing Countries*, pp. 60–91. New York: Oxford Univesity Press.

Stock Markets Fact Book. 1993. Washington, D.C.: International Finance Corporation.

Stork, Joe. 1987. "Arms Industries of the Middle East." *Middle East Report* 12 (January–February): 12–16.

Sunar, Ilkay, and Ziya Öniş. 1992. *Sanayilemede Yönetim ve Toplumsal Uzlama* (Social accord and administration in industrialization). Istanbul: TÜSIAD.

United States Arms Control and Disarmament Agency. 1989. *World Military Expenditures and Arms Transfers.* Washington, D.C.: Government Printing Office.

Vandewalle, Dirk. 1992. "Breaking with Socialism: Economic Liberalization and Privatization in Algeria." In Iliya Harik and Denis Sullivan, eds., *Privatization and Liberalization in the Middle East*, pp. 189–209. Bloomington: Indiana University Press.

Von Sivers, Peter. 1992. *After the Gulf War: Changes in the Politics and Economics of the Middle East.* Unpublished manuscript.

Waterbury, John. 1989. "The Political Management of Economic Adjustment and Reform." In Joan Nelson et al., *Fragile Coalitions: The Politics of Adjustment*, pp. 37–59. New Brunswick: Transaction.

————. 1992. "Export-led Growth and the Center-Right Coalition in Turkey." *Comparative Politics* 24, no. 2: 127–46.

————. 1993. *Exposed to Innumerable Delusions: Public Enterprise and State Power in Egypt, India, Mexico, and Turkey.* Cambridge: Cambridge University Press.

————. 1994. "Democracy without Democrats? The Potential for Political Liberalization in the Middle East." In Ghassan Salamé, ed., *Democracy without Democrats?: The Renewal of Politics in the Muslim World*, pp. 23–47. New York: I. B. Tauris.

Wicksell, Knut. 1988. "A New Principle of Just Taxation." In James Gwartney and Richard Wagner, eds., *Public Choice and Constitutional Economics,* pp. 117–30. London: Jai Press.

Wilensky, Harold. 1976. *The 'New Corporatism,' Centralization, and the Welfare State.* London: Sage.

World Bank. 1990a. *Democratic and Popular Republic of Algeria: A Framework for Adjustment and Reform.* Washington, D.C.: World Bank.

———. 1990b. *Poverty Alleviation and Adjustment in Egypt.* Report no. 8515 EGT. Washington, D.C.: World Bank.

———. 1991. *Lessons of Tax Reform.* Washington, D.C.: World Bank.

———. 1995. *Bureaucrats in Business.* New York: Oxford University Press.

Zartman, I. William. 1993. "State-Building and the Military in Arab Africa." In Rex Brynen, Bahgat Korany, and Paul Noble, eds., *The Many Faces of National Security in the Arab World,* pp. 239–57. Houndmills: Macmillan.

Zayati, Numan al-. 1993. "The First Clash between the Government and the Merchants." *al-Ahram al-Iqtisadi,* November 1, pp. 28–31.

8.

Crises of Money and Power

Transitions to Democracy?

Clement M. Henry

As in the late nineteenth century, the external debt crises of the 1980s provoked major restructurings of the internal financial orders of most of the North African countries. The changes in the nineteenth century led to direct political and military interventions resulting in the colonial conquest of Tunisia, Egypt, and Morocco; but in the late twentieth century such political outcomes are ruled out. The independent political orders established in the 1950s and 1960s are all threatened, to varying degrees, by the burdens of economic adjustment programs, but they will retain their nominal sovereignty. The threat is that they may have to become more democratic.

The question to be addressed in this chapter is how financial reforms encouraged by the International Monetary Fund and the World Bank may transform political power relationships within each state. Specifically, given the authoritarian regimes that presently prevail in the region, how might financial liberalization promote transitions to democracy? Algeria, Egypt, Morocco, and Tunisia offer a fertile field for comparative analysis. Libya must be excluded on several grounds, however. In his *Green Book*, Qaddafi does, to be sure, suggest a certain parallelism between money matters and power hierarchies in keeping with the spirit of the present inquiry, but only because he advocates abolishing both money and power (Qaddafi: 29). While he could not achieve either aspiration, oil wealth shielded Libya from adjustment programs, and international sanctions subsequently isolated Libya in certain respects from the world economy, something that is contrary to the aims of any adjustment program.

The other four countries all experienced debt crises in the 1980s followed by agreements with the IMF and structural adjustment loans from the World Bank, but to date they have experienced little democracy. Let us, with Philippe Schmitter and Terry Karl, define democracy as a mixture of three elements: "1) *contestation* over policy and political competition for office; 2) *participation* of the citizenry through partisan, associational, and other forms of collective action; 3) *accountability* of rulers to the ruled through mechanisms of representation and the rule of law" (which presumably protect the rights "essential to meaningful contestation, participation, and accountability").[1] By these criteria, whatever their respective weights, none of the regimes was democratic. Three of them, Algeria, Egypt, and Tunisia, became noticeably less so after 1991, when each cracked down on its Islamist opposition. Currently—with military rule now fully exposed in Algeria—the climate for democracy seems so wretched in the region that the question this chapter raises may sound surrealistic. Why not argue instead that financial reform promotes political disintegration and civil war?

It must be admitted at the outset that there is as yet no direct evidence that financial reform sets the stage for democratic transitions. The reforms have barely begun to take root, much less lay the ground for political transitions. Yet intuitively, it seems plausible to suppose that altering financial flows will alter power relationships. The political power that does not come out of the barrel of a gun relies directly or indirectly on monetary or moral incentives. Regimes which are suffering losses of legitimacy—the moral incentives—will depend more on money or guns. A regime may survive for a time by multiplying its security services, but brute repression is not a viable long-term political strategy—at least not along the southern shores of the Mediterranean so close to Europe and subject to the pressures of international opinion. Meanwhile, financial liberalization may unravel strategic patronage networks, demoralizing key sources of support for the regime, and may create contending centers of power rooted in the business community. Initially, an authoritarian regime may easily suppress these Lilliputian contenders, but it may be irrational to do so. The international political and monetary costs of terminating structural adjustment programs are likely to outweigh any expected domestic political gains. Eventually, as the new contenders consolidate their business groups, they may find ways of translating their economic power into political power. Business actors are likely to develop an interest in more political contestation and government accountability—two of democracy's three components. Financial liberalization entails a variety of reforms that should eventually constrain the exercise of power.

These reforms come in standard packages which facilitate cross-national comparison. The IMF promotes a standard stabilization package to debtor states, coupled with longer term structural adjustment programs. An Egyptian minister once compared its prescriptions to those doled out by the public hospitals in his country: "iron and arsenic to all, whatever the illness" (Hilal 1987: 171). The IMF's immediate concern is to curtail the patient country's deficits in its international balance of payments and its domestic government budget. It tackles the budgetary deficit by imposing limits on domestic credit and money creation. Governments, including their respective public sectors, are the biggest beneficiaries of easy money—especially in some of the North

African countries, notably Algeria and Egypt. In fact, these countries' governments were not only among the world's largest international debtors, relative to their economic size, but also sustained the largest domestic debt. Table 8.1 ranks forty-seven middle- and lower-middle-income countries by their total domestic credit as a proportion of gross domestic product. In 1987, before embarking on their programs with the IMF, Algeria and Egypt ranked in the top five, and their central governments were among the top borrowers from their respective national financial institutions. When public sectors are also included as government borrowers, Algeria surpassed all the others, including the communist countries that provided sufficient data to the IMF in 1987.[2]

Clamping down on the money supply has the virtue of discouraging government expenditure. If the government is unable to borrow more at home, it cannot spend more unless it taxes more. The IMF also encourages countries to "liberalize" their banking system by increasing domestic interest rates to realistic levels above prevailing rates of inflation. Further, it typically imposes administrative ceilings, monitored every three months during stand-by agreements, on the amounts of credit to be generated by the entire banking system and the amounts to be borrowed by the target governments. To receive stand-by credits, the borrower must meet the IMF's "performance criteria." The stand-by credits really amount to high-powered money because the agreements in turn influence the decisions of commercial banks and official creditors to reschedule loans and grant new credits.

For the longer run, once stabilization is achieved, the IMF and the World Bank promote structural adjustment designed to integrate local financial markets with international ones and alleviate the need for direct controls. Local commercial banking systems are the prime targets of financial reform, pending the emergence or reactivation of stock exchanges. Structural adjustment is designed to render a banking system more efficient and—here is the political rub—more autonomous with respect to its government. Greater autonomy entails not only an enhanced independent status for central banks but also efforts on their part to deregulate credit allocation by replacing direct administrative controls over commercial banks with impersonal market forces. Structural adjustment also supports closer technical supervision of the banks, requiring them to observe various prudential ratios and to undergo external audits. In the long run, each commercial bank is expected to be financially solvent and to allocate credit by standard business criteria. The banking system and its constituent commercial banks must enjoy sufficient autonomy to determine their own credit policies within professional norms. Political interventions in the allocation of credit are ubiquitous, but in the last analysis the individual bank must be free to take its own decisions regarding its loan portfolio.

To the extent that these reforms take root, a commercial banking system will become powerful in its own right, allocating credit in ways that may

Table 8.1. Categories of Domestic Lending as Percentages of GDP, 1987

Country	Total Domestic Credit	Credit to Central Government	Credit to Government and Public Sector
Israel	151.5	74.7	
Egypt	116.0	51.9	77.7
Jordan	105.7	27.4	
Hungary	102.1	48.1	
Algeria	98.6	40.0	95.7
Romania	91.5	nd	
Portugal	88.3	34.1	47.6
Syria	83.5	59.2	76.5
Yemen	81.4	69.4	71.8
Malaysia	76.0	6.2	
Greece	70.1	38.2	
Thailand	69.5	14.0	15.2
Côte d'Ivoire	61.9	8.1	
Tunisia	61.8	9.1	43.2
Turkey	61.7	32.0	
Pakistan	57.4	25.8	
South Korea	55.1	2.9	
Yugoslavia	53.0	1.2	
Nicaragua	50.1	15.3	
Poland	49.7	2.7	45.3
Morocco	48.8	28.2	
Honduras	45.8	12.4	13.6
Jamaica	42.5	15.1	16.8
Tanzania	40.0	16.0	37.3
Mauritania	39.4	7.3	
Senegal	39.2	10.6	
Costa Rica	36.8	6.9	
Nigeria	36.4	19.1	
Sudan	36.2	16.4	23.7
Mexico	35.8	19.5	22.6
El Salvador	35.8	5.7	7.6
Zimbabwe	34.6	7.8	17.2
Venezuela	31.8	0.6	0.8
Yemen PDR	31.8	20.2	29.3
Ecuador	30.4	5.5	
Dominican Rep	30.1	7.9	9.5
Ghana	27.5	21.0	23.7
Papua NG	26.2	-0.2	
Cameroon	23.4	-1.9	
Indonesia	22.6	-5.4	

Table 8.1—*Continued*

Country	Total Domestic Credit	Credit to Central Government	Credit to Government and Public Sector
Colombia	21.4	3.3	
Guatemala	21.4	5.6	5.6
Philippines	21.0	1.3	3.9
Oman	18.9	-4.0	
Peru	18.1	7.0	
Paraguay	13.4	1.0	
Bolivia	8.2	-6.0	

Source: International Monetary Fund, International Financial Statistics; Banque Centrale de Tunisie, Rapport Annuel 1988, p. 173; annual reports of Algeria's commercial banks.

constrain a regime's political choices. Credit constraints alone cannot force a regime to become more democratic, but they render democratic transitions more likely under certain conditions. First and foremost, the incumbent authoritarian regime must already be "weak" in the sense of being riddled with patronage networks and a "class" of crony capitalists (Haggard 1990: 216–17), which marginalizes the regime's technocrats and political cadres. All of the North African regimes have weakened over the years, losing legitimacy and a sense of direction. Algeria, the apparent exception in the 1970s and early 1980s, now seems in retrospect to have nurtured its special forms of patronage and political cronyism as well. Weak regimes are especially vulnerable to financial liberalization because the commercial banks are principal conduits of their centralized patronage systems. If the patronage dries up, the regime may be obliged to seek out the support of and become more responsive to various constituencies, including business.

Second, at least some of the leading banks must be owned predominantly by private shareholders and managed in their own interest as well as that of the general public. International financial institutions encourage the privatization of state-owned banks in the long run, but it is the state managers who are expected to implement the reforms in the short run. It is virtually impossible for these managers to avoid being loyal servants of state patronage machines, thus undercutting private sector autonomy, unless they face the competition of a dynamic private sector in the banking community.

Third, the private business sector must be sufficiently strong and well organized to insist on securing its property rights—typically by supporting a multiparty system and by demanding greater government accountability. And finally, the regime must experience some political crisis that triggers the transition; for while providing incentives for political change, economic constraints do not usually serve as efficient causes. Bankers may be influential but they do not normally engage in the rough and tumble of practical politics.

Even so, a political crisis will not necessarily inspire a democratic transition. Other sectors such as labor and/or the unemployed must not be perceived as sufficiently mobilized in ways that might threaten the vital interests of the business groups. Otherwise the regime may become more repressive rather than more democratic. Indeed, it may co-opt and enlist business to repress the popular sector, giving rise to the sorts of "bureaucratic-authoritarian" regimes that plagued Latin America in the 1960s and 1970s. Or, with a change of political leadership, the regime could conceivably reverse the process of financial liberalization and revert to the populism that prevailed in much of North Africa in the 1960s by mobilizing popular forces against business groups. This alternative seems unlikely today, given the region's substantial international debt and heavy dependence upon European markets. But bureaucratic authoritarianism cannot be ruled out.

In contemporary North Africa the masses are indeed mobilizing, but they are responding to Islamist discourses, which stress moral and cultural grievances, rather than the Marxist ones which invited fascist responses in certain Latin American contexts. Some manifestations of political Islam, to be sure, have threatened business interests, notably tourism in Egypt; but the political thrust of most of these movements lies elsewhere—in the educational and cultural rather than economic spheres. Islamism need not be an obstacle to financial reform. Some regimes, however, have tried to exploit the fears of Westernized elites, in business communities as elsewhere, to delay political reform. Further delay may result in ever more human rights violations and more repressive regimes, which in turn prevent financial institutions from acquiring greater autonomy. Algeria, Tunisia, and Egypt each seem to face this dilemma, as the following discussion of their respective reforms will suggest. Only Morocco, to date, has skirted the dilemma and managed to project an interesting facade of financial and political liberalization. This experience will shed further light on the interrelationships between the two sets of changes.

Algeria

Algeria seemed until 1991 to illustrate simultaneous processes of financial liberalization and democratization. The country had experienced a major political crisis in October 1988, when widespread rioting resulted in hundreds of deaths. The crisis was so severe that the regime subsequently withdrew the police from the streets lest they provoke further popular outbreaks. One sign of the deep political malaise was that normally law-abiding middle class car owners no longer pasted their *vignettes* to their windshields, lest tax resisters break them. The regime had based its legitimacy upon economic performance but literally could no longer deliver the goods after the collapse of oil and gas revenues in the mid-1980s. Heavily indebted, it had drastically cut down on imports rather than reschedule its debt in exchange for agreeing to IMF stabilization and adjustment measures.

In response to the political crisis, President Chadli Benjedid enacted a series of political reforms which destroyed the monopoly of the ruling party, introduced a multiparty system in 1989, encouraged a relatively free press, sponsored free local and regional elections in 1990, and promised free elections to a national legislature in 1991. Plans for economic reform, which had been incubating slowly since 1986, were implemented simultaneously. And just as it was overhauling its party system, Algeria signed its first stand-by agreement with the IMF in 1989.

Algeria had proposed by law in 1986 to restructure its commercial banking system, but the legislation could not be implemented until its borrowers, the public sector enterprises, were also restructured. "Participation funds" were established in the summer of 1988 as state holding companies. Each of the eight funds was concentrated on a particular set of economic sectors, but each enterprise of a given sector was also to be partly "owned" by two other funds so as to diversify their respective portfolios. In 1989 and 1990, most of the enterprises were set loose from their mother ministries and rendered "autonomous," that is, handed over to their respective funds. With government ministers playing the role of shareholders, the participation funds supervised annual meetings of the boards of directors of the enterprises. The funds in turn held their annual assemblies of shareholders, represented by an assemblage of government ministers.

The idea behind the reform was to encourage each enterprise to act like an autonomous, profit-seeking business. The banks, also liberated in theory from the Ministry of Finance, were then to take responsibility for allocating credit to enterprises as they saw fit rather than carry out orders, as in the past, to serve their designated clients. To strengthen their hand, the 1990 Law of Money and Credit freed the Central Bank from the control of the Ministry of Finance and the Treasury. On paper, the Banque d'Algérie became one of the world's most powerful central banks, responsible for the money supply and for maintaining credit ceilings. In this way, the IMF had some assurance in 1991, when a new stand-by agreement was signed, that Algeria's performance criteria could be respected.

The reforms augured radical change from a rigidly managed state economy to a more liberal and competitive one. But, in the words of an astute Algerian commentator, "it is striking to observe that the so-called economic reforms are carried out with the same formalism and dogmatism which inspired the *Gestion socialiste des entreprises* [socialist-managed businesses] and the Agrarian Revolution of yesteryear" (Addi 1991: 120). The freeing of the public enterprises repeated the attempt in 1982 to financially restructure them and encourage them to be independent profit centers.[3] The new participation funds had little staff or expertise, and investment decisions, so far as any funds were available, were still the responsibility of the financial experts in the planning ministry (now relegated to the prime minister's office as a national commission but not downsized). "The year 1989 marked the beginning of implementing a new system of economic planning," the annual report of one of the funds asserted (*Fonds de participation des industries diverses* 1989: 6).

Algeria's five commercial state-owned banks could now in theory choose their clients and make their credit decisions on economic criteria, subject to the Banque d'Algérie's credit ceilings. But in practice they each insisted on keeping their good clients from running off to other banks while refusing each other's less solvent ones. Any competition simply augmented the informal cash economy, which expanded from 40 percent in 1988 to over 50 percent of the M1 money supply in 1990 and 1991. An enterprise seeking loans from a second bank would have to pay that bank off in cash lest the first bank get wind of the deal and insist on its loans being paid off. Free in theory to manage their banks, directors were reshuffled much as before with changing political currents. The banks were themselves in such a precarious financial situation that they did not have the means to survive, much less govern themselves and control their loan portfolios without the support of higher authorities. One look at their financial statements quickly reveals their unhealthy conditions. Table 8.2 presents the ratio of loans to deposits of all five banks. Evidently, only two banks had enough deposits to cover their loans; one bank had loaned out more than three times its deposit base by 1990. The commercial banks merely reflected the crisis of their principal clients, the public sector enterprises.

Table 8.2. Algerian Bank Ratios of Loans to Deposits, 1981–90

	1981	1982	1983	1984	1985	1986	1987	1988	1989	1990
BEA	2.2	1.5	1.4	1.5	1.4	1.2	1.0	0.7	0.9	1.3
BNA	2.0	1.8	1.8	1.5	1.5	1.7	1.5	1.5	1.4	1.5
BADR			2.2	1.9	1.7	2.0	1.6	0.9	0.9	0.9
CPA	1.2	1.0	1.3	1.4	1.6	1.7	2.1	2.3	3.0	3.3
BDL					1.3	1.7	1.7	1.7	1.7	2.0

Source: Annual reports of banks had to be supplemented by Central Bank data for BNA 1989–90, BADR 1988–90, CPA 1990, BDL 1989–90.

In fact, little real liberalization had occurred by 1991, when the political climate deteriorated (Entelis and Arone 1992). The rest of the story is well known: a general strike called by the Islamic Salvation Front (FIS); violence in the streets and military intervention; postponement of the legislative elections until a new government redrew the electoral districts; and finally the army's decision on January 11, 1992, to remove President Benjedid, stop the elections, and suppress the FIS, which had been winning by a landslide. Another casualty of increased military intervention after the summer of 1991 was the financial reform introduced by the previous government. The reformist directors general of two of the major banks lost their jobs for trying to exercise their legal right to stand up to the Treasury. The major bulwark of banking autonomy, the governor of the Banque d'Algérie, risked losing his job, long before completing his six-year term, once the military made his patron, President Benjedid, resign. The governor finally "resigned" on July 20, one day after Prime Minister Belaid Abdesselam constituted his new government in which he concentrated "complete power in the economic sphere" (*MEED*, July 31, 1992: 8).

Although efforts to reform Algeria's statist economy had begun before the crisis of October 1988, which triggered the short-lived democratic transition, it would be wrong to conclude that financial liberalization had any real impact on the transition. Perhaps the prospect of losing power had influenced some elements of the ruling party to withdraw support for Benjedid in 1988 and indirectly to stir up the mass demonstrations that provoked the political crisis. In any event, the financial reforms were not given time to work. Despite some modest legislation favoring joint ventures, the private sector remained weak. It was virtually excluded from commercial banking credit, and the banks remained the servants of the state enterprises.

Algeria neither confirms nor offers evidence against the proposition that financial liberalization can stimulate transitions to democracy. The case suggests, however, that the prospects of economic liberalization may stir up considerable opposition within an authoritarian regime's hard core of supporters. A significant political opening, if not an immediate democratization of the regime, was needed to counterbalance the opposition. Had President Benjedid been permitted to carry out the final round of legislative elections and work out an agreement to share power with the FIS, the financial reforms could have been pursued. There was nothing in the FIS program, published in March 1989, to suggest opposition to these reforms. In addition to favoring free markets, including the realignment of the official exchange rate of the Algerian dinar as per IMF insistence, the FIS advocated the establishment of Islamic banks. Algeria's team of financial reformers had in fact welcomed the initiative of a private Saudi business group to establish an Islamic bank as a joint venture with one of Algeria's state banks.

In desperate financial straits, Algeria finally negotiated an agreement with the IMF in April 1994 and sought to reschedule its foreign debt with foreign official and commercial creditors—an option that previous governments had systematically rejected for the sake of preserving Algeria's sovereignty and dignity. Pursuit of any promised reform program clearly depended, however, on ending the civil war between the government and Islamist oppositions. The new president, retired General Liamine Zeroual, initially signaled his willingness by distancing himself from the other generals who brought him to power and sacking hardline ministers in favor of technocrats and ministers sympathetic to the Islamists. He promoted a controversial referendum in November 1996 opposed by Algeria's principal political parties. However much it was rigged, the vote reinforced his constitutional powers, identified him with the hardliners, and diminished any possibilities of a political solution to the conflict with the Islamists.

Tunisia

Tunisia never experienced the Algerian extremes of a state-run economy, a severe political and economic crisis, and a sudden transition to democracy. Its international debt crisis of 1986 was minor compared to Algeria's, and the tasks of stabilization and adjustment were considerably less onerous. While the country experienced a prolonged political crisis in Bourguiba's declining years, Ben Ali's declaration of November 7, 1987, quickly alleviated it and promised a steady and orderly political transition. The new president declared that "[o]ur people have attained a level of responsibility and maturity that enables all of its elements to contribute constructively to managing its affairs in conformity with the Republican idea, which confers full authority to institutions and guarantees the conditions for a responsible democracy. . . . Our people are worthy of an advanced and institutionalized political life, based on multipartism and a plurality of mass organizations." Ben Ali promised constitutional reform and new laws for political parties and the press, "susceptible of assuring broader participation for constructing Tunisia and consolidating its independence in the framework of order and discipline."

Tunisia indeed appeared to be a fertile field for illustrating a link between financial liberalization and democratization. It embarked on a very serious effort in 1986 to stabilize the economy and embark on structural adjustment, with a special emphasis on reform of the commercial banking system. By the end of 1988, many of the reforms were already in place, including a new money market through which the Central Bank purported to regulate interest rates. In 1993, President Ben Ali was promising a convertible dinar.

How is it, then, that Tunisia displays such an abysmal human rights record, symptomatic of a regression rather than advance along any imagined authoritarian-democratic continuum? Shortly after assuming power, Ben Ali had released and amnestied over 2,000 prisoners, many of whom were Islamists incarcerated by the Bourguiba regime. He promulgated a law in April 1988 that guaranteed Tunisia a multiparty system (not that the one-party state had ever been constitutionally recognized, as is Algeria's). The new regime engaged in political dialogue with the mainstream Islamists, including Rachid al-Ghannouchi, until 1990. Despite the participation of one of its members in the deliberations in the National Pact, however, an-Nahdah was not recognized as a political party. The legislative elections of April 1989 resulted in total victory for the ruling party, but opposition parties and independent Islamist candidates were permitted to contest them and collectively gained up to 41 percent of the vote in some southern and urban constituencies (Moore 1993: 55). The Islamists gained far more votes than the combined totals of all the other opposition groups.

After the elections, however, relations between an-Nahdah and the authorities deteriorated. In early 1991 the director of an-Nahdah's newspaper, *Al Fajr*, claimed to this writer[4] that four to five hundred party members were in jail. In March, some Islamists raided a regional headquarters of the ruling party in downtown Tunis, and a night watchman died under particularly gruesome circumstances. Whether or not the security forces manufactured some of the circumstances (making it appear the assailants had torched a victim whom they had not intended to harm, some neutral observers believe), they took advantage of the incident to crack down on moderates and extremists alike in a tense political climate aggravated by the Gulf War. In late summer, the authorities purported to discover a new plot against the regime, though the evidence did not convince the international press. The crackdown on Islamists intensified, and by 1992 thousands had been in and out of jail— between 3,000 and 8,000 at any given time, well-informed Tunisians suggested. Amnesty International conservatively estimated in a report released on January 12, 1994, that at least 1,020 political prisoners were in jail, and arrests were continuing on a regular if less frequent basis. Amnesty International also inferred from documented instances of torture that the practice was widespread and systematic (Fischer and Henry 1994: 12–13). Others reported that brothers and sons of Islamist opponents were subject to various forms of administrative harassment including arbitrary arrest and loss of employment.

These political developments bore an eerie resemblance to those in neighboring Algeria. Tunisia had moved much more cautiously than Algeria toward multiparty politics but had experienced a similar breakdown in political dialogue with the Islamist opposition. While Tunisia did not face a civil war like that in Algeria, it was reliving its recent history just as Algeria, too, seemed to return to its colonial past. Each country in its own way was replicating the struggle for national liberation against French colonialism. But this time the Islamists occupied the political ground that the nationalists had successfully held several decades earlier, against states now dominated by indigenous rather than foreign elites. Just as Algeria's military republic recalled the military regime of French Algeria beefed up by the Mollet government in 1956, Ben Ali's regime was reminiscent of the Corsican police state managed by hardline French residents such as Marcel Peyrouton in 1934 and Jean de Hautecloque in 1952.

Ben Ali, possibly influenced by his military intelligence and police background, considerably expanded the police and security forces. Though the exact numbers were not a matter of public record, one knowledgeable informant's guess is that their number had almost tripled from approximately 15,000 in Bourguiba's day. Ben Ali's regime also developed its covert as well as overt activities—in France as well as in Tunisia. Many Tunisians believe that their telephones are tapped; recently a Tunisian businessman overheard making deprecatory comments about the presidential cavalcade over his car telephone was subsequently arrested and fined for his remarks. The police have become omnipresent in Ben Ali's Tunisia, so much so that measures have recently been taken to curb police abuses. The human rights section recently established in the Ministry of Justice claims to have investigated 140 cases brought to its attention in the past year and to have taken action in 60 of them. The ostensible reason for the huge police build-up was to combat Islamist terrorism.

As in Algeria, the polarization between government and Islamist opposition has blocked any transition toward greater accountability, contestation, or political participation, at least for the time being. And Tunisia, like Algeria, has not yet undergone sufficient financial liberalization to confirm or disprove the hypothesis that such liberalization tends to encourage political transitions toward greater democracy. Rather, a political opening of the regime to the Islamist opposition may be a prerequisite for continued financial liberalization in Tunisia as well as Algeria.

Financial reform has obviously not given rise to an independent business sector committed to greater government accountability, much less willing to finance a multiparty system. Some opposition parties were permitted to compete in the parliamentary elections held in 1989 and 1994, but they fared poorly. They had little time to campaign and only token access to the media. Private businesses were perhaps less loathe in 1994 than in 1989 to be perceived as supporting these parties, after the regime had officially endorsed the token oppositions and entitled them to a small share of the parliamentary seats. Collectively, they won less than 3 percent of the vote in 1994—an even weaker showing than that of Tunisia's principal opposition party in 1989. The strongest opposition candidates in 1989 were the independent candidates fielded by Islamists. They ran as independents because their party was not officially recognized; the official business community also seems to have shunned them. Some small local businesses may have lent them informal support, and private Saudi businessmen may also have contributed to the Islamists' nationwide campaign; most of the Tunisian private sector was too vulnerable—beholden to the government for credit and other favors—to be associated with any opposition candidates. For electoral and other purposes, the ruling party's patronage networks remained largely in place, channeled through a state banking sector that still held well over half of the total assets of the commercial banking system.

Efforts to reform the banking system foundered on the same obstacles that had inhibited reform in Algeria. Though the Tunisian public sector was smaller and less financially troubled than that of Algeria, the state banks remained saddled with many bad debts and could not be rapidly transformed, as reformers had hoped, into responsible and autonomous allocators of credit. One result of the financial reforms was that they were obliged to reveal more information about their loan portfolios in their published annual statements.

From these statements, published by the Professional Association of Banks of Tunisia, it is possible to infer how much capital would be needed to cover outstanding loans that were not being serviced and probably deserved to be written off.[5] Table 8.3 presents the capital shortfalls of Tunisia's commercial banks as reflected in their balance sheets of December 31, 1989. The shortfalls are the additional capital that would be needed to write off all of the "problem loans" reported at the end of the year, after first spending the provisions set aside as reserves for such loans and the capital not already tied up in fixed assets such as bank buildings and equipment. By the author's count, over 400 million dinars (about $500 million in 1989) would have been needed, and the situation only worsened in the early 1990s.

Tunisia's private sector banks, the bottom five reported in table 8.3, nevertheless manifested some dynamism and independence. With the exception of the Banque de Tunisie, a private sector bank that had always curried favor with Tunisia's political establishment and was now apparently paying the price, they were much less saddled with doubtful loans than the public sector banks. They were also gradually gaining market share at the expense of some of the more troubled public sector banks and further, displayed greater profitability and growth potentials. But Ben Ali's regime has apparently set limits on their growth and autonomy.

In fact, Tunisia offers at least one perverse illustration of the link between financial liberalization and political change. Ben Ali targeted the Banque Internationale Arabe de Tunisie (BIAT), Tunisia's leading private sector bank and the one that seemed in table 8.3 to be the most effective in controlling its

Table 8.3. Tunisia's Problem Loans and Capital Shortfalls, 1989

Bank (mm TD)	Problem Loans*	Problem Loans as % of All Loans	Equity[†]	Provi- sions[a]	P Loans /(E+P)	Immobilized Capital as % of All Equity[§]	Capital Shortfall
STB	244	25.9	68	42	2.2	84.2	190.8
BNA	135	11.9	83	50	1.0	49.8	43.8
UIB	92	23.3	14	14	3.3	113.2	79.7
BS	71	20.3	23	27	1.4	57.1	34.0
BFT	21	32.8	6	4	2.2	30.2	13.0
BT	54	16.5	30	26	1.0	72.4	19.7
CFCT	23	8.8	19	4	1.0	77.4	14.2
BIAT	37	8.8	32	17	0.7	87.7	15.7
UBCI	23	9.1	22	20	0.5	74.1	-2.5
ATB	13	11.0	18	0	0.7	74.2	8.7
TOTALS	712	15.8	316	204	1.4	71.3	418.1

Source: Association Professionnelle des Banques de Tunisie, Annual Reports; Banque Centrale de Tunisie, *Statistiques Financières*, various issues; writer's data base of commercial bank reports.

*"Autres crédits" from Reports of APBT, slightly reduced by weightings to the totals presented by BCT, *Statistiques Financières*. The Banque de Tunisie's (BT) "autres crédits" for 1990 are reported here because they were not fully disclosed in 1989.
[†] Includes net income for 1989.
[a]Projected from APBT data and verified by Statistiques Financières.
[§] Capital funds tied up in fixed assets on 12/31/89 and in shares in other companies. Since some of the shareholdings were unavailable, the capital shortfall was actually higher.

loan portfolio. Its autonomy, buttressed by private enterprise based in Sfax, threatened the government's informal control over the private sector through selective credit incentives. On May 11, 1993, *Le Monde* cited its chairman, former Finance Minister Mansour Moallah, as calling Tunisia "more IMF than the IMF." By May 19, parastate organizations such as Tunis Air began to withdraw their deposits from the bank, obliging Moallah to resign from the honorary chairmanship of the bank as well as from other public positions in order to save the bank. BIAT lost 20 percent of its deposits within a week but managed to survive by borrowing expensive funds from the Central Bank. The real issue behind the affair was that BIAT, Tunisia's third largest commercial bank, had grown economically too powerful; but there is a political interpretation that sheds further light on the link between political and financial reform. Some weeks earlier, Moallah is reported to have responded to a former French prime minister in an informal conversation overheard at a reception that yes, he supposed that he too might be *"présidentiable."* Moallah's elimination from public life was viewed by many Tunisians as part of Ben Ali's preelectoral campaign to preempt any presidential opposition in the 1994 elections (though Moallah's associates indicate that he did not harbor any presidential ambitions); other aspiring candidates were subsequently jailed. In the elections Ben Ali, uncontested, received 99.9 percent of the vote.

Egypt

Financial reform has a longer history in Egypt—where it dates from the *infitah* [economic liberalization] of the mid-1970s—than it has in the other former one-party states of North Africa. It also should be recalled that Nasser's command economy lasted for a relatively brief period in Egypt's modern history, from roughly 1961 to 1974. Consequently, memories of a somewhat independent banking system were still fresh, and many of Egypt's leading bankers of the 1980s and 1990s had begun their careers under the old regime or in the early and relatively liberal Nasser years. Yet the financial liberalization of the 1970s and 1980s is associated at best with very tentative and inconclusive efforts to promote a very modest degree of political pluralism consonant with an authoritarian regime. Since 1992, moreover, systematic government efforts to repress moderate as well as extremist wings of Islamist movements have rendered any political pluralism and contestation in Egypt almost as meaningless as Tunisian variations on this theme.

The banking system, which had been inherited from Nasser and the heady unregulated days of *infitah,* was in worse financial shape than Tunisia's; financial liberalization could therefore not result in a truly autonomous banking system. Throughout the entire period from 1974 to 1996, moreover, Egypt's four public sector banks have held over 60 percent of the commercial banking system's deposits and indirectly (at least in theory) controlled an additional 20 percent through joint ventures with the private sector. Private capital remained highly fragmented. Only three of Egypt's seventy-three new private sector banks were fully owned by private investors, and only two of them survived without an infusion of public sector capital. The typical investment strategy of a private investor was to buy a very small share of a bank's capital and then use the investment as leverage to extract loans. For example, Osman Ahmad Osman, Egypt's premier private capitalist, generated large amounts of finance capital in this way with minimal personal risk. The banks serviced the extensive patronage networks he had developed as a public sector contractor, housing minister, and close friend and advisor of Nasser and Sadat. Egypt's private sector investors had short time horizons and sought quick profits; they preferred milking the commercial banking system to building durable financial empires. Therefore, most of the private sector banks were in no better shape than the state banks. Financial liberalization could not result in a strong private sector committed to greater government accountability or prepared to invest in a multiparty system.

For a time in the late 1970s and early 1980s, however, the banks promoted a pluralism of sorts within Egypt's political elite. Sadat's strategy of presidential rule thrived on elite factionalism, and small banks in the hands of former ministers served his purpose of breaking up some of the coalitions which had served his predecessor. They also exercised significant influence over economic policy, under both Sadat and Mubarak. Despite the efforts of one of Mubarak's governments, for example, some of the banks were sufficiently influential, with help from foreign partners and their bank branches, to sabotage plans to resuscitate state control over foreign exchange markets. Financial deregulation led to virtual anarchy in the banking sector because the attractions of jobs in the Gulf as well as in Egypt's many new banks depleted the ranks of Central Bank supervisors. The banks freely financed shaky business combines in a parasitical private sector, but their new freedom lacked an economic base. Far from acquiring genuine autonomy, most of the banks and the businesses they supported barely managed to survive.

Like Tunisia's banking system, the Egyptian banks were submerged in nonperforming loans. An official study of the National Bank of Egypt recognized a total value of "sick balances" in the commercial banking system amounting to £ E 5.3 billion as of June 30, 1989—15 percent of the total outstanding loans—and claimed that only 104 clients were responsible for 56.4 percent of them.[6] Their real value was probably much higher, depending upon one's definition of a "sick balance." The banks did not disclose information about their loan portfolios in their annual reports, but it was possible to infer some information about them. The banks did report net income after taxes, interest revenues and expenses, loans, deposits, and total assets. From these data it was possible to calculate their net return on assets (ROA), the average rate they received on their loans, and their "spreads," or the difference between the rate they charged on loans and the rate they received for deposits.[7] Table 8.4 presents these summary measures of financial performance, averaged over the years for which data on each bank were available.

Egypt's four big public sector banks fared poorly. The average return on assets was only .37 percent, and the average interest rates charged on loans was only 1.19 percent higher than the interest offered depositors. Returns

Table 8.4. Financial Indicators of Egyptian Commercial Banks, 1985–91

Banks	ROA	Lending Rates	Spreads	Average For the Years
		as Percentage		
Public Sector Commercial	0.37	7.11	1.19	
Banque Misr	0.44	7.81	1.79	1986–91
National Bank of Egypt	0.27	5.92	0.89	1986–91
Banque du Caire	0.54	7.21	1.26	1986–91
Bank of Alexandria	0.24	7.52	0.81	1986–91
Infitah Banks				
I. Big Banking Joint Ventures	1.53	8.71	3.09	
Misr International Bank	0.68	8.26	2.46	1988–90
Commercial International Bank (ex Chase)	1.71	9.42	4.39	1985–90
Egyptian American Bank	2.18	8.45	2.43	1985–90
II. Other Joint Ventures	0.96	7.94	2.28	
Arab Investment Bank	0.19	8.72	1.62	1988–90
Cairo Barclays	0.17	7.35	0.94	1985–90
Misr Iran Development Bank	0.77	8.59	0.80	1985–90
Misr American International Bank	0.88	7.41	0.87	1987–90
National Société Générale	0.76	9.21	4.34	1985–89
Export Development Bank of Egypt	2.68	7.48	3.75	1986–90
Caire Paris	1.12	9.98	4.27	1987–90
Crédit International d'Egypt	0.98	6.23	0.87	1988–89
Misr Romanian	1.10	6.46	3.02	1986, 1988–90
III. With Egyptian Private Ownership	0.83	8.28	2.00	
A. *General*	0.86	8.60	2.32	
Suez Canal Bank	0.50	6.75	0.81	1985–90
Bank of Credit & Commerce Misr	0.50	8.63	3.03	1985–90
Delta Bank	0.25	7.86	1.78	1985–90
Nile Bank	2.00	9.59	3.49	1985–90
Alexandria Kuwait International Bank	0.00	7.21	1.11	1985–89
Misr Exterior	1.07	9.06	2.60	1985–86, 89–90
Egypt Gulf Bank	0.95	9.08	1.32	1985–90
Egypt Arab African Bank	0.81	8.11	2.93	1985–90
Hong Kong Egyptian Bank	0.88	11.63	5.07	1985–90
Alexandria Commercial Maritime Bank	2.41	9.35	2.09	1985–86, 89–90
Al Watany	0.77	9.13	2.85	1985–90
Société Arabe Internationale (SAIB)	1.02	7.03	2.77	1985–86, 88–89
Cairo Far East	0.07	8.36	0.28	1985–90

Table 8.4.—*Continued*

Banks	ROA	Lending Rates	Spreads	Average For the Years
		as Percentage		
B. Development Banks	1.01	8.40	1.89	
National Development Bank	0.49	6.42	0.97	1985–90
Assiut	0.17	8.80	0.56	1987–88, 90
Behera	1.76	7.36	3.00	1987–88, 90
Damietta	-0.01	8.41	2.28	1987–88, 90
Fayoum	-1.82	5.76	-1.29	1987–88, 90
Gharbiya	1.25	10.57	2.65	1987–88, 90
Giza	0.91	7.43	2.26	1987–88, 90
Ismailiya	-0.17	9.07	-1.40	1987–88, 90
Kafr el Sheikh	1.85	9.40	2.70	1987–88, 90
Minya	0.74	9.97	3.61	1987–88, 90
Mounoufeya	1.51	7.77	3.16	1987–88, 90
Port Said	1.60	8.82	1.83	1987–88, 90
Qalyoubeya	1.27	6.65	0.14	1987–88, 90
Qena	3.53	8.16	4.50	1987–88, 90
Sharqiya	0.81	8.42	1.64	1987–88, 90
Sinai	5.23	8.77	7.69	1987–88, 90
Souhag	1.62	10.65	1.95	1987–88, 90
Dakahlia Development Bank	-2.02	3.79	-3.71	1989–90
Housing & Development Bank	0.58	13.46	3.41	1988–90
C. Professional Unions	0.64	9.67	3.33	
BCD Tegariyoon	-0.84	8.14	1.40	1985–86, 89–90
Mohandes Bank	-0.70	9.42	2.58	1985–86, 88–89
Workers Bank	3.47	11.46	6.00	1989–90
D. Islamic Banks	0.01	5.21	0.19	
Faisal Islamic Bank of Egypt	0.50	7.35	1.24	1985–90
Islamic International Bank for				
Investment & Development	-0.60	4.76	1.20	1985–90
Egyptian Saudi Finance Bank	0.13	3.54	-1.88	1987–90
Major Arab "Offshore" Banks				
Arab African International Bank	-1.83	7.95	-0.73	1985–86, 89–90
Arab International Bank	0.58	8.36	1.78	1986–91

Source: Annual reports of the banks; Egyptian Banks' Directory; writer's data base of commercial banks.

and spreads calculated from the banks' published annual reports were higher in the private sector. Commercial International Bank and Egyptian American Bank set a relatively high standard and were generally considered to be Egypt's most solid joint venture banks. But many of the private sector banks seemed to be experiencing difficulties. Even the Misr International Bank, Egypt's largest joint venture, seemed overextended. Some of the smaller banks owned in part by Egyptian shareholders as well as other banks and public sector companies were in dire straits by 1990. As the table shows, Cairo Far East had averaged only a .07 percent return on assets and enjoyed very meager spreads; and some of the provincial development banks (sponsored by Osman Ahmad Osman) were in the red and, for all practical purposes, bankrupt. For that matter, the much larger Suez Canal Bank, which Osman had also helped establish, was in a precarious situation as well, burdened by a number of his projects that had gone sour. The banks of the professional syndicates (Tegariyoon and Mohandes) were in grave difficulty, and Tegariyoon, like a number of other private sector banks, received an injection of public sector capital to keep it afloat. With few exceptions, such as the Nile Bank (totally owned by private individuals), the private sector showed little dynamism or staying power.

Despite its longer experience with financial liberalization, Egypt offered no more evidence than Tunisia of any potential for financial change to encourage a transition toward more democracy. Indeed it was only during the build-up to the Gulf War, in early 1991, that Egypt took decisive steps to adjust foreign exchange and domestic interest rates to market rates and to embark on structural adjustment of the sort that Tunisia had undertaken earlier. To the extent that deteriorating economic conditions triggered popular unrest associated with Islamism, Egypt's further efforts to liberalize its banking system had perhaps indirectly contributed to sharper authoritarian practices against the Islamists in 1992 and 1993. However, the Egyptian *infitah* had also previously unleashed another potential link between finance and politics—a political economy of Islam.

What follows is at best speculation, because it deals with what might have been, not what actually happened. By the mid-1980s, Islamic finance had become a significant force in commercial banking, and the new Islamic financial institutions might have mediated the growing confrontations between the Mubarak regime and its Islamist opposition rather than exacerbating them. *Infitah* had facilitated the emergence of two official Islamic banks, the Faisal Islamic Bank of Egypt and the Islamic International Bank for Investment and Development. Recognized as such by both Islamic transnational authorities and the Egyptian government, they controlled roughly one-quarter of the private sector's deposits and represented about one-quarter of the new private capital that had been funneled into the banking system. In addition, the money changers who had defied government efforts to control foreign exchange were able to amass vast amounts of remittances from Egyptians working in the Gulf. They gradually developed new financial institutions in the early 1980s to invest the funds rather than immediately exchange them. The new investment companies called themselves Islamic so as to gain people's trust and confidence, though only a small number of their owners had any ties with Islamic banks or with Islamist political movements. While competing successfully with the Islamic banks for deposits—because they offered higher returns to investors—these companies also tried to achieve official recognition by the Islamic banking community. Though they failed to convince Prince Mohammed al-Faisal of their Islamic credentials, the owner of the most senior and respectable, if not quite the largest, of them acquired a commanding share of one of the official Islamic banks. Abd al-Latif Al-Sharif, unlike the young upstart money changers, was an experienced entrepreneur with a substantial business group that included at least nine factories, mostly producing plastics. He was reputed to be a former member of the Muslim Brotherhood, and he had set up Islamic investment companies to finance his businesses.

Had the other "Islamic" investment companies enjoyed comparable business leadership and political affiliations, the Egyptian remittances might have financed durable private sector enterprises. They could have offered certain Islamist political movements important material support—in exchange for a willingness to compete and coexist with other parties in a pluralist political system—just as the Islamic banks competed and coexisted with conventional banks. Perhaps it was just this prospect that encouraged the Egyptian government, intent on retaining its shreds of authority, to crack down on these companies in ways that prevented the legitimate ones, like Sharif's, from restructuring themselves. As in Tunisia, any appearance in the private sector of a financially viable actor intent on exercising autonomous economic activity had to be suppressed. That is why the argument developed in this chapter may still carry weight in the long run: as private business groups do eventually emerge (as they did in pre-Nasser Egypt and in post-statist Turkey), they will be committed to more democracy.

Morocco

Finally it is Morocco, which never experienced a one-party system or a command economy, that best illustrates the argument. It meets most of the conditions conducive to democratic transitions. Morocco delayed much of its financial reform until 1991, despite experiencing a severe debt crisis earlier than its North African neighbors. In the late 1970s, its debt service ratio surpassed Egypt's, and it then stumbled through a series of agreements with the IMF in the 1980s. Gradually, Morocco brought its fiscal and foreign trade deficits to manageable proportions and then, in careful sequencing following IMF recipes, launched its reform of financial structures. Graced, like Egypt, by IMF and Arab windfalls from the Gulf War, Morocco was able, in 1991, simultaneously to control its credit ceilings and deregulate interest rates. Credit quotas, which had prevented its commercial banks from seriously competing with one another, were finally lifted in 1991.

When Morocco finally underwent financial liberalization, it quickly caught up with Tunisia and Egypt (not to mention Algeria) because its commercial banking system had never experienced as much state intervention. The banks, with two major exceptions, were privately owned—partially Moroccanized in the 1970s. Once the Bank al-Maghreb, Morocco's central bank, lifted the credit restrictions imposed in 1976 on the commercial banks, they could freely compete for clients and enjoy full autonomy in managing their loan portfolios. Moreover, strong and relatively autonomous private sector business groups flourished. Some, including the leading Omnium Nord Africain (ONA), had survived intact from the colonial era under new Moroccan owners, while others resulted from the Moroccanization of French businesses in the 1970s (Saâdi 1988: 140–53). They seemed too powerful, however, to need more accountable government, however much they supported the various parties that contested Moroccan elections.

The Moroccanization policies of the 1970s, in fact, had rearranged the king's patronage networks. The king's problem was not so much the multiplicity of new generations of potential actors whom clients of clients could not quite absorb (Leveau 1985: 266–67), as the diminishing resources needed to fuel the networks (Leveau 1987). Deep and durable networks require alienable riches as well as intimidation to keep clients in line. Patronage was indeed perfected: A veritable treasure of crown jewels, it ran deepest and was most centralized in Morocco, because the monarchy had shepherded more strategically the resources left by departing colonists than the Algerians or Tunisians. Two-thirds of the colonial lands, for instance, were distributed surreptitiously to the king and his followers rather than politically wasted away in state farms or sales on the open market (Leveau 1985: 247). French commerce and industry were barely touched until 1973, when Moroccanization could serve a useful political purpose. Senior administrators could then be shuffled off to the private sector, opening the way to government promotions for a new generation of king's men (Leveau 1985: 255). But once production was in native hands, there was little left to redistribute. Dramatic rises in world phosphate prices kept the *makhzan*'s (royal household's) coffer supplied a while longer, but then prices collapsed and budget deficits had to be brought under control.

Cheaper forms of patronage had to be discovered, but the IMF straitjacket diminished the government's margin for maneuver. After 1983, freezes on government employment, tariff reductions, and freer trade; elimination of most price controls and some state trading monopolies; and various other measures of economic liberalization required by either the IMF or the World Bank tended to undercut the traditional sources of patronage that relied on selective implementation of government regulations. The international agencies were in effect devaluing the treasure of crown jewels. Yet the king, an astute political actor, acted as if he wished to give some of his jewels away. His official application to join the European Community, for instance, had the response been favorable, would have further opened up Moroccan economic decisionmaking to European as well as international pressures for deregulation (Leveau 1987).

King Hassan was able, in fact, to adapt his patronage system to the new international rules. Tactically, for instance, support for small and medium enterprises satisfied foreign lenders insisting upon export-oriented growth as it rebuilt clienteles to offset "legitimacy deficits" (Doumou 1987: 212). Strategically, Morocco's largest party, the Union Constitutionelle (UC), favored both economic liberalism and political restructuring—to consolidate "democracy." The makhzan seems to have devised a scheme to control political and economic reform simultaneously while sticking to Morocco's international commitments.

On this reading, the makhzan's purchase in 1980 of the ONA was the key to the new political strategy. This holding company is Morocco's most powerful conglomerate and the one best positioned to compete in liberated internal markets. Since gross revenues amounted to 5.5 percent of Morocco's GDP, the new potential for patronage seemed enormous. In 1987, the ONA added Morocco's top performing bank to the portfolio of banks under its direct control or influence. Significantly, too, the first thrust of "privatization" was the sale of a government sugar refinery to the ONA. The makhzan now seemed in position to repeat the political achievements of the 1973 Moroccanization campaign alluded to earlier. To avoid unseemly appearances, however, the king's son-in-law, who headed the ONA, disclaimed further interest in acquiring state enterprises. When procedures for privatization were accelerated in 1991, the owners of two other major conglomerates, Ali Kittani and Mohammed Karim Lamrani, also excluded themselves from acquisitions by agreeing to join the Privatization Council, which was to evaluate enterprises up for sale. These three king's men, however, already controlled much of Morocco's banking system and could veil any direct control of business enterprises in banking secrecy.

As privatization picked up momentum in 1993, the makhzan seemed to have adapted elegantly to the new international pressures placed on the Moroccan economy. By waiting until 1991 to proceed with financial reform, the government not only followed good financial advice but also gave the makhzan time to consolidate its command over the heights of a liberated economy. After acquiring a one-quarter stake in Morocco's best-performing private bank, the Banque du Commerce Marocain (BCM), the ONA proceeded in 1991 to buy 15 percent of the Banque Marocaine du Commerce et de l'Industrie (BMCI) and rejuvenate its management. Subsequently, the ONA took over half the shares of Morocco's eighth largest bank, the Société Marocaine de Dépôt et de Crédit (SMDC). In 1992, the ONA encouraged the merger of the Société de Banque et de Crédit (SBC) with the BCM. Thus, as the financial reforms went into effect, the ONA controlled almost one-quarter of the total assets of Morocco's commercial banking system and close to half of those of the private sector (that is, all banks excepting the Banque du Crédit Populaire and the Banque Marocaine du Commerce Extérieur). As table 8.5 indicates, two of the other leading private sector banks were also controlled by Moroccan private sector groups. These groups were headed by Lamrani and Kittani, individuals who enjoyed particularly close relations with the palace. In 1991 Kittani's Wafabank was especially well positioned to benefit from the lifting of credit restrictions, and it increased its loan portfolio by over 40 percent, well above the average rate. In league with foreign owners, principally French banks, the king's men thus controlled over three-quarters of the private sector's total assets.

Table 8.5. Capital Structure of Moroccan Commercial Banks, 1990

			Percent Shares Held by			
				Moroccan Private Sector		
	Total Assets	Capital				
Bank	(Million Dirhams)		Public Sector	Groups	Misc.	Foreign
BCP	35136	2340	100.0			
BMCE	22817	1262.6	58.7		28.7	12.6
BCM	13930	1049		32.7	42.5	24.8
Wafa	10011	617		100.0		
BMCI	7235	321		19.7	27.3	53.0
SGMB	7785	506			50.0	50.0
CDM	6713	455	26.5	17.7	12.6	43.2
SMDC*	3600	174			50.0	50.0
UNIBAN	1979	182				100.0
SBC	1556	99		54.0	46.0	0.0
Algemen	1502	99			50.0	50.0
BMAO	1448	109			100.0	
Arab Bank	794	106	50.0			50.0
Citibank*	800	56			50.0	50.0
Totals	115306	7376				

Source: Groupement Professionnel de Banques du Maroc, Annuaire des Banques du Maroc, 1991–92.

*Total assets are estimated from data for prior years.

By disengaging the state from the economy, King Hassan not only developed new clienteles but lightened his political responsibilities. Financial reform was obviously critical—and it was brilliantly timed. A more systematic, "Turkish" approach to constitutionalism would now be in keeping with the new strategy. The electoral law, which promotes bipartism under normal conditions (Charlot and Charlot 1985: 501, 511), might even give rise, under pressures to reform the constitution, to alternating UC and Union Socialiste de Forces Populaires (USFP)/Istiqlal (Independence) governments. The 1993 legislative elections seemed a step in this direction, but Morocco still awaited some political crisis that might further push the king or his successor toward greater democracy.

Morocco is presently no more democratic than its neighbors. Its astute king, however, offers good evidence of the possibility that financial reform may ultimately drive political change there as elsewhere in the region. His awareness of the challenge drove him to preempt it by dominating the private sector that might otherwise have challenged his authoritarian regime.

Conclusion

North Africa, then, offers some evidence that the financial reforms encouraged by the IMF and the World Bank may push incumbent regimes toward greater accountability and political contestation. So far as they gain real autonomy, with freedom to manage their loan portfolios, commercial banks may foster business groups and encourage a potential for collective action in their respective business communities. In Tunisia, the Ben Ali regime seems to have become aware of the danger when it attacked a leading private sector bank. In Egypt, the potential threat was more visible. The Islamic investment companies accumulated financial resources that were at least as substantial as those of the official Islamic commercial banking sector. The informal Islamic business sector was acquiring increasing prestige and influence in the mid-1980s, until the regime cracked down on the free-wheeling investors. While many of the investment companies were poorly managed, so also were many of the non-Islamic commercial banks. The regime protected the latter while making it impossible for the former, even relatively well-managed companies with substantial tangible assets, to restructure themselves. As in Tunisia, the authorities could not tolerate the specter of a relatively independent business constituency. Across North Africa, only in Morocco did private sector banking and business groups gain sufficient shares of the market to enjoy a significant degree of financial autonomy. Yet here, too, the autonomy was in a sense fictitious, at least for the time being, because it reflected the fusion of public and private property characteristic of a patrimonial regime. A recent initiative to deflect criticism by selling about 10 percent of the shares of the

ONA to the public, including small investors (*MEED,* April 29, 1994: 6), will not alter the group's management structure.

So far, then, North Africa illustrates only a negative relationship between economic and political change: Financial reform cannot give rise to independent business constituencies because the incumbent regimes remain authoritarian and can tolerate only crony capitalism. Of the four regimes, however, Morocco appears to have come closest to meeting the conditions postulated at the outset of this chapter as favoring a political transition toward greater accountability and contestation. Its banking system displays a relatively strong and autonomous private sector, and private business supports a variety of political parties. But the businesses themselves depend upon Morocco's principal ruling institution, the makhzan, and the regime of crony capitalists still awaits a crisis—perhaps a royal succession—that might spark significant change.

Morocco seems best positioned to enjoy an internally generated transformation—wider public ownership of the business groups accompanied by more constitutional political practices. The business histories of the other three countries are very different. Algeria and Tunisia lack a tradition of private sector business conglomerates, either under the French or subsequently, when statist regimes nationalized most of the colonial assets. Egyptian capital did generate a number of private business groups before Nasser's time, but Sadat's *infitah* did not give rise to new conglomerates, only to numerous and fragmented private capital holdings feeding off Nasser's big public enterprises. When a financial liberalization of sorts—workers' remittances escaping formal controls—threatened to generate new autonomous private holdings, the regime stopped them. Perhaps the stimulus to further liberalization and privatization, pushed since the Gulf War in return for debt relief, will eventually give rise to a more dynamic private sector; but a major opportunity was lost.

The current confrontations between regimes and Islamist opposition does not bode well for any easy political transitions. The Islamist phenomenon also points to the vulnerability of any theory that tries to link financial reform to democratization. However consonant with greater accountability and political contestation, capital concentration in strong private sector groups would appear to be incompatible with the widespread participation that democratization also entails. How can business constituencies relate to, much less encourage, a mobilization of masses consonant with electoral participation and other forms of democratic participation? Business may favor political contestation so as to make any incumbent government more responsive to its interests, but why might it reach out to broader constituencies?

Algeria and Egypt offer partial answers to these questions in Islamic contexts. As discussed earlier, the program of the FIS, Algeria's principal

Islamist party, seemed quite compatible with financial liberalization. The principal economic innovation proposed by the FIS was to convert the commercial banking system into Islamic banks. These, as experiences in Egypt and other Arab countries have demonstrated, are compatible with market economies. Indeed, Islamic banking in theory requires closer relationships between the banks and business enterprises than conventional banks. Practices deemed "Islamic," moreover, may engender greater trust among Muslim populations. Islamic banks in Egypt were remarkably successful in attracting deposits that otherwise might have been withheld from a banking system perceived by many as Western and alien. The money changers who converted their operations into investment companies also projected themselves as "Islamic" to cultivate trust among the professionals and workers who were remitting hard currency from the Gulf. "Islamic" capitalism had a mass appeal that Western capitalism and commercial banking lacked. But Muslim businesses, whether banks or Sharif's plastics industry, were capitalist nonetheless, and they shared an interest in greater government accountability (see Richards 1993: 225). Although few of them were engaged in the country's Islamist political movements, their wealth added political weight within these movements to the relatively liberal elements (including the Muslim Brotherhood mainstream) committed to working within the political system. Despite lost opportunities, Islamic finance might yet stimulate democratization. Change in this direction will depend in part upon the incumbent regimes' strategies of survival. But in part it will also depend upon the liberal Islamists' ability to consolidate themselves within their respective oppositions.

Notes

1. See Collier and Mahon 1993: 851; for a similar, slightly narrower definition of democracy, see Rueschemeyer et al. 1992: 43–44.
2. In the *International Financial Statistics* reports published by the IMF, some countries provide explicit information about credit to public enterprises as well as to the central government. As can be seen from table 8.1, Poland did, but Hungary and Romania did not. Unfortunately, only Egypt, among the North African countries, offered such data. The author estimated comparable Algerian and Tunisian data from annual reports of commercial and central banks but could not find similar information concerning the Moroccan public sector.
3. Brahimi 1991: 291, indicates that 172 out of 480 state enterprises became profitable as a result of the earlier efforts under his administration. He served as prime minister from 1984 to 1988.
4. Interview with Hamadi Jabali, January 11, 1991.
5. These doubtful loans were reported as "Other Credits to Clients." Technically this rubric was expanded after February 1987 to include loans backed by certain types of deposits, syndicated loans, and loans to bank personnel; but these additional items did not add much to the totals. Presumably this rubric still consists mainly of loans that have been frozen and on which interest is not being paid. More detailed records from individual banks corroborate this assumption.

6. National Bank of Egypt, *Economic Bulletin* 42, no. 3 (1989): 143–46.

7. However, until 1991 most banks declared interest revenues on nonperforming loans, thereby inflating their spreads. ROA was a somewhat more reliable measure, but some banks inflated their net income by omitting deduction of the fictitious interest revenues from their bottom line. After capitalizing them (adding the "interest" to the outstanding loan), the public sector banks "correctly" deducted them from their net income as provisions against loan write-offs. Consequently, they displayed very low ROA results. But some of the private sector banks did not make these "correct" deductions.

References

Addi, Lahouari. 1991. "Les réformes économiques et leurs limites." *Les Cahiers de l'Orient* 23 (3rd trimester.): 115–22.

Brahimi, Abdelhamid. 1991. *L'Economie algérienne: défis et enjeux.* 2nd ed. Algiers: Editions Dahlab.

Charlot, Jean, and Monica Charlot. 1985. "Les groupes politiques." In M. Grawitz and J. Leca, eds., *Traité de Science Politique,* vol. 3, pp. 429–536. Paris: Presses Universitaires de France.

Collier, David, and James E. Mahon, Jr. 1993. "Conceptual 'Stretching' Revisited: Adapting Categories in Comparative Analysis." *APSR* 87, no. 4 (December): 845–55.

Doumou, Abdelali. 1987. *Etat et Capitalisme au Maroc.* Rabat: Edino.

Entelis, John, and Lisa J. Arone. 1992. "Algeria in Turmoil." *Middle East Policy* 1, no. 2: 23–35.

Fischer, Jeff, and Clement M. Henry. 1994. *Pre-Election Technical Assessment: Tunisia.* Washington, D.C.: International Foundation for Electoral Systems, January 31.

Fonds de participation des industries diverses [Annual Report]. 1989. Algiers.

Haggard, Stephan. 1990. "The Political Economy of the Philippine Debt Crisis." In Joan Nelson, ed., *Economic Crisis and Policy Choice: The Politics of Adjustment in the Third World,* pp. 215–55. Princeton: Princeton University Press.

Hilal, Rida. 1987. *Sinat Al-tabaiyah* [The construction of dependency]. Cairo: Dar Al-Mustaqbal Al-Arabi.

International Financial Statistics. Washington, D.C.: International Monetary Fund.

Leveau, Rémy. 1985. *Le fellah marocain défenseur du trône.* 2nd ed. Paris: Fondation Nationale des Sciences Politiques.

———. 1987. "Stabilité du pouvoir monarchique et financement de la dette." *Maghreb-Machrek* 118 (October–December): 5–19.

MEED (Middle East Economic Digest). London.

Moore, Clement Henry. 1993. "Political Parties." In William M. Habeeb and I. William Zartman, eds., *Polity and Society in Contemporary North Africa,* pp. 42–67. Boulder, CO: Westview.

Qaddafi, Muammar. N.d. *The Green Book.* Part 2, "The Solution of the Economic Problem." Tripoli, Libya: Public Establishment for Publishing, Advertising, and Distribution.

Richards, Alan. 1993. "Economic Imperatives and Political Systems." *Middle East Journal* 47, no. 2 (Spring): 217–27.

Rueschemeyer, Dietrich, Evelyne Huber Stephens, and John D. Stephens. 1992. *Capitalist Development and Democracy.* Chicago: University of Chicago Press.
Saâdi, Mohamed Saïd. 1988. *Les groupes financiers au Maroc.* Rabat: Editions Okad.

9.

The International Politics of Democracy in North Africa

I. William Zartman

Democracy is a lonely business. Self-government is an exercise in internal politics. When people take their own destiny in their hands, that act cannot be tainted by external involvement in it, or it is, by definition, no longer democratic. Other types of government do not have the same inhibitions; authoritarian governments, for example, can form their Holy Alliances without impinging on the nature of their authority. Still other types of government actually depend for their legitimacy on their international nature. Communist regimes proclaimed their basis in international proletarian solidarity, and Islamic regimes declare themselves to be a local branch of an international community on whom Westerners have imposed an alien concept of boundaries.

Against such movements and alliances, democracies stand alone. Rooted in the national community—the national self of the self-determination exercise—democracy regards internationalism in governance as interference. Democratic governments charged with conducting relations among states can of course cooperate together as a perfectly normal exercise of their functions, and they can band together in collective defense agreements to hold off a nondemocratic onslaught. But external support for democratic parties and movements supposedly operating within their states only is suspect, and the thin line that separates policy cooperation and collective defense from interference is sometimes hard to see. This contradiction was long an aspect of the Cold War, where democratic regimes often felt besieged by an international conspiracy that could pool greater resources, invoke broader solidarity, and claim higher legitimacy. Three events reversed these conceptual standards, just at the time of the final paroxysms of communism.

One was the Reaganite notion of "our Freedom Fighters," suggesting that there was an operational legitimacy in superpower support for rebellion against established but leftist regimes. This notion suggested that international support of revolt was legitimized by international support of revolutionary regimes, and therefore that democracy (the presumed goal of the revolt) need not rely only on its own means. The second was the creation—under a curious melange of Carterite and Reaganite populism—of the National Endowment for Democracy and the attendant party institutes to assist democratization and democratic parties abroad. The effort was inspired by the work of Christian Democratic parties and of labor unions (including the AFL-CIO), hitherto the only free world activity in foreign political support (see, e.g., Douglas 1972 and Douglas 1976).

The third, of a different sort, was the discovery by political scientists that democracies do not go to war against each other (see Mansfield and Snyder 1995: 79–97; Kant 1795: 100; Muravchik 1992: 8–10; Diamond 1992: 25–46; and Lane 1994). The putative evidence ignited a wide-ranging debate over definitions, causes and effects; but it also took another page from the communist handbook on political relations and suggested that democracy creates a special type of international politics that is by nature cooperative, in contrast both to Marxist claims that capitalist relations are by nature conflictual and to general, almost definitional, notions that democratic politics is necessarily conflictual because competitive (see, e.g., Schattschneider 1960).

Thus, the movement toward democratization returns the nature of international politics to earlier eras, when interstate relations also had to include the politics of movements—such as those of nationalists and Communists—aspiring to hold state power (Zartman 1987). Although these developments open up the relations between international politics and democracy (or democratization), they do not remove the inherent "contradictions" (also a term inherited from the communist handbook). External support delegitimizes democracy, yet democratic movements—or rather political movements aspiring to create or benefit from democracy—are vulnerable to nondemocratic authorities and international movements.

Since there is no full-fledged democracy in North Africa, it would be premature to investigate the effects of democracy on international politics. But it could be interesting to study the effects of international politics on democratization and to examine the efforts of aspiring democratic movements to utilize international relations to strengthen their claim to power without at the same time delegitimizing that claim. This discussion will focus on the international relations of cooperation in the process of democratization and on the effects of cooperation between movements and between states. The international relations of conflict, from the struggle for self-determination to the fight against enemies of democracy, are more straightforward and less paradoxical, and hence less interesting.

Nationalism: The First Phase of Democracy

There is no need to repeat the arguments of the many inspiring discussions of democracy; but it is important to highlight two ostensibly contradictory but defining elements. Essentially, democracy is a procedure, not a substance. It provides for choice of rulers, at regular intervals, from among contending candidates. It carries no guarantee of substantive results at any particular time; it is not synonymous with good government in the short run; and the procedure cannot be invalidated or annulled merely because of the bad choice of a given moment. Indeed, from time to time democracy will produce bad choices, which are bearable only because the procedure guarantees a chance to reverse them the next time around.

Procedure is, in fact, the only known guarantee of good government in the long run. Through its provision for the accountability and responsibility of the governors, it provides the only way of correcting mistakes—the only way both to get the rascals out and to reduce rascaldom while they are in. Democracy is the ability to choose *and* the ability to repent and choose again. But democracy can also serve to keep the incumbents in and the minorities out.

On the other hand, democracy is not just procedure. It is government conducted by democrats, by people who live within the rules that provide for repeated choice and who believe that losing does not threaten their security and that winning does not guarantee their privilege. While it does not guarantee good results at any one election, it is based on the deeper belief that only open debate can and will bring the best alternative to light—though perhaps with some delay. Democracy is built on a blind and dogmatic faith in the ability of the public to make enlightened choices and to prevent demagoguery from prostituting the process of public discussion. Thus, democracy depends, in a complex and reasoned way, on enabling attributes that are neither necessary nor sufficient but that are nonetheless helpful. These attributes include social preconditions such as literacy and urbanization (see Lipset 1960) but also adherence to such democratic ideals and values as those indicated above. Literacy and urbanization have their own causes and processes, but adherence to democratic values is hard to come by without experience in democracy, posing a chicken-and-egg dilemma.

Colonialism worked to resolve this dilemma by giving triple training in democracy to its subjects—sometimes, but not always, on purpose. In the Maghreb, France taught colonial peoples about French ideals of governance, in terms of parliamentary democracy, for example, or liberty, equality, and fraternity, and then made these ideals even more tantalizing by withholding them from colonial populations. It gave the colonial populations an example to emulate by showing how the French government was responsible to settler populations—a process from which the colonized peoples were excluded. And it forced colonial populations to create nationalist movements as the means of achieving national self-determination. For unlike arms, money, organization, and international support, the population and legitimacy itself were the only instruments of power that the colonial ruler could not monopolize. Nationalist movements embodied the mass democracy of Rousseau's General Will, targeted against foreign rule (see Rousseau 1762). They were an instrument of national self-determination, taking government into their own hands and restoring it to the nation that they represented.

Nationalist movements in North Africa felt no ambiguity about the national self that they represented. But they also had positive and negative reasons to justify collaboration as North Africans without diminishing their identity as Moroccans, Algerians, and Tunisians. On the one hand, they were united in a common Muslim Arab North African condition that allowed for mutual support. On the other hand, their nationalism was partly negative, a mutual refusal to be the "Other" (Memmi 1967) that all North Africans shared, even if they were less clear about the positive identifying characteristics that distinguished them from each other.

As a result, the democratizing nationalist movements of North Africa acted as protostates and developed their own international relations even before independence (Zartman 1987). The point here is not to develop the historic record but simply to recall the international relations of democratization in an earlier era. If the cornerstones of North African nationalism were the North African Star, founded in 1927, and the Moroccan Action Committee and the Neo-Destour Party, both founded in 1934, the keystone was the Association of North African Muslim Students (AEMAN), also founded in 1927. It remained the nursery for nationalist leadership in the Maghreb for over thirty years, raising leaders for the three national organizations. Once they won independence for Tunisia and Morocco, the movements, as new governments, supported the nationalist movement of Algeria in its struggle for self-determination. After 1957, both the Independence (Istiqlal) Party of Morocco and the New Constitution (Neo-Destour) Party of Tunisia were preoccupied with establishing their predominance as the single party and voice of the general will in their respective countries—unsuccessfully in Morocco and successfully in Tunisia—but both were continually reminded by the Algerian National Liberation Front (FLN) of their duty to sacrifice their independence to support the yet unachieved cause of national self-determination in Algeria. It has taken a long time for Algerians to get over the idea that their part of the common struggle did not receive sufficient support from their neighbors.

But nationalist governments were so heavy with legitimacy and unity that they were unable to carry the democratic argument to its operational conclusion. They were unable to condone division, debate, competing parties, and repeated elections among opposing candidates. As a result, three decades after independence, with three-quarters of the population born after the nationalist struggle was over, a new demand for democracy is sweeping North Africa as part of a larger world movement, mobilizing renewed pressure for popular sovereignty. Democracy is the fulfillment of the logic and promise of the nationalist movement and the culmination of self-determination; under democracy, the people determine the government at regular intervals, not merely the independence of the state in a one-time vote. But democratization also engenders a new dimension in the international politics of the region as democratizing states consort among themselves to control the movement toward their own democratization, and opposition movements cooperate among themselves and with foreign governments to hasten their accession to power.

Democratization: Internationalizing Independence

Like the postwar nationalist movement for colonial independence, the current wave of democratization, which began in the late 1980s, is a move for domestic political change born of international inspiration. It draws major impetus from the collapse of the communist system of social or totalitarian democracy in the former Soviet Union and Eastern Europe and from the exhaustion of the apartheid system of hijacked democracy in South Africa. Although it is a move to internalize the promise of independence by enlarging the "self" of self-government to the entire nation, it is also—paradoxically perhaps—a move involving the internationalization of that move, in its causes and its effects. Several general factors beyond the world events of the late 1980s have made the pressure for change particularly acute.

On one hand, the functions of the state have expanded enormously, extending into areas of socioeconomic services and regulations that far exceed the scope of state activities in precolonial or even colonial times. Typically, in the Maghreb, the state is the largest employer and the largest investor; nearly all religious officials, schoolteachers, and university faculties are civil servants; and all students live on state subsidies, expecting (and sometimes being guaranteed) state jobs upon graduation. Basic food staples have long been subsidized to maintain low consumer prices, and medical treatment, like education, is free or low in cost. But the state is also a source of intrusive regulations, such as labor laws, religious organization, currency and import controls, exit visas, curriculum content, and social norms. As a result, political control of the state is an important prize, posing the problem of beneficiaries and criteria.

On the other hand, the state has come to be treated as the hunting preserve of the few—alienated from the people, ruled not so much by coercion as by manipulation, and closed to the charismatic leaders of the nationalist movement. The ruling elite has been seen to rule for itself, conspicuously improving its own position but doing little for the rest of the nation (see Dawisha and Zartman 1988). The decade of the 1980s saw significant outbursts of popular disapproval in the Maghreb, with protests not only against shortfalls in goods and services provided by the government but a lack of trust and faith in the leaders themselves. Riots—in 1981 and 1984 in Casablanca, and in 1990–91 in northern Morocco; in 1986 in Constantine, and in 1988 throughout Algeria; and in 1984 in Tunis—were all strident and bloody instances of popular protest against the successors of the nationalist generation (see Zartman and Habeeb 1993). These negative protests have been complemented by a movement that seeks to give guidance and content to the selection process by isolating one part of the national culture as the essential criterion of rulership—adherence to a selection of Islamic beliefs.

In the Muslim world, including in the Maghreb, the pressure for democratization has become entangled with a concomitant movement arising in the region. In the broadest sense, the historic current of political Islamism is merely the latest phase in the cultural dialectic between secular modernism and authentistic tradition within the Arabo-Muslim world (see, e.g., Zartman 1985 and Zartman 1992). At identifiable moments in the past, as at the present time, the confrontation between a culture viewed as modern but foreign and another viewed as traditional but backward has produced a synthesis that lays claim to the positive values of authentistic modernity, only to be confronted again at a later moment by a challenger that blames it for its foreignness in the name of a new authenticity. The Islamic movement today challenges the secular modernist syntheses of the 1960s in these very terms. It provides an ideology for the disillusioned, a set of values for the uprooted, a sense of identity for the disoriented—all of whom constitute ready audiences produced by the failures of socialism, "Westernism," statism, and other failed formulas of the recent past.

Despite the similarity of their causes and their appeals, the Islamist movements of the North African countries are national responses to an international inspiration and a domestic opportunity, not local branches of an organized international movement. In addition, each of them was fostered in the 1970s by its own government as a way of building up domestic support for a national sense of values and identity against a growing leftist opposition, and as a way of taming the domestic religious order (Tozy 1993: 102–22). Each is a product of its country's national political tradition and development—local rebellions against the monarchy in Morocco, revolutionary protest in Algeria, evolutionary political organization in Tunisia. Though they exhibit a common purpose individually applied, their fortunes are intertwined, and so they offer mutual support. Notable examples are the self-exile in Algeria of Rachid al-Ghannouchi of an-Nahdah in the early 1990s after he lost hope and faith in the Tunisian regime, and the refuge taken by Islamic Salvation Front (FIS) leaders from Algeria in Morocco. None of the organizations, however, presents itself as a pan-Maghrebi party or movement, either in platform or in structure.

In this situation, both sides seek to internationalize the domestic process of democratization. Both sides view internationalization as part of their nature—the incumbent authorities as part of their interstate relations conducted through foreign policy, and the Islamic movements as part of their international character. At the same time the two have been the most visible parties in a fragile domestic process of broadening political participation as well as in the struggle to control that process. Secular democratic movements other than the original single parties have had little role to play in this contest (see Zartman 1994), though they may well be its major beneficiaries in the long run. Nor have they been players in the process of internationalization, despite the few efforts of the U.S. National Endowment for Democracy to assist the democratization process (McMahon 1992). That process involves, above all, the Maghrebi governments and their countries' Islamist movements.

Islamist movements and North African governments reach out and sometimes cross each other's lines in their search for external support. Saudi Arabia, a close monarchical ally of Morocco, has long supported Islamic movements throughout the Arab world, in much the same way that North African governments in the 1970s built up domestic Muslim groups to counter leftist agitation (Black, Pugh, and Tisdall 1992). The major source of the Islamist groups' support, however—probably exceeding the *zakat* [alms] they receive from their followers—is Iran. No reliable figures are available, however, and confirming the accuracy of this information is beyond ordinary research capabilities. Nonetheless, there is consensus that a large amount of Iranian financial support reaches followers of the Algerian FIS and that smaller amounts reach followers of the Tunisian Nahdah. The Tunisian government charges that a plot by an-Nahdah to kill President Ben Ali in mid-1991 was to have been accomplished by means of a Stinger missile acquired from Afghanistan via Algeria (Dunn 1994: 161). Iran is alleged to have "provided $3 million in campaign aid" to the FIS in the 1990 elections (Mohandessin 1993: 88). Further away, Pakistan was the site of a crucial meeting of the Islamist movement on July 3, 1991, when Algerian former participants in the Afghan war came together in Peshawar during a conference to support the "Muslims of Algeria," which was organized by the Arab Information Club, and to challenge the political (electoral) orientation of the leaders of the FIS.[1] Following the meeting, agreement was reached on an attack on the military post of Guemmar, on November 28—the anniversary of the death of one of the militants—well ahead of the 1991 elections. The absence of a single dominant Islamist organization makes Morocco a less attractive target for external support.

The international politics of internal movements participating in the process of democratization in turn impinge on the international politics of the states themselves. During the Afghan War, the North African governments opposed the Soviet-installed government and backed the efforts of the Mujahideen to overthrow it. Islamists from Algeria above all went to Afghanistan to join the Mujahideen of Gulbuddin Hekmatyar[2] and his Islamic Party (*Hizb i-Islami*), particularly in the mid- and later 1980s. They returned to provide dynamic leadership to the militant wing of the FIS and the Islamic Armed Groups (GIA).[3] Islamic movements met their first challenge in choosing foreign allies in the second Gulf War, when they rallied in tardy disorder behind the cause of Saddam Hussein. Their actions and reasoning provide a good example of the process of choice of foreign issues and allies in a context of democratizing competition, where that choice is determined above all by the image the movements and governments wish to present to their people. The popular quip in Tunisia was that, confronted with the Gulf War, the Islamic movement "first missed the train, then turned around and tried to take over the locomotive," a judgment that applies to Algeria as well. An-Nahdah and the FIS were both shocked by the Iraqi attack on a fellow Arab state and condemned the aggression. But they soon sensed a potential for wrenching public support away from the governments when the Western coalition joined Arab states in repelling the invasion. Both movements organized units of their citizens to go to Iraq and join the fighting, although neither arrived in time.

Rachid al-Ghannouchi saw the Western intervention as "the greatest affliction . . . since the fall of the Khalifate" for the Muslim *umma* (community), and he portrayed the war as the epitome of the conflict between the proud and powerful North and the "humble South armed [only] with its faith" (*Le Monde*, November 21, 1990). Ali Laaridh, spokesman for an-Nahdah, called for a *jihad* against the "regimes militarily and politically allied with American imperialism in its conspiracy against our umma . . . [and its efforts] to destroy the potential of the umma and to suffocate and marginalize its life forces, above all the Palestinian intifada and the Islamic dawa" (al-Ahnaf 1990). Hammadi Jebaili was more lenient in his judgment of Saudi Arabia only because he felt that the Saudis must have been forced to call on Western assistance since they could not possibly have done so on their own (*Le Monde*, August 24, 1990).

At the same time, most of the other parties in all three countries, both in government and in opposition, supported the regime of Saddam Hussein and its actions; also, massive demonstrations in favor of Iraq in early 1991 in Rabat and Algiers indicated where public sentiment lay. Political parties rose to tap this sentiment and the governments persisted in their policies—ranging from support for Saudi Arabia, if not Kuwait, to attempts at mediation between the two sides—only by allowing an unusual degree of free speech in public and in the press. Whatever the substantive merits of the debate, the opposition, and indeed the cause of democracy in general, benefited from the open atmosphere (see *Middle East Insight,* February 8 and 22, 1991).

Thus, movements as well as governments make foreign policy decisions for triple reasons: because of the need for mutual support, because of the values they proclaim, and because of the image they wish to present to the public whose support they solicit. Usually, governments and opposition end up with different allies and supporters; but sometimes, these reasons converge to bring all political forces in a country into competition for sustenance at the same trough.

Security: The Dynamics of International Politics

Just as democratization has led some of the parties taking advantage of the new opening to develop international support and relations, so too have the governments of North Africa turned to international politics to strengthen their domestic position throughout the time of change. International agreements and cooperation are usually undertaken for purposes of external security. But when domestic change is so great as to alter the system of government and threaten the positions of the incumbents, then domestic security becomes a major motive behind the politics of states. Neighboring North African countries have tightened their relations and overcome their hostilities on occasion over the last decade in order to help each other meet the challenge of democratization, notably in regard to the Islamist movements.

After 1988, the three Maghrebi countries reacted differently to the rising internal opposition coming from the Islamic movements, with legalization in Algeria, repression in Tunisia, and cautious control in Morocco. But they all saw these internal movements as a politico-economic problem with security dimensions and decided to treat it as such. Each of them engaged in a vigorous search for foreign aid and foreign investments. (See the "Chronologies" in *Maghreb-Machrek,* 123 [January 1989]: 64, 85, 97; 124 [April 1989]: 126, 138, 146.) But they also realized that the economic development necessary for national security could not be obtained without regional collaboration. The signing of the treaty of the Arab Maghreb Union (UMA) in February 1989 was the fruit of this understanding (see Zartman forthcoming).

Tunisia under Ben Ali started to move the conflictual alliances in North Africa toward Maghreb unity by convincing Chadli Benjedid that unity would be impossible without the participation of Morocco (see Zartman 1989: 67–

68). The main obstacle to Maghrebi cooperation was the rivalry between Algeria and Morocco, the most tangible manifestation of which was the Western Saharan dispute. On May 16, 1988, Algeria and Morocco restored diplomatic relations. Benjedid agreed to rapprochement with Morocco without receiving from King Hassan any firm guarantee on the specifics of a solution to the Western Saharan problem or of direct talks between Morocco and the POLISARIO. Diplomatic relations between Morocco and Algeria were renewed and important steps were taken toward settling the thirteen-year-old conflict over the Western Sahara. The Algerian-Moroccan rapprochement enabled an all-Maghrebi summit to be convened on June 10, 1988, to inaugurate planning for the creation of a formal institutional structure for the Greater Arab Maghreb.

Less important than the Western Saharan issue as a cause of rapproachement, however, was the internal security question. Rather than "one of several factors" (Mortimer 1992: 252), the growing Islamist pressure was the primary issue pushing the Maghrebi leaders along the path to the constitution of the UMA. The absence of a Saharan solution has led the UMA to be considered a failure, but in internal security matters it has shown much greater—though uneven—cooperation and greater success (Daoud 1989: 120).

In this same period, bilateral security cooperation contributed to building the multilateral web. Following the "constitutional coup" of November 7, 1987, Tunisia moved toward liberalization of its political life (see Zartman 1990). On the first anniversary of his rise to power, Ben Ali announced a "National Pact," which was designed to present Tunisia as a country ready for democracy. Basic freedoms were guaranteed, and political parties could be formed if not rejected for cause by the Minister of the Interior. Elections, which were not due until 1991, were moved forward to April 1989. The Tunisian government vigorously debated legalizing the MTI, but hardliners participating in the internal discussions (Minister of the Interior, ruling party officials) were strengthened by Algerian warnings not to do so. In July 1988, Cherif Messaadia, representing the FLN at the congress of the Democratic Constitutional Rally (RCD), openly warned the Tunisian regime that the legalization of the MTI would constitute a bad example for the Algerian opposition—an example that the Algerian government would not be able to ignore. The Algerian disorders of October 1988 heightened Algerian concerns; it was evident that the recognition of the MTI at this point would weigh on the political equilibrium inside Algeria. Tunisia depended on Algeria too much as a counterweight against the threat coming from Libya to be able to ignore Algerian pressures (Leveau 1989: 15). The episode demonstrates the growing concern of the two Maghrebi regimes over the development of the Islamic movements in the area and over the necessity of cooperating to overcome or control the risk.

The cooperation did not work both ways, however. A year later, the Algerian government of Chadli Benjedid reversed its policy and recognized its own Islamist movement, the FIS, in order to counterbalance its earlier decision, in the October riots, to call out the army. Ben Ali did not appreciate the Algerian decision, taken without consulting or even forewarning him of this decision (Grimaud 1992: 37).

In the following years, the internal security issue continued to dominate Maghrebi cooperation. On October 11, 1988, following the Algerian disorders the king of Morocco sent military columns to supply Algerian cities with food ("Chronologie," *Maghreb-Machrek*, 124 [April 1989]: 84). General statements of support also came from Tunisia (*FBIS* 1988: 21). On April 19, 1989, Algeria and Morocco signed a treaty of cooperation in the field of Islamic and religious affairs; it includes a program on the exchange of information on their Islamic heritage and the elaboration of a joint program of religious manifestations (*Annuaire de l'Afrique du Nord* 1989: 501).

Riots in Morocco and Tunisia and the results of the June election in Algeria brought an intensification of visits of security personnel and Ministers of the Interior toward the end of 1990. On December 5, 1990, the Tunisian Minister of the Interior went to Algeria, and three weeks later the Algerian Prime Minister was in Tunis. Strikes and incidents with many casualties took place in all three countries in December 1990, and in early 1991 there were terrorist attacks against European offices and companies ("Chronologie," *Maghreb-Machrek*, 132 [April 1991]). During this same period, Algerian Prime Minister Mouloud Hamrouche and King Hassan spoke out in favor of closer economic and social cooperation. The two countries signed an agreement on extending the permits of residency for their citizens to ten years and a convention on social security. The same kind of agreement was signed between Algeria and Tunisia on February 6, 1991 ("Chronologie," *Maghreb-Machrek*, 132 [April 1991]). Islamist disorders in Algeria in early June coincided with government charges of a fundamentalist plot to kill Ben Ali, pointing up parallels between the Algerian and Tunisian events (*FBIS*, June 6, 1991, p. 14). King Hassan and his Interior Minister met with the Algerian President to issue a declaration on March 30 on bilateral relations and freedom of circulation, among other things ("Chronologie," *Maghreb-Machrek*, 133 [July 1991]). Interviewed on the Algerian situation on December 24, 1991, Moroccan Foreign Minister Filali expressed support for Benjedid's position (*FBIS*, December 24, 1991, p. 13).

The Tunisian Minister of the Interior visited Algiers on September 9, 1991, as al-Ghannouchi continued his verbal attacks, from Algiers, against the Tunisian government. At the end of the month, the Tunisian UGTT (Tunisian Labor Union) urged Algiers to act on the security threat, in particular calling on Algeria to put an end to "the terrorists' use of Algerian soil to execute attacks against Tunisia" (*FBIS*, October 1, 1991, p. 13). An "understanding" was reached with Algeria a week later on its hosting of elements from the Nahdah movement (*FBIS*, October 9, 1991, p. 15); a month later al-Ghannouchi left Algiers. Thus, by the fall of 1991, close antifundamentalist cooperation had developed between the two governments (*FBIS*, October, 9, 1991, p. 33).

After the resignation of Chadli Benjedid and the military coup d'etat, the reactions of Tunisia and Morocco were complex. In an interview on January 9, the king praised the electoral process in Algeria and declared himself a partisan of multipartyism (as he had already said in his constitution), and on February 24 he said he would have preferred that the electoral process not be interrupted in Algeria (*FBIS*, February 24, 1992, p. 25). This view has been repeated a number of times since then (bringing, in turn, an increasing number of Algerian leaders' pronouncements in 1994 that reaffirmed a hard line on the Western Sahara). The king sees the Algerian army as his nemesis and the Algerian Islamists as the opponents of the army in power; he appears to believe that, as "Commander of the Faithful," he has nothing to fear from Moroccan Islamists.

The new Algerian head of state, Mohammed Boudiaf, had long been an exile in Morocco and was favorable to Algerian-Moroccan cooperation, as well as to cleaning out corruption in the Algerian system. Soon after coming to office, he called for a solution to the Saharan issue, declaring that for the sake of full collaboration with Morocco, his country had decided to abandon totally the policy of putting up obstacles to a solution (*FBIS*, February 25, 1992, p. 15). On May 28, the Moroccan Official Bulletin published the ratification of the 1972 treaty delimiting the borders between the two countries (*Maghreb-Machrek*, 137 [June 1992]: 98). Cooperation among the Interior Ministries over internal security matters, the heart of the common interest in the UMA, continued for a number of years after the overthrow of Benjedid. The day after the king's original statement in February 1992, his closest advisor and Minister of the Interior, Driss Basri, was in Algiers; in March the Algerian Minister of the Interior visited Morocco in order to discuss the coordination of security measures ("Chronologie," *Maghreb-Machrek*, 136 [April 1992]). Regularly thereafter, until mid-July 1994, the Interior Ministers of the Maghreb states met to discuss internal security, visits and migration, and a Maghrebi identity card ("Chronologie," *Maghreb-Machrek*, 146 [October 1994]).

Conflictual relations overtook cooperation, however, on August 24, 1994, with the terrorist attack that killed two Spanish tourists in Marrakesh. Franco-Moroccan cooperation swung into action to arrest and then sentence a number of Islamists, mainly of Algerian origin. It remains unclear, however, which of the two conspiracy theories gets to the bottom of the matter—that the terrorists were an emanation of the Algerian Military Security (SM), or of the FIS or of the GIA (Ouazani 1996). The border between the two countries was closed for several months and visas were required when border crossing was resumed. The affair spilled over into Tunisia when over 300 Moroccans were expelled from Tunisia in September 1994 for illegal entry, despite provisions in the UMA treaty. Internal security matters brought the neighbors together and, six years later, restored the normal pattern of conflicting relations within the Maghreb.

In Tunisia, the reaction to the Algerian situation was more direct. The overthrow of Benjedid occasioned a meeting of the Supreme Council of the Tunisian internal security forces, which conducted "an appraisal of the program of international cooperation among the various security forces and their counterparts in the sisterly countries[;] . . . Algeria was in the forefront of the sisterly countries" (*FBIS*, January 14, 1992, p. 21). Soon after, Tunisia's Minister of the Interior, Abdallah Kallel, praised the policy pursued by the new Algerian leadership and expressed his appreciation for what he defined as the "corrective action" that Algeria was then undergoing (*FBIS*, February 14, 1992, p. 19). The continuing incidence of Islamic fundamentalist terrorism led Algeria and Tunisia to begin closer collaboration with Egypt, especially after the determination that Iran had been actively supporting terrorism within their countries and using the Sudan as a training center and arms conduit. Mohammed Ben Yahya, Tunisia's Foreign Minister, declared in October 1992 that his country was involved in "extensive consultation" with the Algerian and Egyptian governments in the field of security and antiterrorism, coordinating positions on many regional and international issues in an effort called "Pan-Arab Security." This is a new concept that says much about the current level of regional cooperation among Arab governments on issues related to democratization.

Security cooperation between the Islamic movements and oil states of the Mashreq is harder to document, even for Western or Maghrebi intelligence sources (*International Herald Tribune*, January 24, 1994). The arms itinerary is relatively well known, though it is very poorly controlled. It begins in the open arms markets of the former East European countries, runs through Germany, Switzerland, and France, then passes through either Marseilles or Spain, and ends in a North African harbor (*Libération*, January 4, 1995). The discovery of several large arms caches in France and the arrest of a few of the transporters involved in late 1994 and early 1995 drew attention to arms supplies procured with Iranian money and sent principally to Islamic groups in Algeria (*Le Figaro*, November 9, 1994, and March 1, 1995; *Libération*, January 4, 1995). The Moroccan and Algerian Interior Ministries worked in close cooperation with French authorities on these matters, but German and Swiss governments have been slower in monitoring the arms traffic through their territories. The Algerian government broke off diplomatic relations with

Iran on March 27, 1993, after several months of warnings (*FBIS,* October 7, 1992: 14; November 25, 1992: 90; December 28, 1992: 3; *al-Watan,* January 29, 1994).

Security relations would seem to be marginal to normal democratization processes. Yet opening up the political field of competition touches on vital stakes of power, representation, and allocation—crucial areas that people vote on and fight over. Under normal conditions and established rules of the game, internal security is neither a matter of regional alliances nor of clandestine armament. But when the rules are suddenly up for change, law and order are necessary to assure a peaceful transition, even to the point of requiring cooperation among states in a similar situation; and violence is invoked by those who seek to seize the transition as well as its results, even to the point of requiring external assistance for their efforts.

The Internationalization of Domestic Change

In the name of domestic sovereignty and self-determination, states and movements seek allies for outside support. The effects of this phenomenon are contradictory, as might be expected, but not necessarily negative for the process of democratization. First, it enhances the sense of regional unity and its operationalization on both sides. Islamist movements, while not formally pan-Maghrebi, reject boundaries as a Western imposition on the Muslim umma and cooperate with one another. Too much should not be made of this; nationalist movements also cooperated with each other, and the result was the same kind of "selfish states acting in a system of anarchy" that could be found anywhere else in the world (see Waltz 1979: iii). But some cooperation is present. Similarly, the states of North Africa have temporarily put aside their alternating pattern of alliances and conflict for cooperation on internal security matters (Modelski 1964: 549–60; see also Zartman 1987: 13–27). In the absence of a common external enemy, they have united for a while against a common internal threat; when one (or more) feels that a threat is manageable, it weakens the urge to work together. The consequent dampening of intra-Maghrebi conflict in the late 1980s and early 1990s was salutary, even if temporary. If, in addition, security cooperation also could foster economic collaboration and common efforts to improve socioeconomic conditions, no one would be the loser. However, security enjoys top priority, and in times of crises, the neofunctionalist notion of cooperation always falls before the neorealist notion of selfish security.

Second, in a paradoxical way, collaboration on both sides has aspects that further democracy. It may well be that without the international dimension to their activity, Islamist movements would be seen as less of an internal threat to incumbent regimes; but this is in no way certain. Rather, as seen in regard to the Gulf War, the international politics of the Islamist opposition, coupled with currents of public opinion, actually led to an opening of political space throughout North Africa. Whatever the deplorable state of democratic proclivities in the Islamist parties, they do bring real grievances of the public to government attention in a powerful way. Caveat governor.

On the state side, no government—despite appearances—has reacted in a fully and permanently antidemocratic way. Every regime knows full well that it has to find ways of coming to terms with the democratization movement, of sorting out democrats from autocrats, and of providing a transition into legitimizing democracy. This is not to say that any government's intentions are benign; every government has its own interests and the interests of those who run it as well, and no incumbent likes to guarantee his own imminent retirement. At the same time, the Algerian regime looks for ways to undo Benjedid's "error" and its own—to restore its legitimacy through elections but to limit political competition to democratic parties—those who will permit future rounds of elections. The Tunisian regime has long wrestled with the recognition issue and has finally overcome the opposition of its dominant party—called "quasi-unique" by the Tunisians—to electoral law changes in order to pass a law that practically guarantees third party representation in parliament, as after the April 1995 elections. The Moroccan monarchical regime, in the September 1992 and 1996 referenda, introduced constitutional changes making the government responsible to the elected parliament as well as to the king; the June 1993 elections saw a return of the nationalist parties to prominence (even if their majority was denied in the indirect part of the elections in October 1993). There has been coordination among the North African states on these issues.

Third, the internationalization of democratization also allows for external pressures from beyond the Arab world. Attention from both Amnesty International and from the U.S. government to Moroccan, Tunisian, and Algerian civil rights abuses are integral components of the move toward democracy. It is appropriate to insist that such attention be directed as much to the would-be participants in the political process as to the governments. In general, the bumpy progress of North Africa—and it would be blind or partisan to deny that progress exists—plays back to Western countries already dedicated to maintaining a democratic system and leads to a fruitful debate over the meaning of democracy and the ways to attain it, a debate that goes beyond the mechanical formalism of either elections alone or immediate alternance of parties in power.

Notes

1. Labat 1995: 436–37, 456; information taken from a videotape of the meeting.
2. For an interesting interview with Hekmatyar, see Rose 1992.
3. Labat 1995: esp. 433–38, including a biography of Si Ahmed Mourad (Jafar al-Afghani).

References

Ahnaf, M. al-. 1990. "L'opposition maghrébine face à la crise du Golfe." *Maghreb-Machrek* 130 (October): 110.

Black, Ian, Deborah Pugh, and Simon Tisdall. 1992. "Militant Islam's Saudi Paymasters." *Guardian,* February 29.

Daoud, Zakya. 1989. "La création de l'union du Maghreb arabe." *Maghreb-Machrek* 124 (April): 120.

Dawisha, Adeed, and I. William Zartman, eds. 1988. *Beyond Coercion: The Durability of the Arab State.* London: Croom Helm.

Diamond, Larry. 1992. "Promoting Democracy." *Foreign Policy* (Summer): 25–46.

Douglas, William A. 1972. *Developing Democracy.* Washington, D.C.: Heldref.

———. 1976. *Fundamentos de la Democracia.* Washington, D.C.: Instituto Americano para el Desarollo del Sindicalismo Libre.

Dunn, Michael. 1994. "The Al-Nahda Movement in Tunisia: From Renaissance to Revolution." In John Ruedy, ed., *Islamism and Secularism in North Africa.* New York: St. Martin's.

Grimaud, Nicole. 1992. "Prolongements externes des élections algériennes." *Les Cahiers de l'Orient* 23: 37.

Kant, Immanuel. 1795 [1970]. In Hans Reiss, ed., *Kant's Political Writings.* New York: Cambridge University Press.

Labat, Séverine. 1995. "Les islamistes algériens à la conquête du pouvoir." Paris: Institut d'études politiques, doctoral thesis.

Lane, Christopher. 1994. "Kant or Cant: The Myth of the Democratic Peace." *International Security* 19 (Fall).

Leveau, Rémy. 1989. "La Tunisie du Président Ben Ali." *Maghreb-Machrek* 124 (April): 15.

Lipset, Seymour Martin. 1960. *Political Man.* New York: Doubleday.

Mansfield, Edward D., and Jack Snyder. 1995. "Democratization and War." *Foreign Affairs* 74, no. 3 (May–June): 79–97.

McMahon, Ned. 1992. *Democratization in Tunisia.* Washington, D.C.: NED.

Memmi, Albert. 1967. *The Colonizer and the Colonized.* Boston: Beacon.

Modelski, George. 1964. "Kautilya: Foreign Policy and International System in the Ancient Hindu World." *American Political Science Review* 57, no. 3 (September): 549–60.

Mohandessin, Mohammed. 1993. *Islamic Fundamentalism.* Washington, D.C.: Seven Locks Press.

Mortimer, Robert. 1992. "Algerian Foreign Policy in Transition." In John P. Entelis and Phillip Naylor, eds., *State and Society in Algeria*. Boulder, CO: Westview.

Muravchik, Joshua. 1992. *Exporting Democracy*. Washington, D.C.: AEI Press.

Ouazani, Cheril. 1996. "UMA Gesticulations." *Jeune Afrique*, no. 1857 (August 7): 19–20.

Rose, Carol. 1992. "Gulbudeen Hekmatyar in Person." *Institute for Current World Affairs Report*, CVR–22, March 21.

Rousseau, Jean-Jacques. 1762 [1962]. *The Social Contract*. New York: Oxford.

Schattschneider, E. E. 1960. *The Semi-Sovereign People*. New York: Holt, Rinehart and Winston.

Tozy, Mohammed. 1993. "Islam and the State." In I. William Zartman and William M. Habeeb, eds., *Polity and Society in Contemporary North Africa*. Boulder, CO: Westview.

Waltz, Kenneth. 1979. *Theory of International Relations*. New York: Random House.

Zartman, I. William. 1985. "The Cultural Dialectic." In Halim Barakat, ed., *Contemporary North Africa*. London: Croom Helm, pp. 20–36.

———. 1987. "Foreign Relations of North Africa." *Annals of the American Academy of Political and Social Science* 489 (January): 13–27.

———. 1987. *The International Relations of the New Africa*. 2nd ed. Lanham, MD: University Press of America.

———. 1989. *Ripe for Resolution: Conflict and Intervention in Africa*. New York: Oxford University Press.

———. 1992. "Democracy and Islam: The Cultural Dialectic." In Charles Butterworth and I. William Zartman, eds., "Political Islam," *Annual of the American Academy of Political and Social Science* 524 (November): 181–91.

———. 1994. "The Challenge of Democratic Alternatives in the Maghreb." In John Ruedy, ed., *Islamism and Secularism in North Africa*. New York: St. Martin's.

———. Forthcoming. "The Ups and Downs of the Arab Maghreb Union." In Michael Hudson, ed., *The Arab World in the Middle East: Problems of Integration and Interdependence*. Washington, D.C.: Georgetown University.

Zartman, I. Willaim, ed. 1990. *Tunisia: The Political Economy of Reform*. Boulder, CO: Lynne Rienner.

Zartman, I. William, and William M. Habeeb, eds. 1993. *Polity and Society in Contemporary North Africa*. Boulder, CO: Westview.

Index

Abd al-Latif, Shaykh Soltani: and official Islam opposition, 58–59

AIS. *See* Islamic Salvation Army (AIS, Algeria)

Algeria, 3; anti-West sentiment in, 104; Armed Islamic Group (GIA) in, 65–66; democratization in, xxiv–xxv, 7, 182–83; domestic discontent in, x, xvi, 82, 98–100; economic reforms in, 183–86; elections in, x, 36, 57, 69–71; financial liberalization in, xxiv–xxv, 182–86, 184(table), 200–202; government investment policy in, 163–64; Gulf War and, 212; human rights in, xv–xvi, 75, 87; inflation taxes in, 159; internal security of, 77–78, 214–17; Islamic revivalism in, xx, 57; Islamic Salvation Army (AIS) in, xx, 46, 63–65, 70, 168; military control in, xv, 146–47, 170*n*4; military expenditures in, 147(fig.), 148; modernization in, 15; nonviolent Islam in, 66–67; per capita real GNP growth in, 167(fig.); political Islam in, x, 17, 43, 57–71; political reforms in, 183–84; political systems in, xix, 6, 12, 142, 182–83; populist Islam in, 58–62; radical Islam in, 62–66; radical secularist authoritarianism in, xi, 4; revolution failure in, 5; Rome Platform and, 68–69; state Islam in, 58; Liamine Zeroual and, 57

Algerian Military Security (SM), 216–17

Amnesty International: human rights issues and, xv, 47, 187

Arab states: democracy prospects in, xii, xxiv–xxv, 19–20, 30–35; revenue and expenditure trends in, 145(fig.)

Arab-Israeli war, 107–108, 148

al-Arabi, Mahmud, 165

Armed Islamic Group (GIA, Algeria): and Algerian presidential election, 70; internationalism of, 212; and religious protest in Algeria, 65–66

Armed Islamic Movement (MIA), 58, 63

Association of Algerian Ulema, 57

Association of North African Muslim Students, 208

Authoritarianism: democratic revolution and,

xii, 7–8, 15*n*2, 19–20, 30–35; financial crisis solutions of, 143–44; foreign powers and, 9; Islamic opponents of, 9; liberal secularism and path to, 5; political culture and, xi–xvii; political economy and, xvii–xxv, 141–45, 145(fig.); taxation and, 149, 152–53, 171*nn*11–13

Ben Ali (president, Tunisia), 191; financial liberalization under, 186; human rights and, xvi, 75, 88, 187; Liberalism and, 128; national security and, 211, 213–16; as presidential advisor, 75; as ruling power, x, 46–50, 147, 186; security forces expansion and, 188. *See also* RCD (Tunisia)

Ben Badis, Shaykh Abdelhamid, 57

Ben Bella, Ahmed (president, Algeria), ix, 12, 58

Ben Boulaïd, Mustafa, 59

Benhadj, Ali: FIS and, xv; history of, 64; political Islam and, 43; populist Islam and, 60–61; as stabilizing force, 59

Benjedid, Chadli (president, Algeria): financial liberalization and, 183–85, 184(table), 202*n*3; as human rights minister, 75; Islamic conduct and, 17; national security and, 213–16; political reforms of, 183–84; as ruling power, xii, 58, 62

Benkirane, Abdellah, 53

Bennabi, Malek, 58

Bitat, Rabat, 59

Boudiaf, Mohammed, 216

Boumedienne, Houari (president, Algeria), 12, 58, 77

Bourguiba, Habib (president, prime minister, Tunisia), ix, xvi, 1; authoritarianism opponents and, 9; internal security agencies and, 78; Islamic democracy and, 14; liberal secularism of, 4–5; military of, 146; an-Nahdah and, 47; political crisis under, 186; *president for life* concept and, 12

Bouyali, Mustafa, 58, 62–63

CCDH (Consultative Council on Human Rights, Morocco), 75